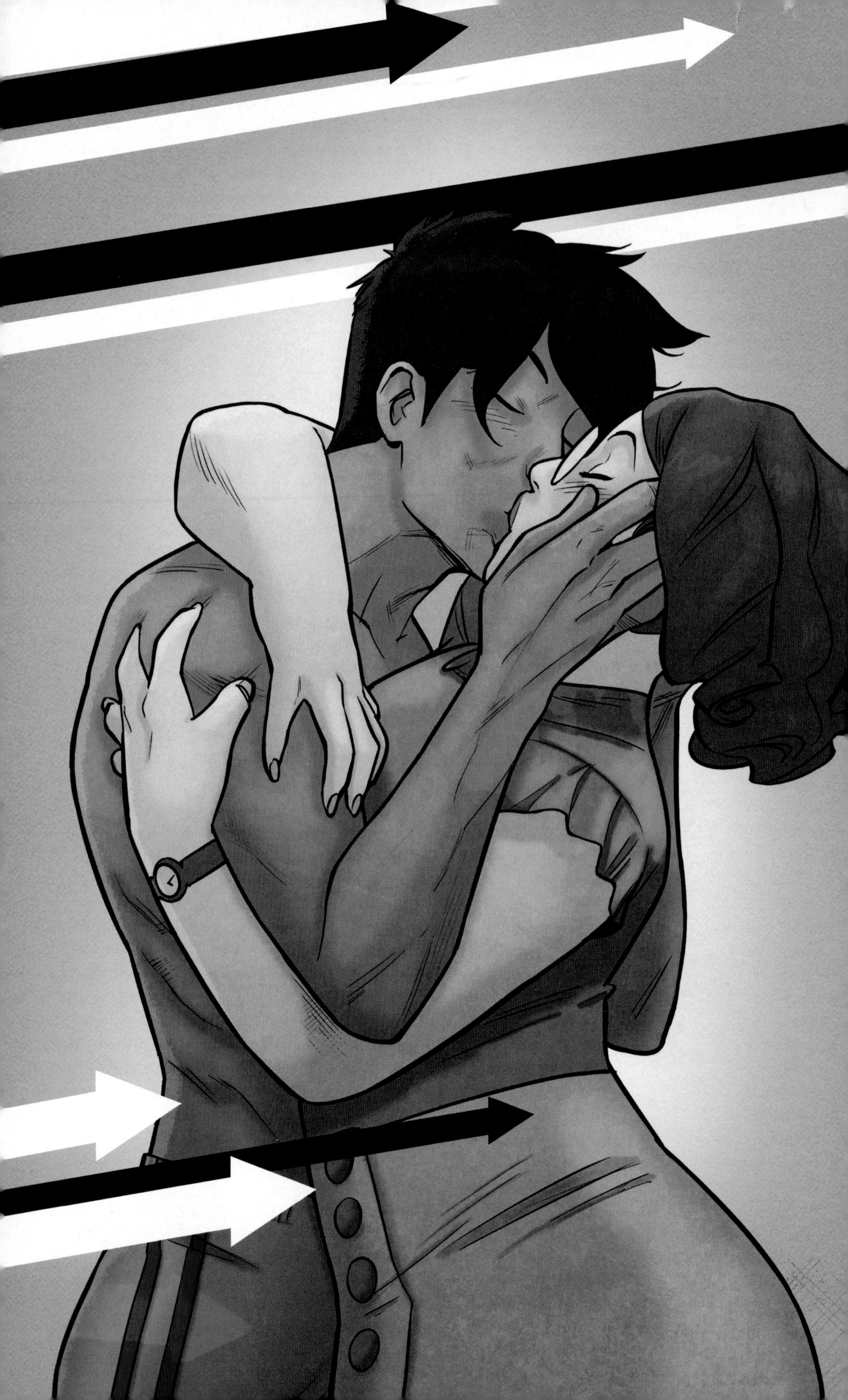

RUNAWAYS
But You Can't Hide

WRITER **RAINBOW ROWELL**

ARTISTS **ANDRÉS GENOLET**

WITH **NIKO HENRICHON** *(#22-23)*

COLOR ARTISTS
TRÍONA FARRELL *(#19-20)*, **CHRIS O'HALLORAN** *(#21)*,
MICHAEL GARLAND *(#22)* & **MATTHEW WILSON** *(#23-24)*

LETTERER **VC'S JOE CARAMAGNA**   COVER ART **KRIS ANKA**

ASSISTANT EDITOR **KATHLEEN WISNESKI**   EDITOR **NICK LOWE**

RUNAWAYS CREATED BY **BRIAN K. VAUGHAN & ADRIAN ALPHONA**

COLLECTION EDITOR JENNIFER GRÜNWALD | ASSISTANT EDITOR CAITLIN O'CONNELL | ASSOCIATE MANAGING EDITOR KATERI WOODY
EDITOR, SPECIAL PROJECTS MARK D. BEAZLEY | VP PRODUCTION & SPECIAL PROJECTS JEFF YOUNGQUIST | BOOK DESIGNER JAY BOWEN
SVP PRINT, SALES & MARKETING DAVID GABRIEL | DIRECTOR, LICENSED PUBLISHING SVEN LARSEN
EDITOR IN CHIEF C.B. CEBULSKI | CHIEF CREATIVE OFFICER JOE QUESADA
PRESIDENT DAN BUCKLEY | EXECUTIVE PRODUCER ALAN FINE

RUNAWAYS BY RAINBOW ROWELL VOL. 4: BUT YOU CAN'T HIDE. Contains material originally published in magazine form as RUNAWAYS #19-24. First printing 2019. ISBN 978-1-302-91801-9. Published by MARVEL WORLDWIDE, INC., a subsidiary of MARVEL ENTERTAINMENT, LLC. OFFICE OF PUBLICATION: 135 West 50th Street, New York, NY 10020. © 2019 MARVEL No similarity between any of the names, characters, persons, and/or institutions in this magazine with those of any living or dead person or institution is intended, and any such similarity which may exist is purely coincidental. **Printed in the U.S.A.** DAN BUCKLEY, President, Marvel Entertainment; JOHN NEE, Publisher; JOE QUESADA, Chief Creative Officer; TOM BREVOORT, SVP of Publishing; DAVID BOGART, Associate Publisher & SVP of Talent Affairs; DAVID GABRIEL, SVP of Sales & Marketing, Publishing; JEFF YOUNGQUIST, VP of Production & Special Projects; DAN CARR, Executive Director of Publishing Technology; ALEX MORALES, Director of Publishing Operations; DAN EDINGTON, Managing Editor; SUSAN CRESPI, Production Manager; STAN LEE, Chairman Emeritus. For information regarding advertising in Marvel Comics or on Marvel.com, please contact Vit DeBellis, Custom Solutions & Integrated Advertising Manager, at vdebellis@marvel.com. For Marvel subscription inquiries, please call 888-511-5480. **Manufactured between 8/23/2019 and 9/24/2019 by LSC COMMUNICATIONS INC., KENDALLVILLE, IN, USA.**

10 9 8 7 6 5 4 3 2 1

PREVIOUSLY

WHEN YOUNG ALEX WILDER LEARNED THE ANCIENT GIBBORIM PLANNED TO DESTROY ALL HUMANITY EXCEPT FOR SIX SERVANTS, HE DID WHAT WAS NECESSARY TO ENSURE THEY'D SPARE THE PEOPLE DEAREST TO HIM — HIS MOTHER, FATHER AND NICO. THE OTHER RUNAWAYS REFUSED TO BARGAIN AND SAVED THE WORLD — EXCEPT FOR THEIR OWN PARENTS…AND ALEX. SOMEHOW ALIVE AGAIN AND PURSUED BY THE GIBBORIM'S OFFSPRING, ALEX FOUND THE OTHERS SO THEY COULD SAVE EACH OTHER. HE WAS PREPARED TO SACRIFICE ANYONE TO PROTECT THE ONLY FAMILY HE HAD LEFT, BUT INSTEAD, GERT BANISHED HER PARENTS' INVALUABLE TIME MACHINE AND THE MOST DANGEROUS GIBBORIM CHILDREN TO THE DISTANT FUTURE. AGAIN THEY REJECTED PRAGMATISM…AND ALEX. MORE ALONE THAN HE'S EVER BEEN, ALEX LEFT. BUT SOMEONE FOLLOWED HIM…

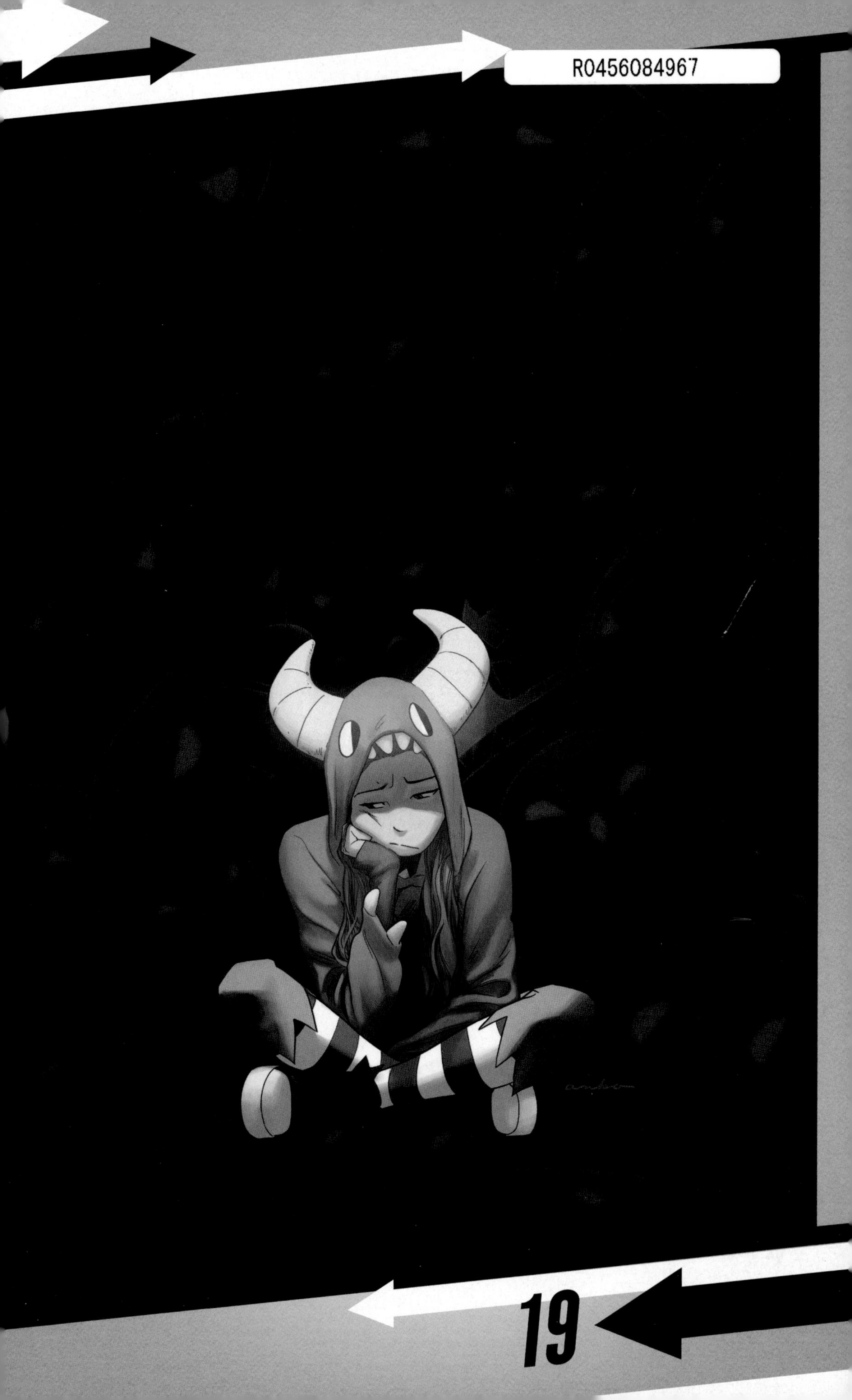
19

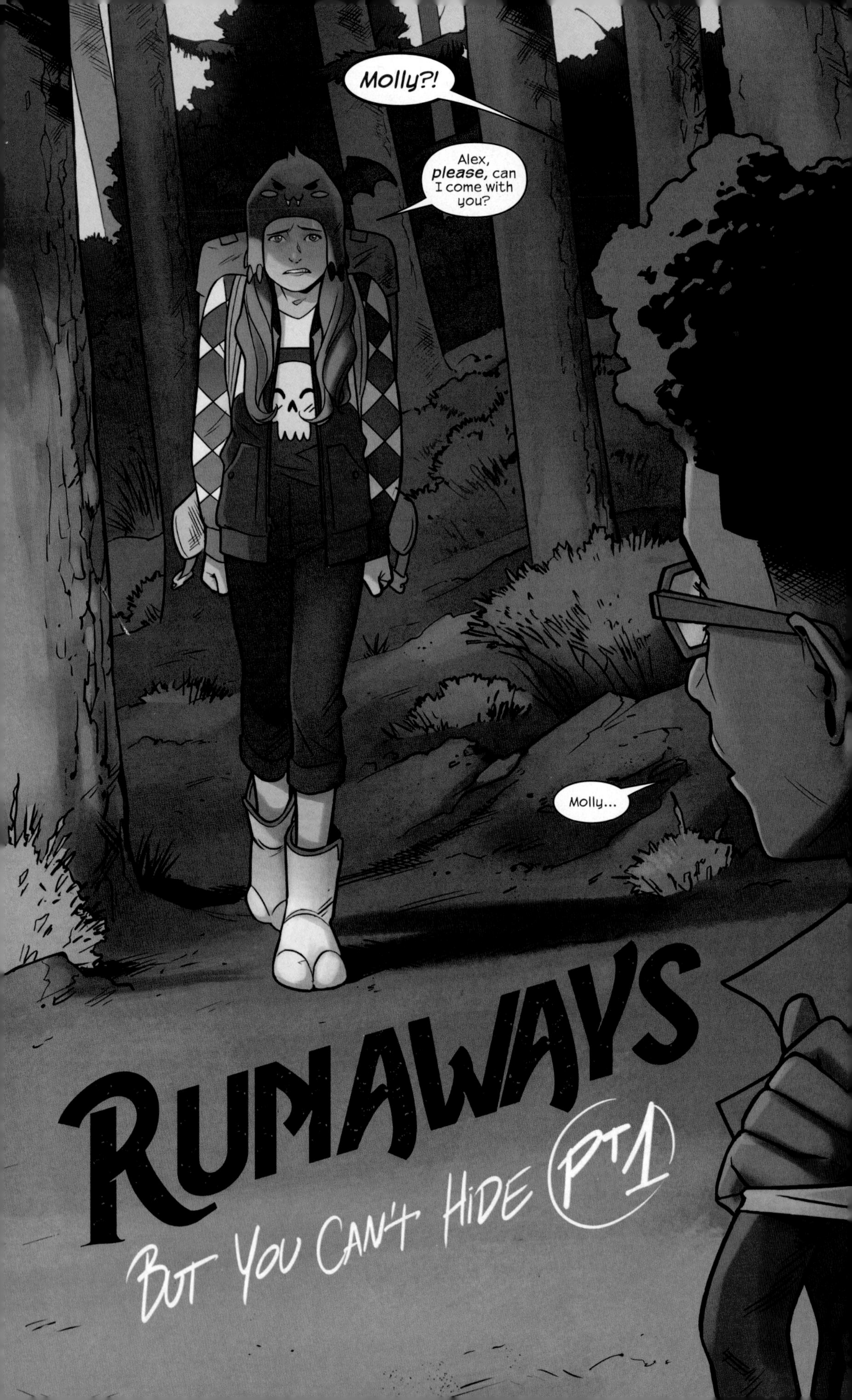
Molly?!
Alex, please, can I come with you?
Molly...
RUNAWAYS
BUT YOU CAN'T HIDE PT 1

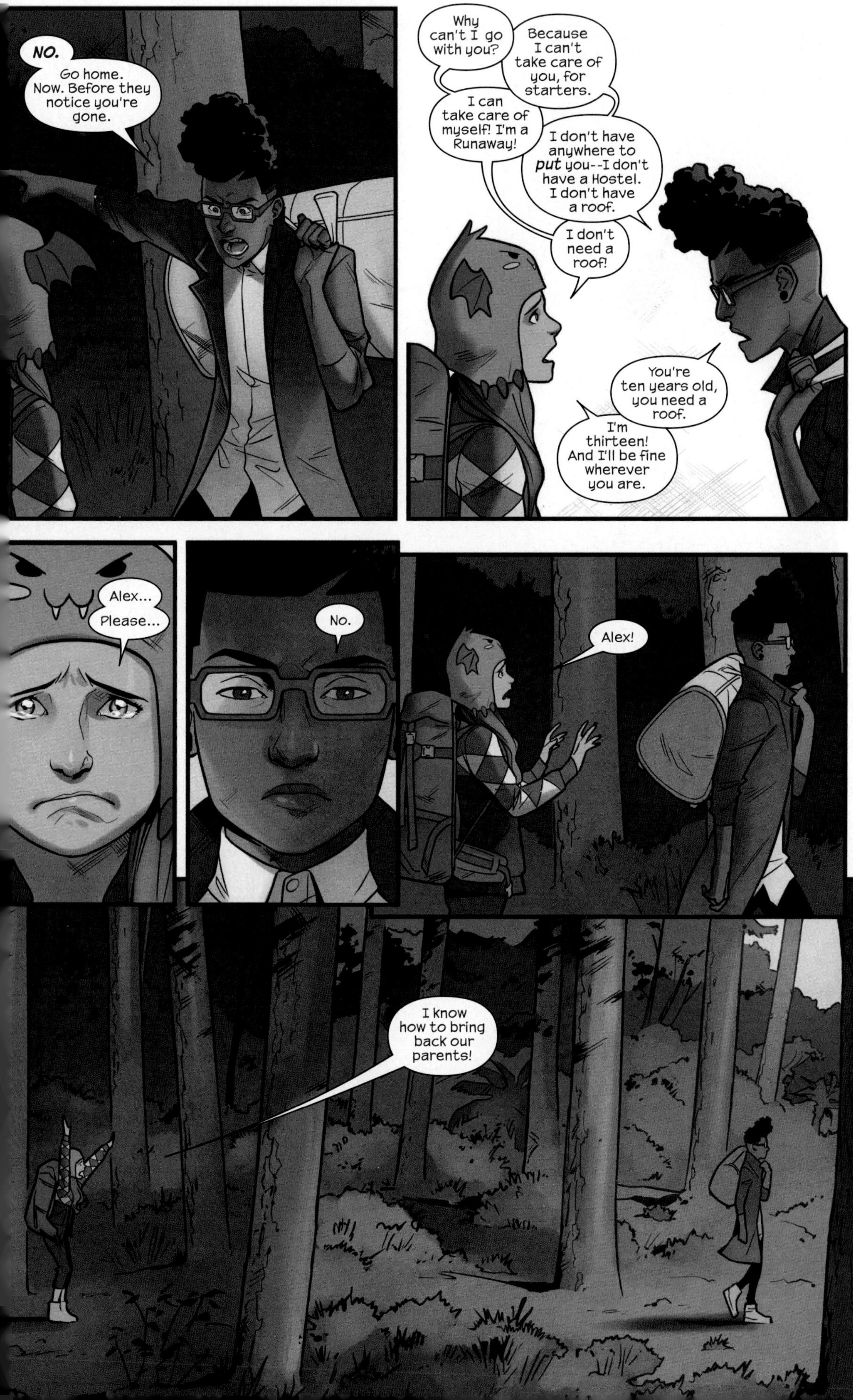
NO.
Go home. Now. Before they notice you're gone.
Why can't I go with you?
Because I can't take care of you, for starters.
I can take care of myself! I'm a Runaway!
I don't have anywhere to *put* you--I don't have a Hostel. I don't have a roof.
I don't need a roof!
You're ten years old, you need a roof.
I'm thirteen! And I'll be fine wherever you are.
Alex... Please...
No.
Alex!
I know how to bring back our parents!

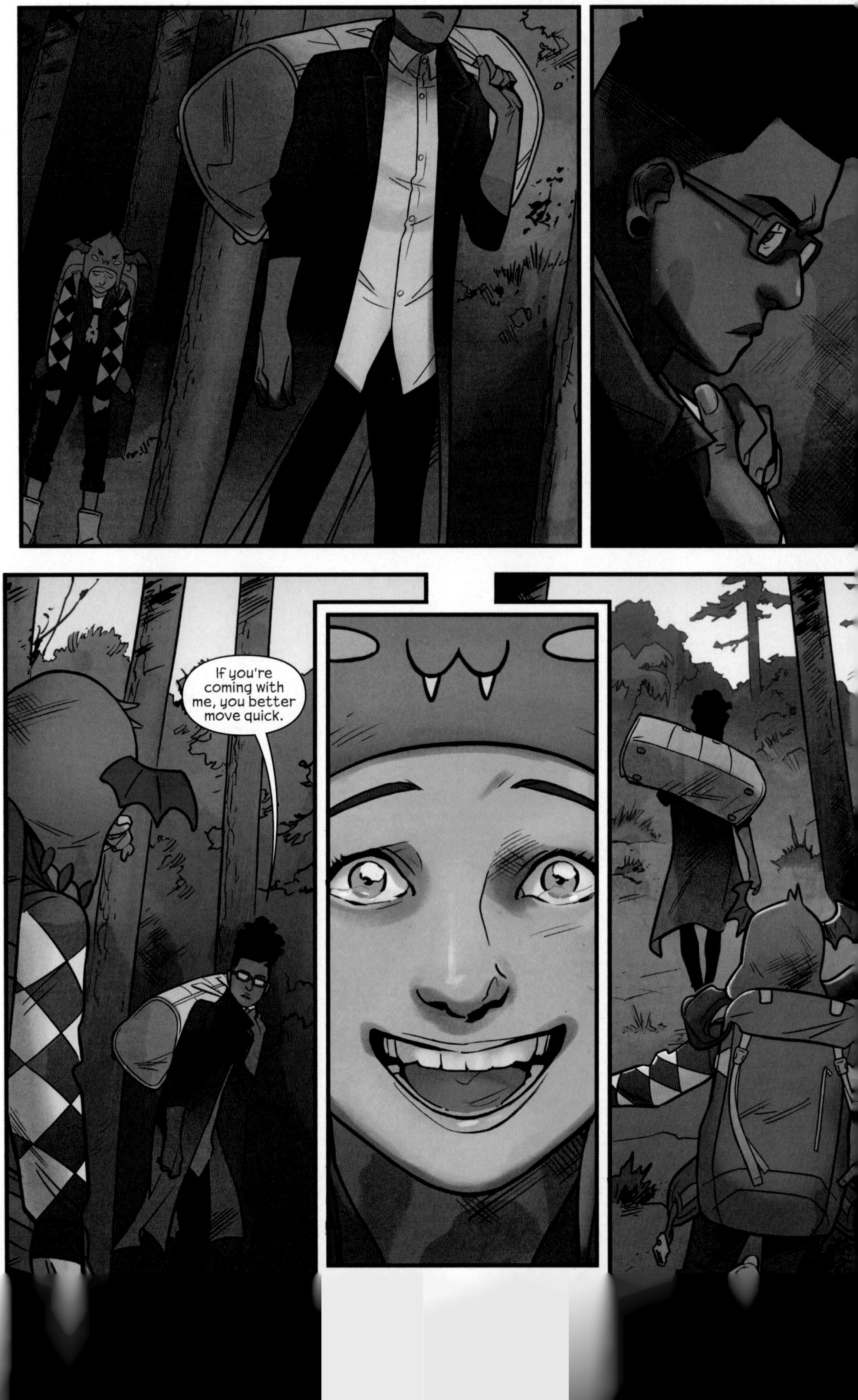
If you're coming with me, you better move quick.

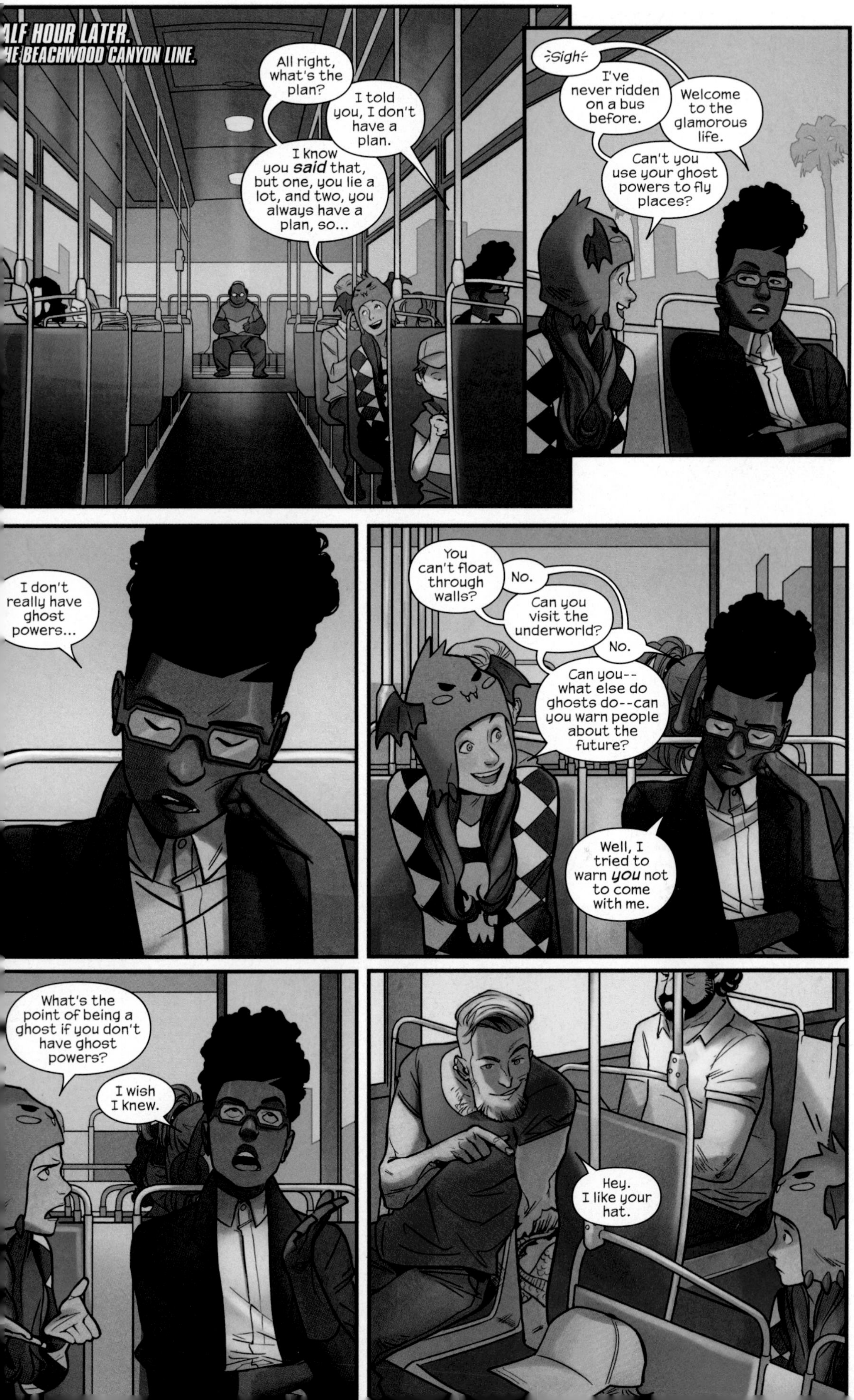
ALF HOUR LATER.
HE BEACHWOOD CANYON LINE.
All right, what's the plan?
I told you, I don't have a plan.
I know you *said* that, but one, you lie a lot, and two, you always have a plan, so...
-Sigh-
I've never ridden on a bus before.
Welcome to the glamorous life.
Can't you use your ghost powers to fly places?
I don't really have ghost powers...
You can't float through walls?
No.
Can you visit the underworld?
No.
Can you-- what else do ghosts do--can you warn people about the future?
Well, I tried to warn *you* not to come with me.
What's the point of being a ghost if you don't have ghost powers?
I wish I knew.
Hey. I like your hat.

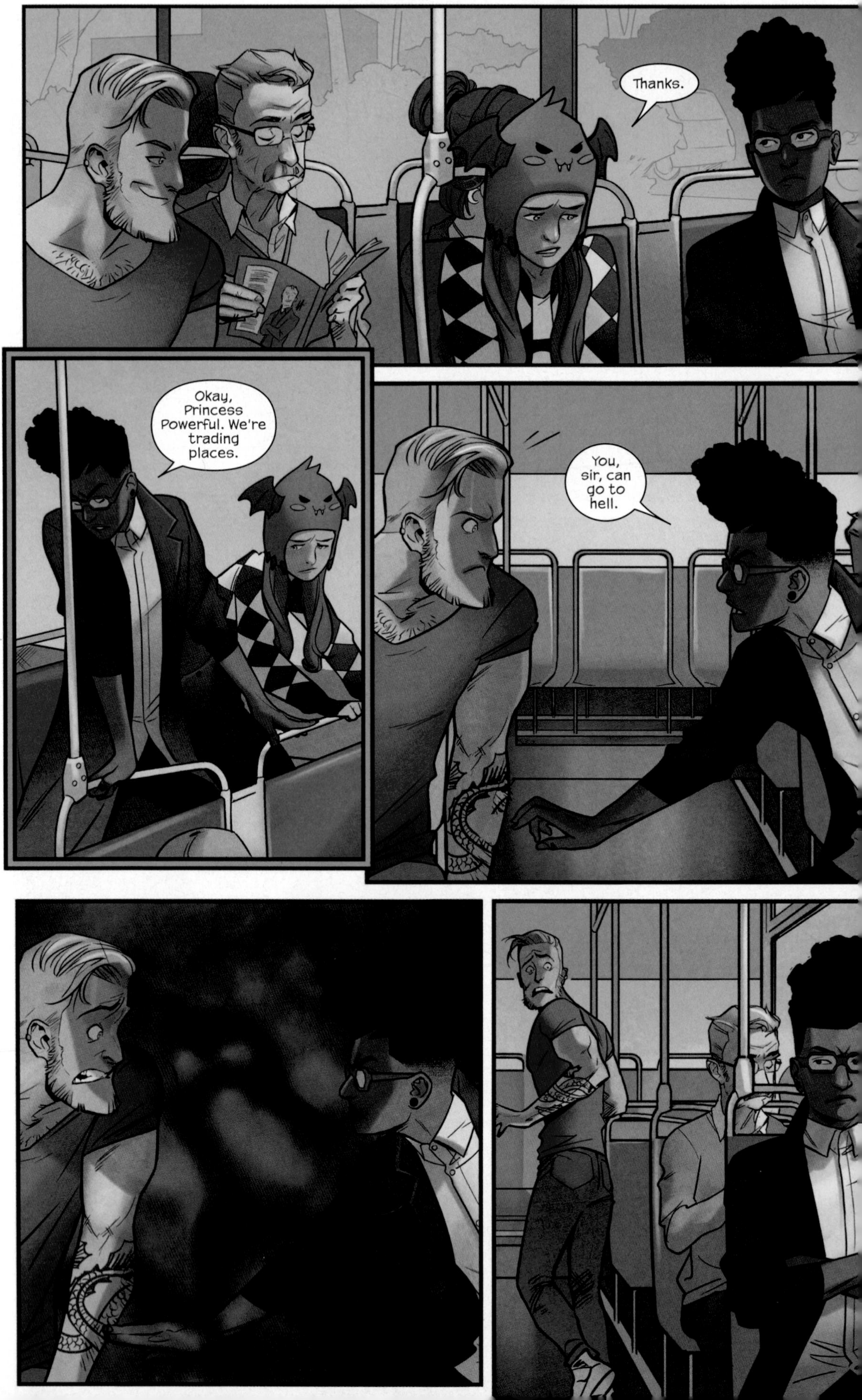
Thanks.
Okay, Princess Powerful. We're trading places.
You, sir, can go to hell.

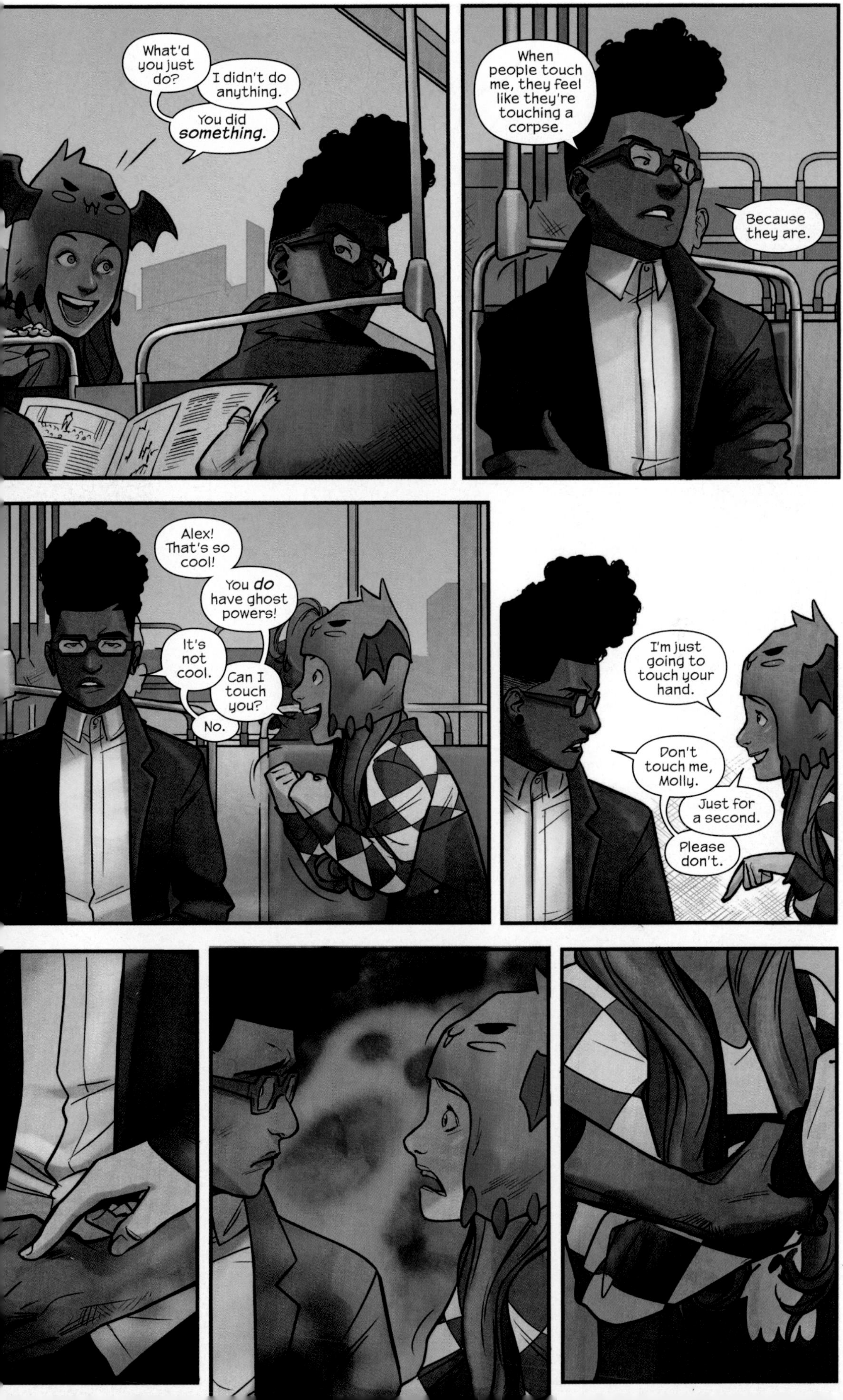
What'd you just do?
I didn't do anything.
You did *something.*
When people touch me, they feel like they're touching a corpse.
Because they are.
Alex! That's so cool!
You *do* have ghost powers!
It's not cool.
Can I touch you?
No.
I'm just going to touch your hand.
Don't touch me, Molly.
Just for a second.
Please don't.

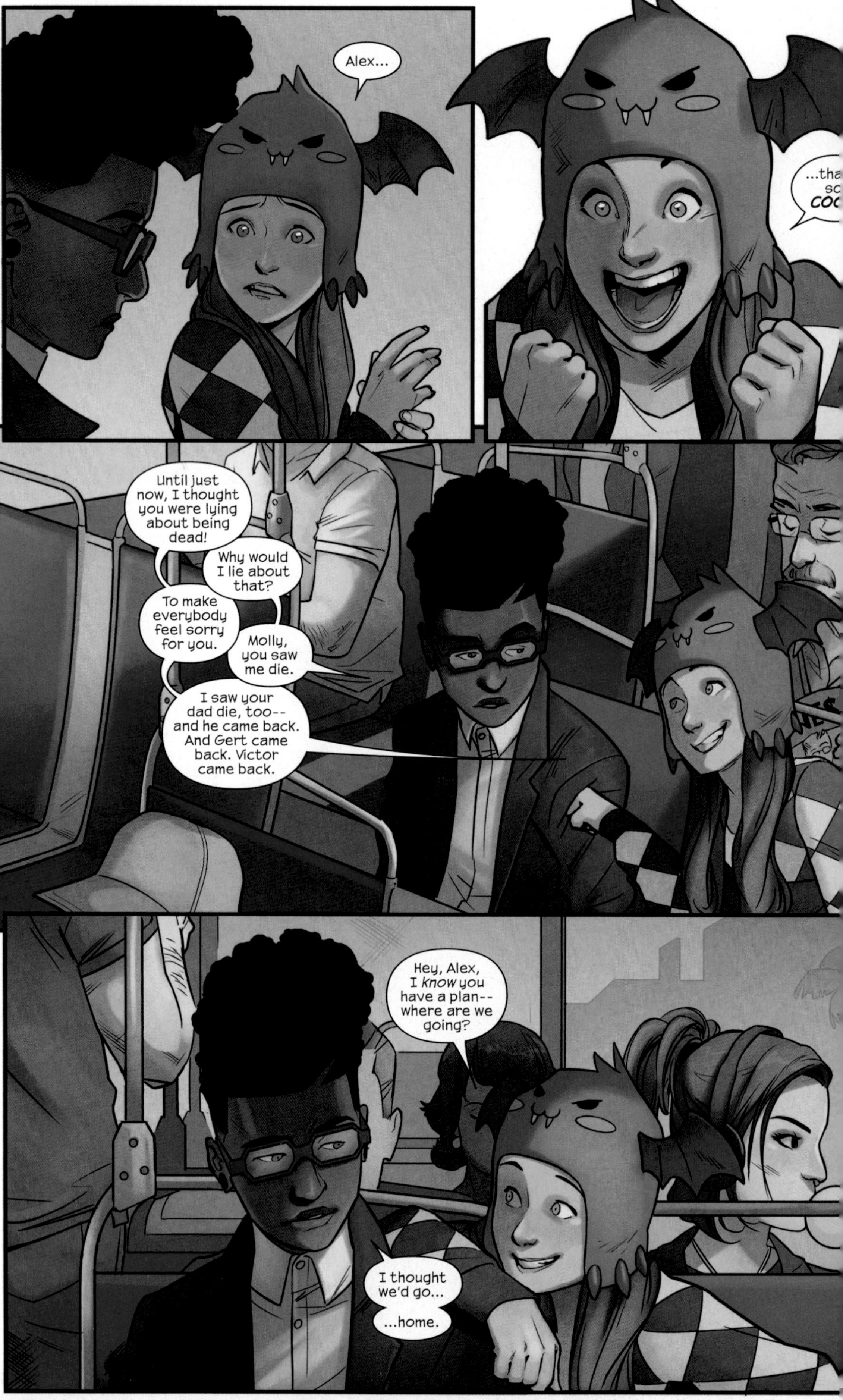
Alex...
Until just now, I thought you were lying about being dead!
Why would I lie about that?
To make everybody feel sorry for you.
Molly, you saw me die.
I saw your dad die, too-- and he came back. And Gert came back. Victor came back.
Hey, Alex, I *know* you have a plan-- where are we going?
I thought we'd go...
...home.

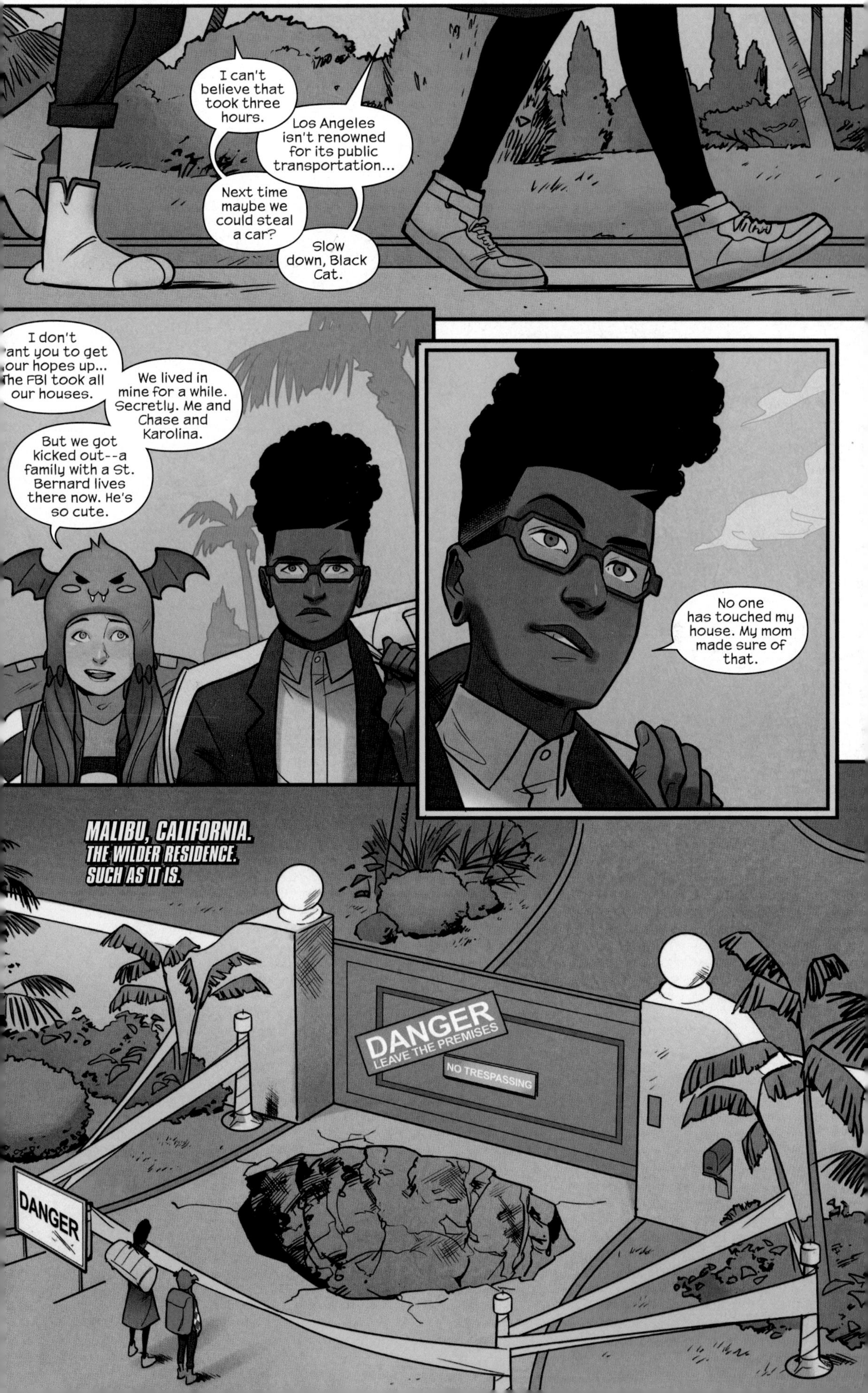
I can't believe that took three hours.
Los Angeles isn't renowned for its public transportation...
Next time maybe we could steal a car?
Slow down, Black Cat.
I don't ant you to get our hopes up... The FBI took all our houses.
We lived in mine for a while. Secretly. Me and Chase and Karolina.
But we got kicked out--a family with a St. Bernard lives there now. He's so cute.
No one has touched my house. My mom made sure of that.
MALIBU, CALIFORNIA.
THE WILDER RESIDENCE.
SUCH AS IT IS.
DANGER
LEAVE THE PREMISES
NO TRESPASSING
DANGER

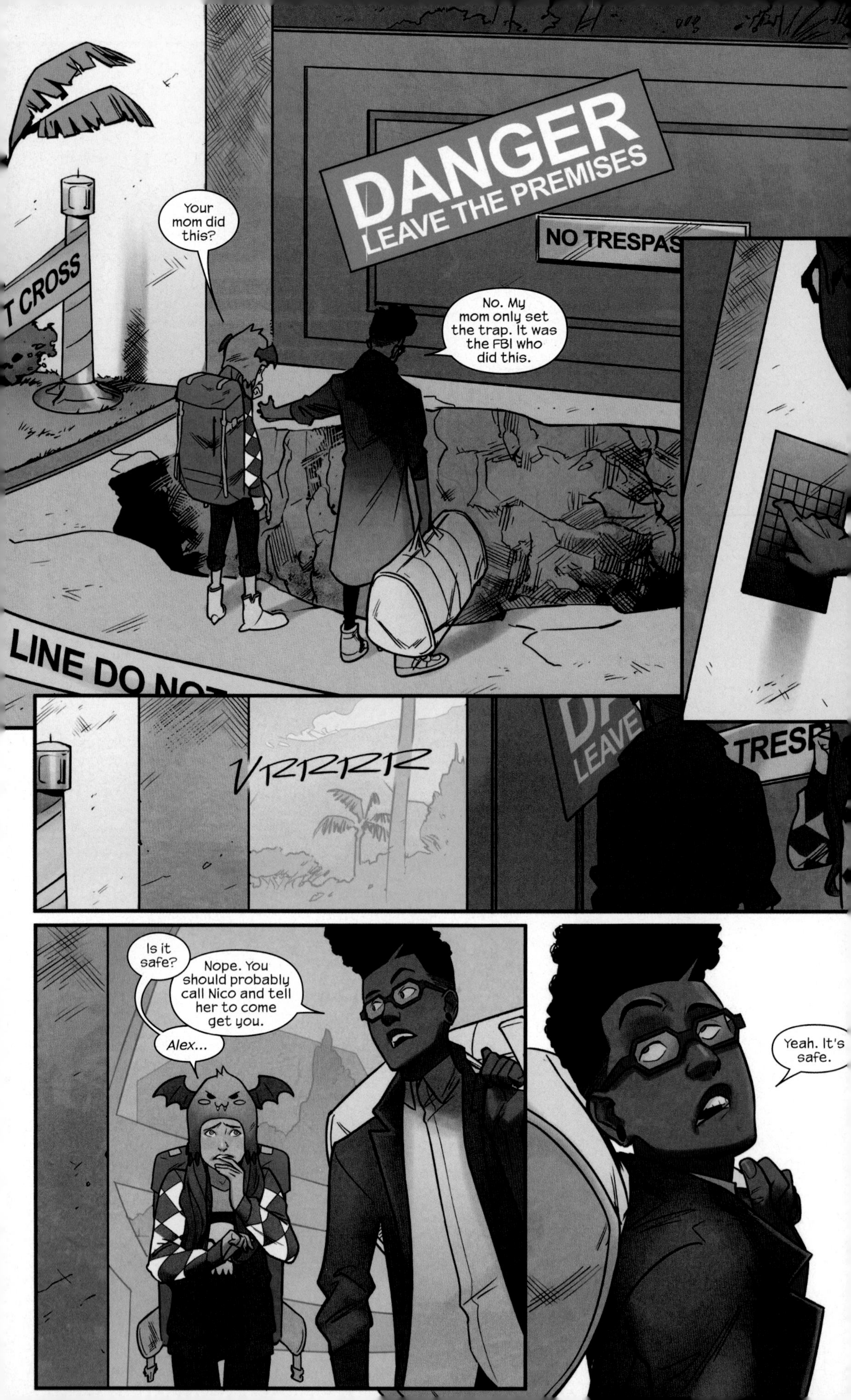

DANGER
LEAVE THE PREMISES
NO TRESPAS
T CROSS
Your mom did this?
No. My mom only set the trap. It was the FBI who did this.
LINE DO NOT
VRRRR
LEAVE
TRESP
Is it safe?
Nope. You should probably call Nico and tell her to come get you.
Alex...
Yeah. It's safe.

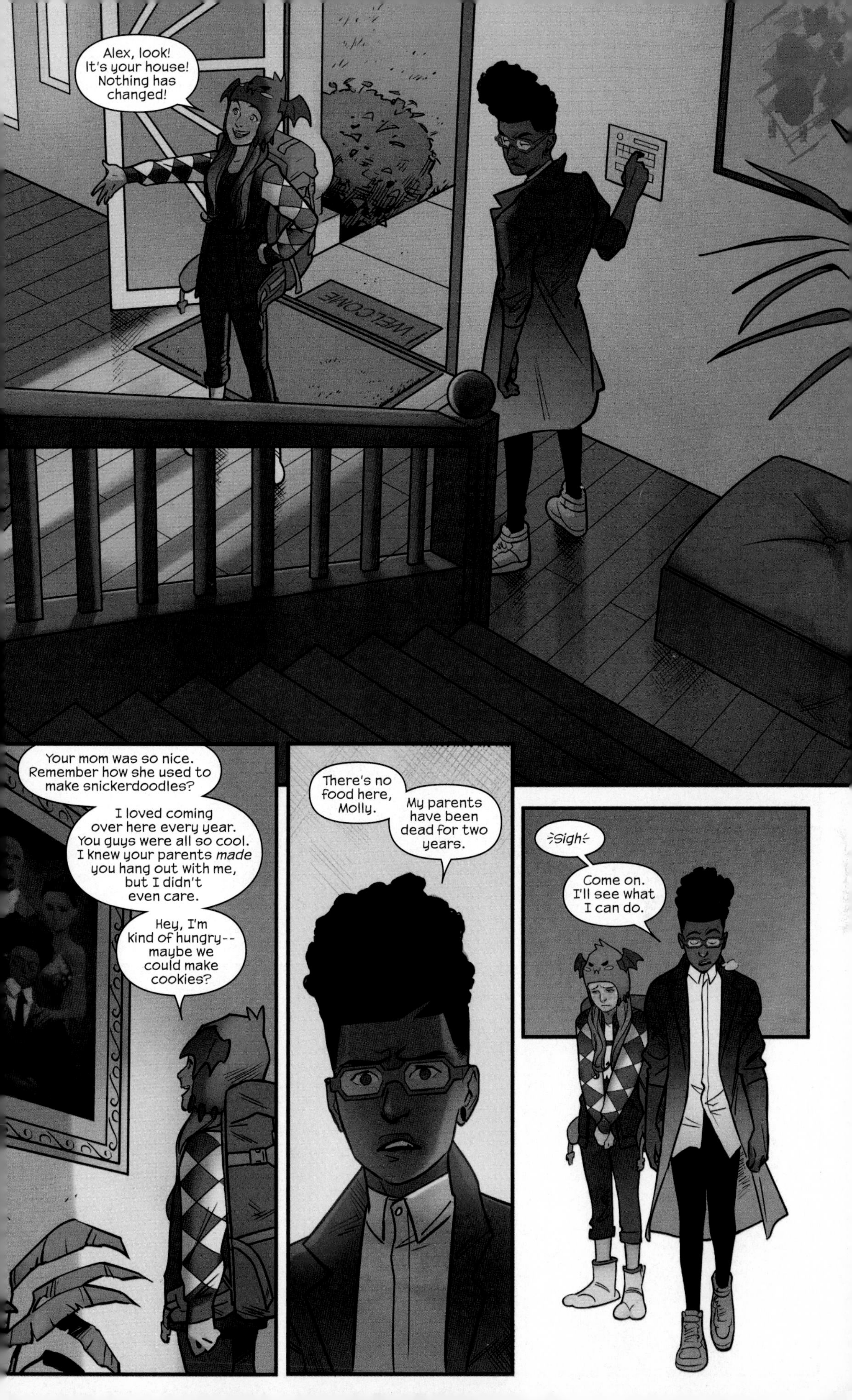
Alex, look! It's your house! Nothing has changed!
WELCOME
Your mom was so nice. Remember how she used to make snickerdoodles?
I loved coming over here every year. You guys were all so cool. I knew your parents *made* you hang out with me, but I didn't even care.
Hey, I'm kind of hungry--maybe we could make cookies?
There's no food here, Molly.
My parents have been dead for two years.
Sigh
Come on. I'll see what I can do.

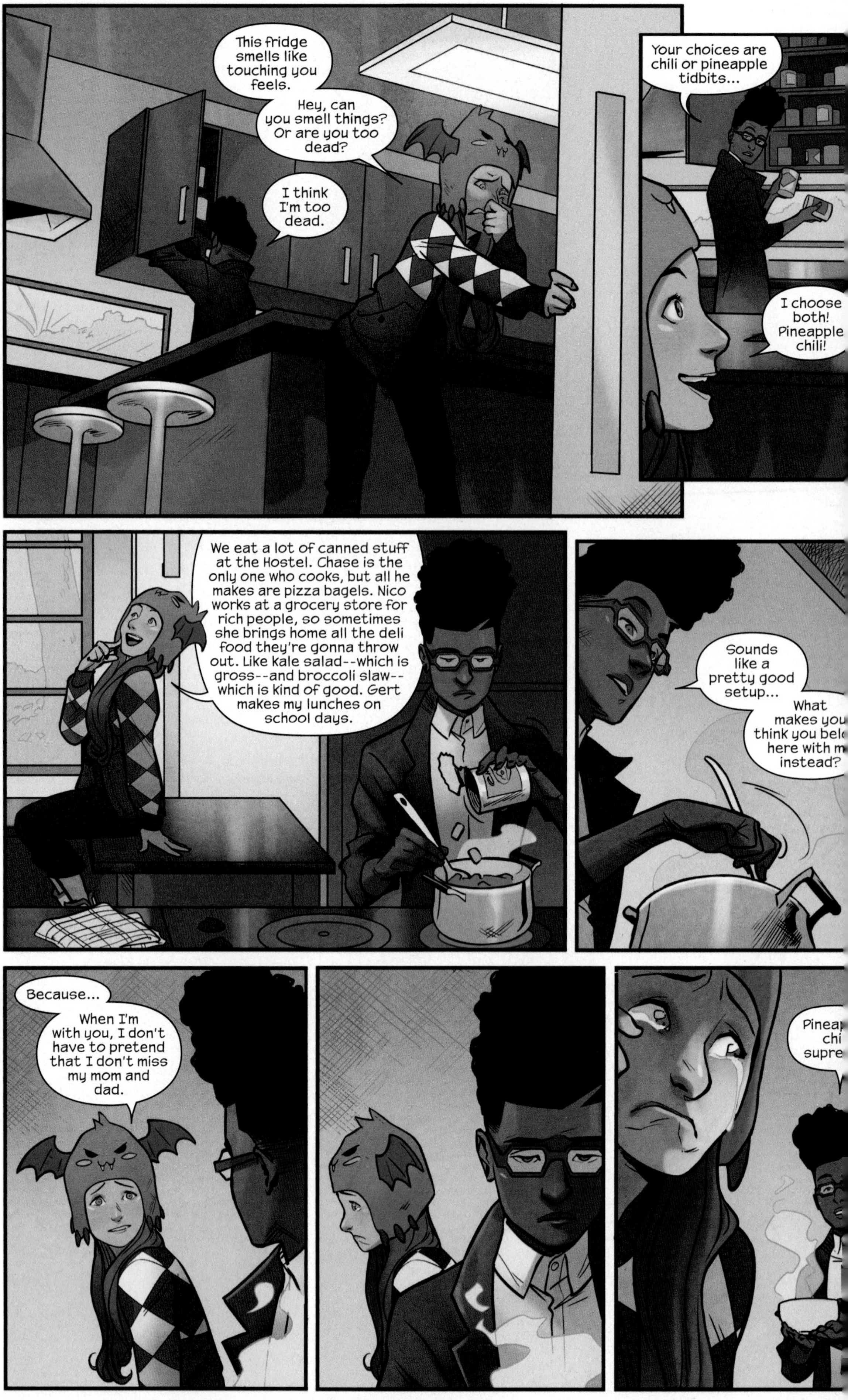
This fridge smells like touching you feels.
Hey, can you smell things? Or are you too dead?
I think I'm too dead.
Your choices are chili or pineapple tidbits...
I choose both! Pineapple chili!
We eat a lot of canned stuff at the Hostel. Chase is the only one who cooks, but all he makes are pizza bagels. Nico works at a grocery store for rich people, so sometimes she brings home all the deli food they're gonna throw out. Like kale salad--which is gross--and broccoli slaw--which is kind of good. Gert makes my lunches on school days.
Sounds like a pretty good setup...
What makes you think you bel here with m instead?
Because...
When I'm with you, I don't have to pretend that I don't miss my mom and dad.
Pinea chi supre

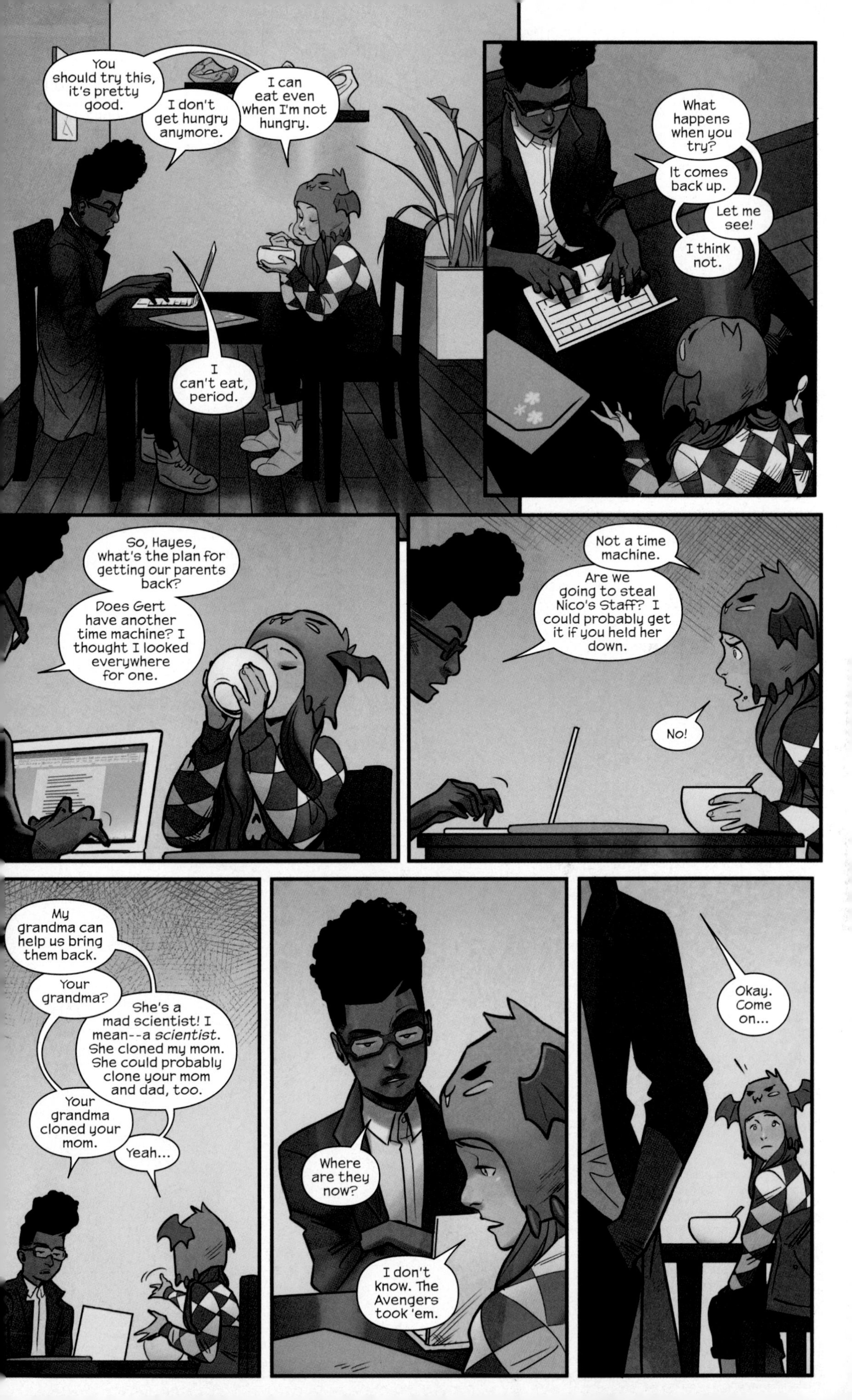
You should try this, it's pretty good.
I don't get hungry anymore.
I can eat even when I'm not hungry.
I can't eat, period.
What happens when you try?
It comes back up.
Let me see!
I think not.
So, Hayes, what's the plan for getting our parents back?
Does Gert have another time machine? I thought I looked everywhere for one.
Not a time machine.
Are we going to steal Nico's Staff? I could probably get it if you held her down.
No!
My grandma can help us bring them back.
Your grandma?
She's a mad scientist! I mean--a *scientist*. She cloned my mom. She could probably clone your mom and dad, too.
Your grandma cloned your mom.
Yeah...
Where are they now?
I don't know. The Avengers took 'em.
Okay. Come on...

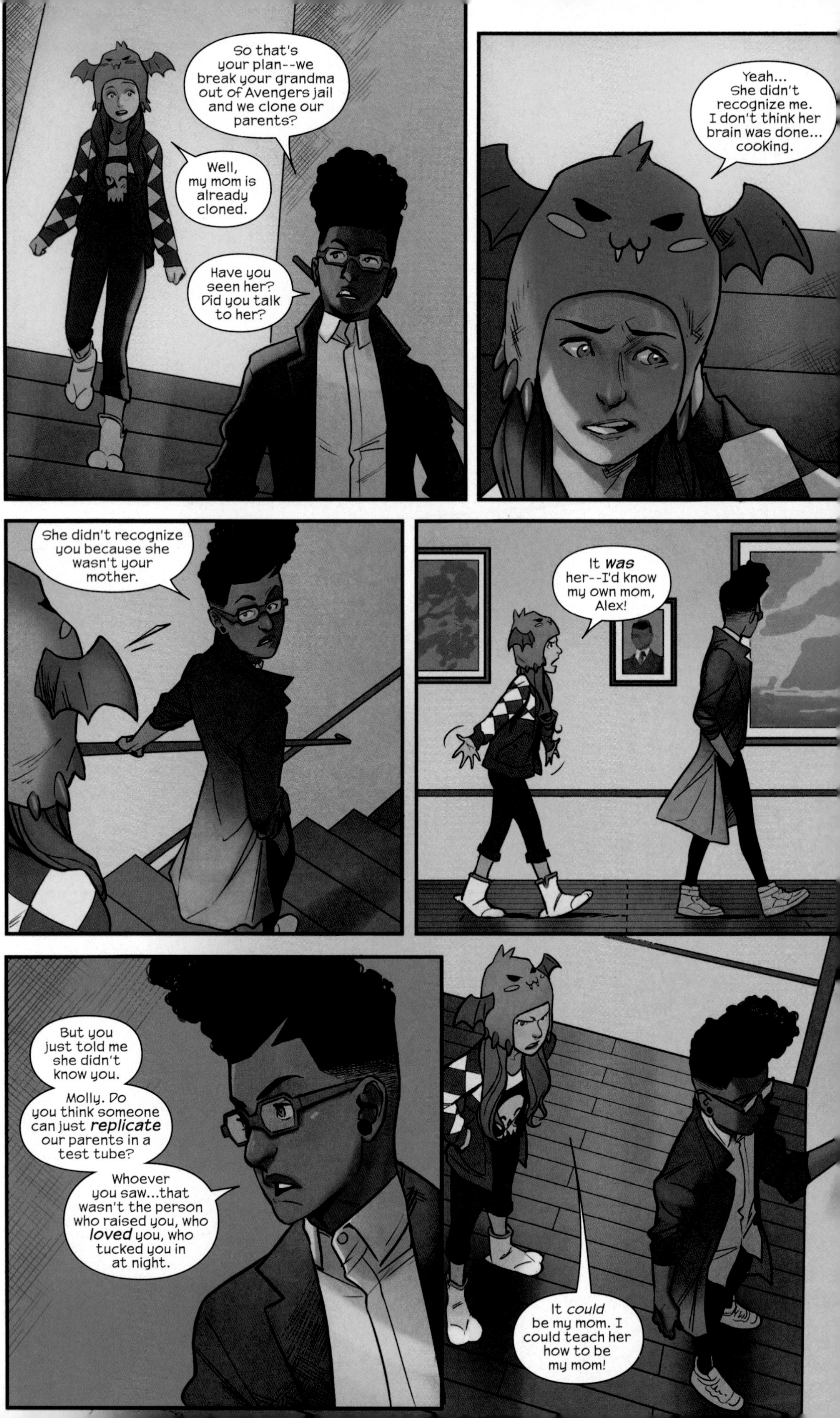
So that's your plan--we break your grandma out of Avengers jail and we clone our parents?
Well, my mom is already cloned.
Have you seen her? Did you talk to her?
Yeah... She didn't recognize me. I don't think her brain was done... cooking.
She didn't recognize you because she wasn't your mother.
It *was* her--I'd know my own mom, Alex!
But you just told me she didn't know you.
Molly. Do you think someone can just *replicate* our parents in a test tube?
Whoever you saw...that wasn't the person who raised you, who *loved* you, who tucked you in at night.
It *could* be my mom. I could teach her how to be my mom!

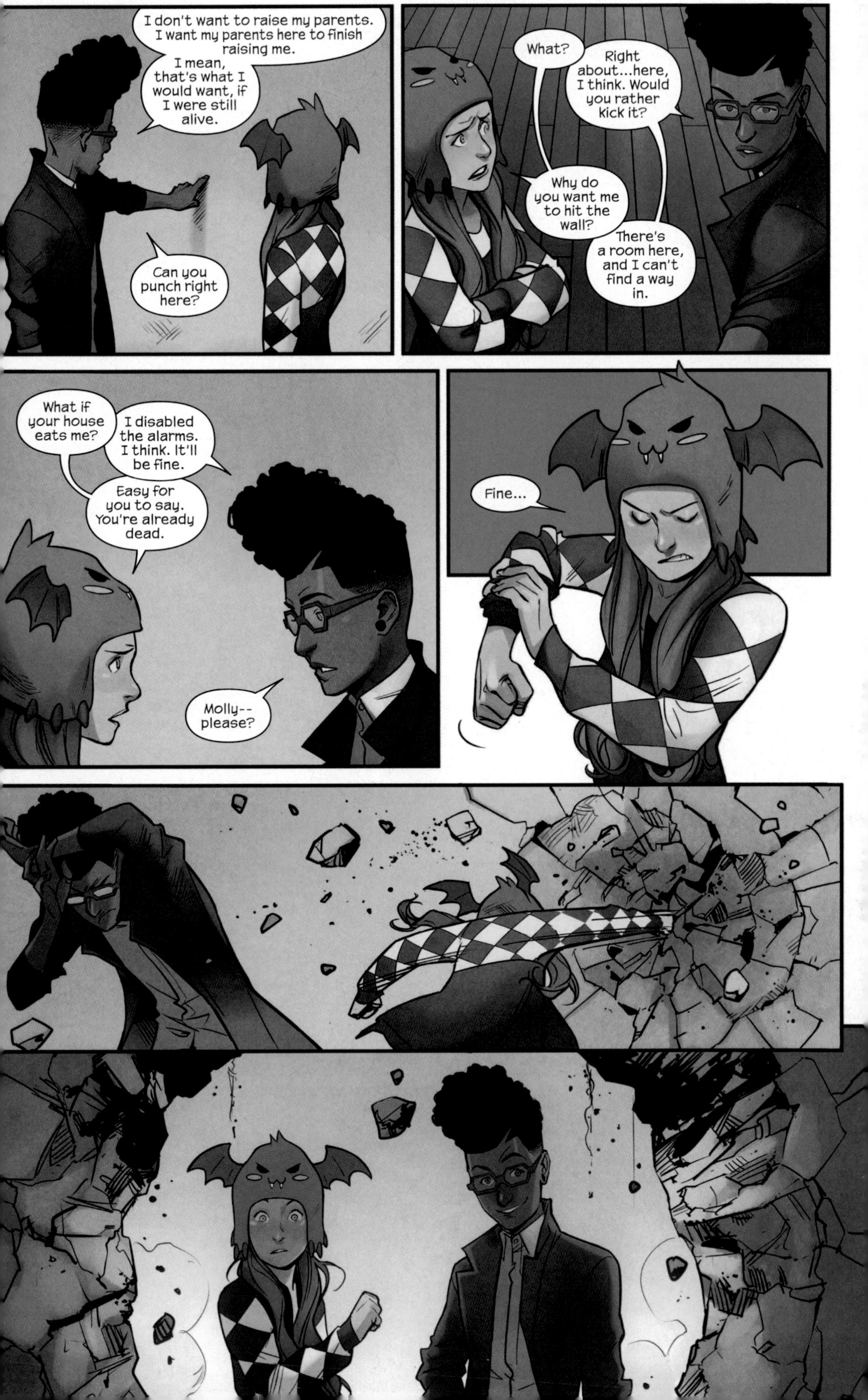
I don't want to raise my parents. I want my parents here to finish raising me.
I mean, that's what I would want, if I were still alive.
Can you punch right here?
What?
Right about...here, I think. Would you rather kick it?
Why do you want me to hit the wall?
There's a room here, and I can't find a way in.
What if your house eats me?
I disabled the alarms. I think. It'll be fine.
Easy for you to say. You're already dead.
Molly--please?
Fine...

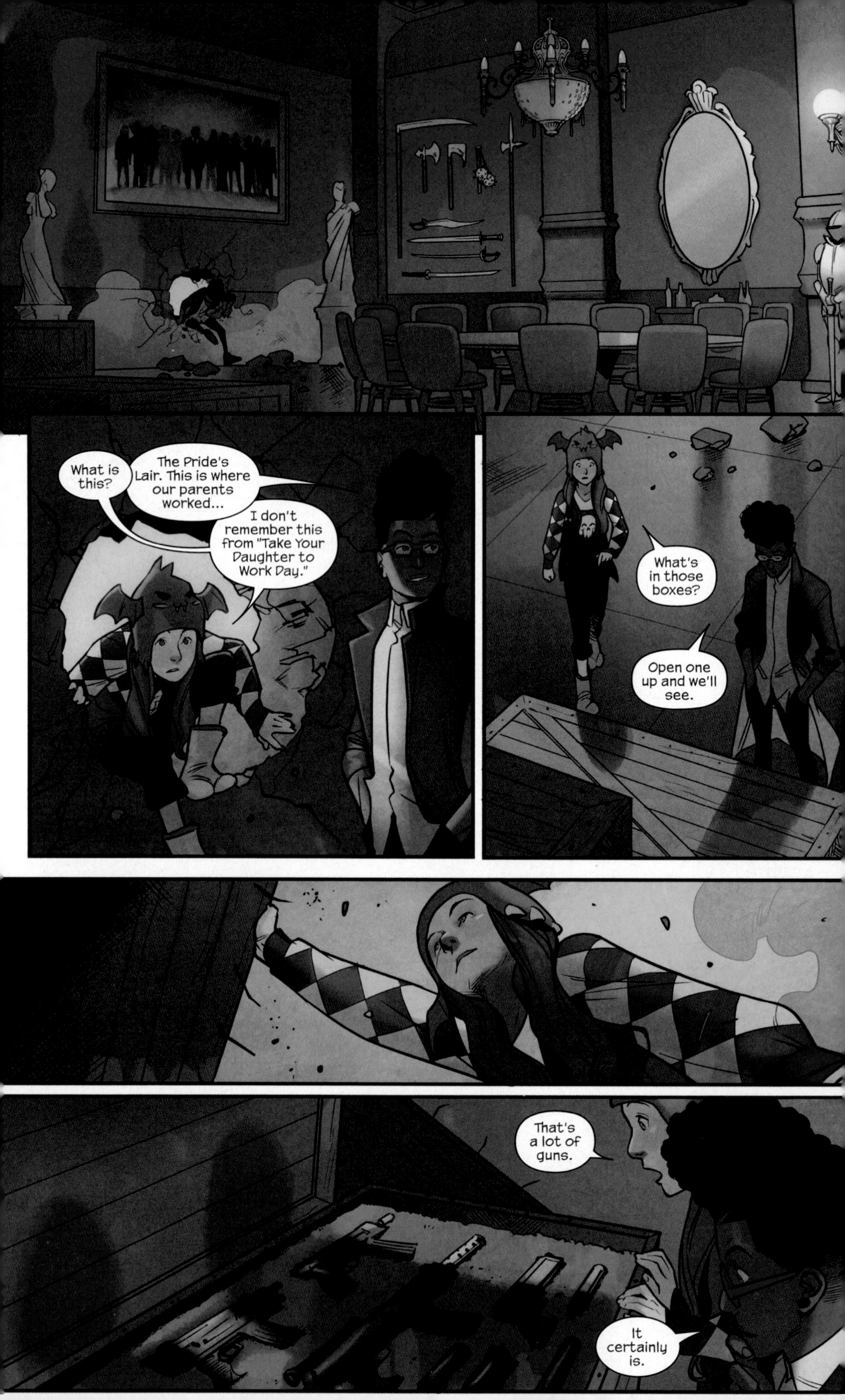
What is this?
The Pride's Lair. This is where our parents worked...
I don't remember this from "Take Your Daughter to Work Day."
What's in those boxes?
Open one up and we'll see.
That's a lot of guns.
It certainly is.

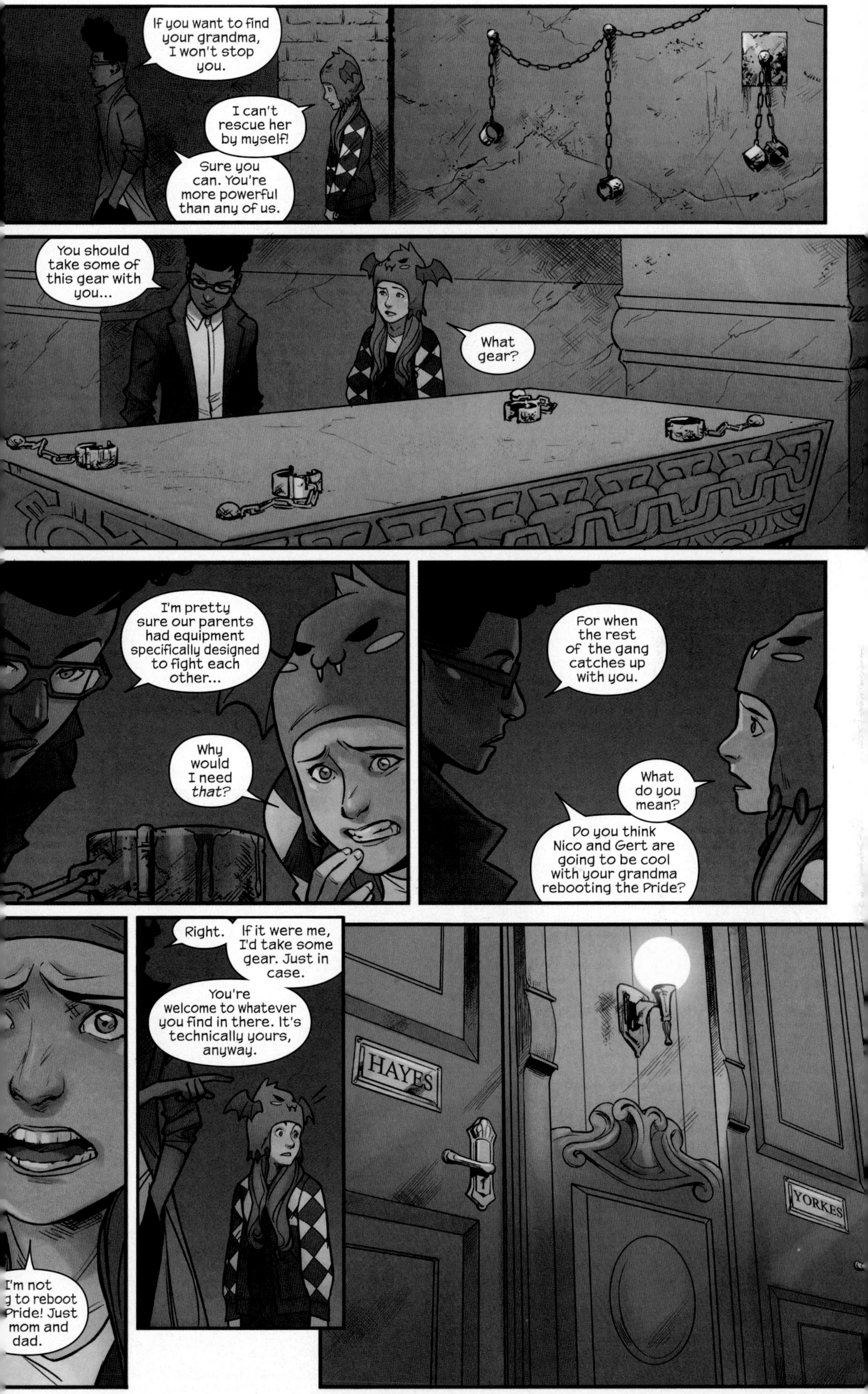
If you want to find your grandma, I won't stop you.
I can't rescue her by myself!
Sure you can. You're more powerful than any of us.
You should take some of this gear with you...
What gear?
I'm pretty sure our parents had equipment specifically designed to fight each other...
Why would I need *that*?
For when the rest of the gang catches up with you.
What do you mean?
Do you think Nico and Gert are going to be cool with your grandma rebooting the Pride?
I'm not
g to reboot
Pride! Just
mom and
dad.
Right.
If it were me, I'd take some gear. Just in case.
You're welcome to whatever you find in there. It's technically yours, anyway.
HAYES
YORKES

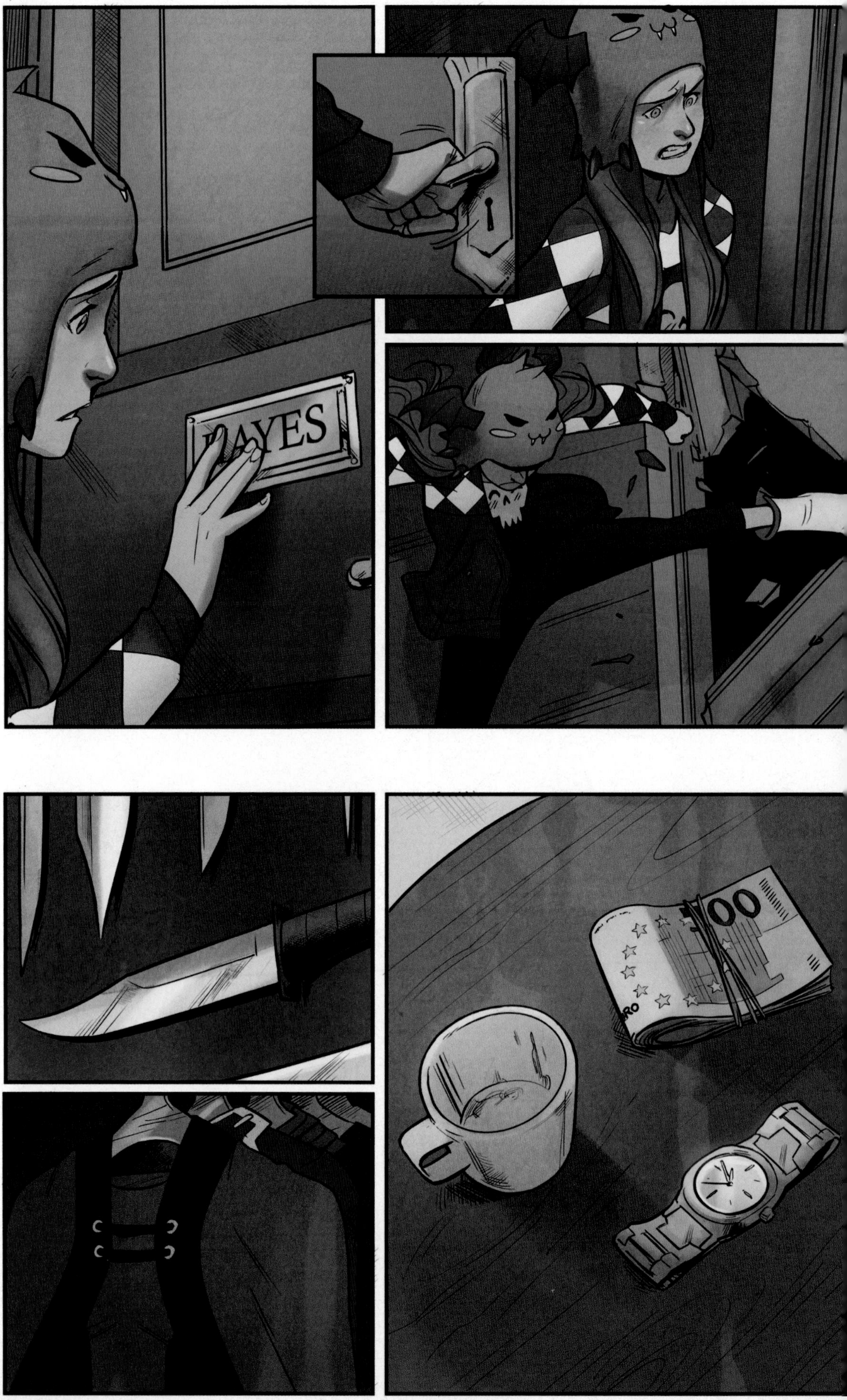

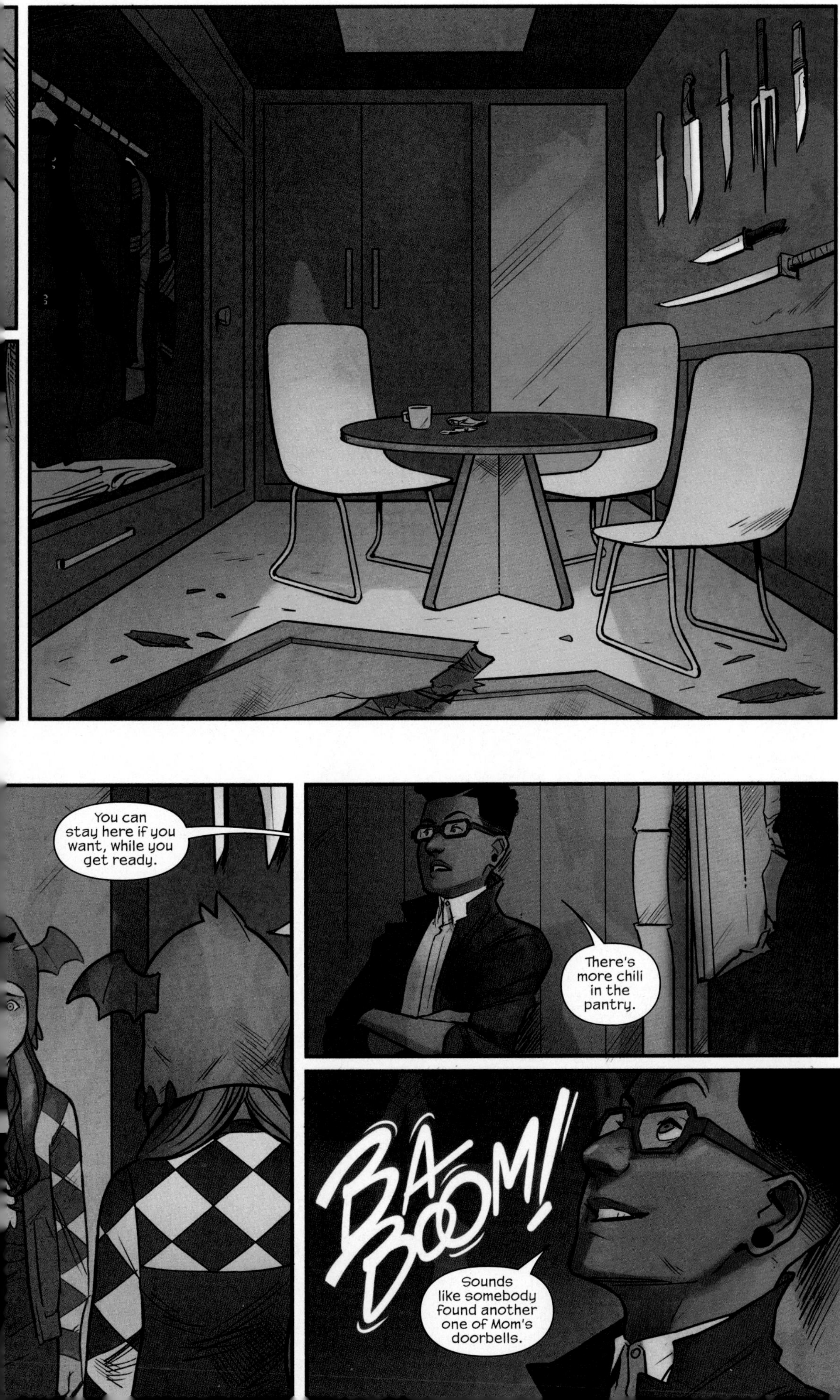

You can stay here if you want, while you get ready.
There's more chili in the pantry.
BA BOOM!
Sounds like somebody found another one of Mom's doorbells.

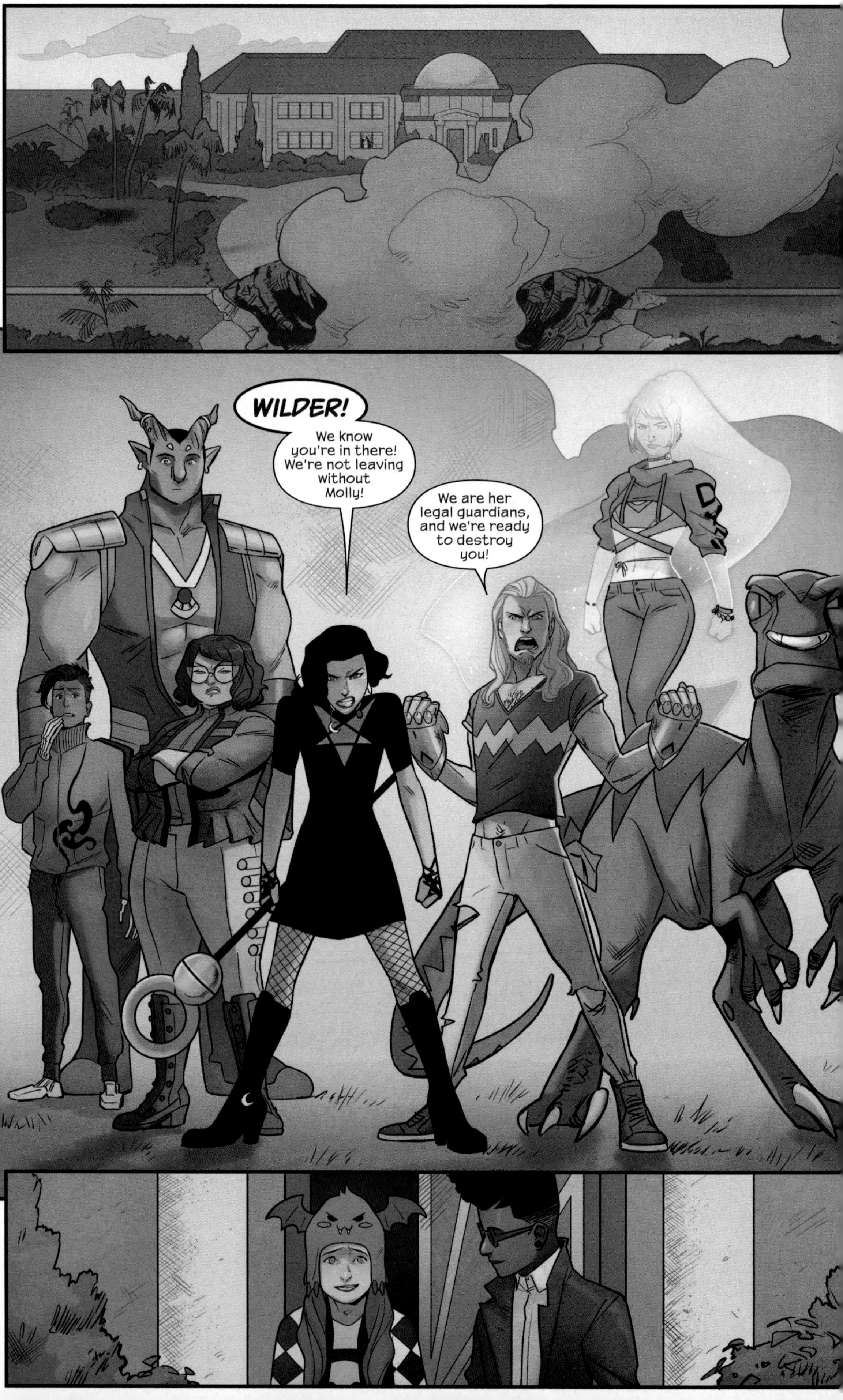
WILDER!
We know you're in there! We're not leaving without Molly!
We are her legal guardians, and we're ready to destroy you!

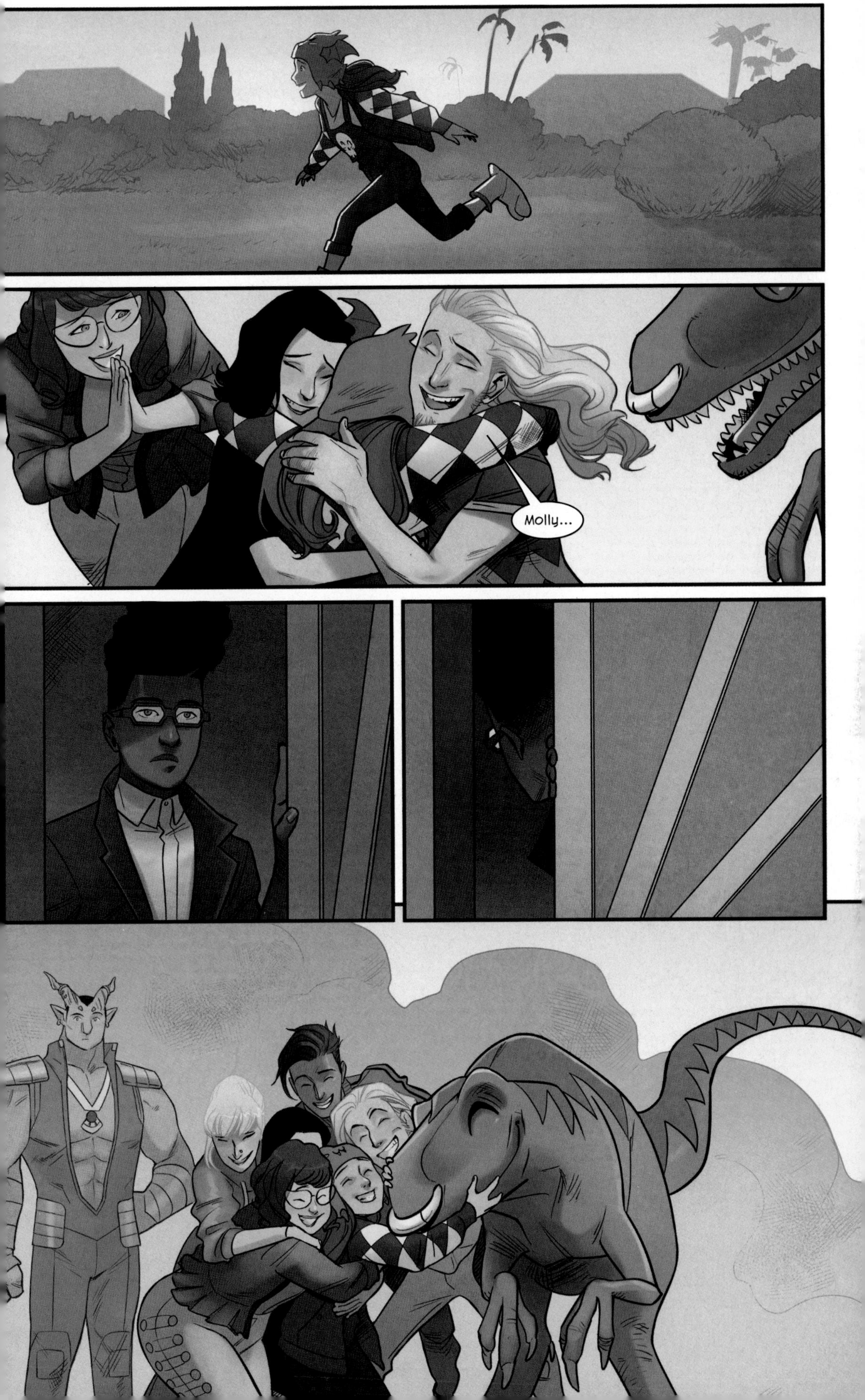
Molly...

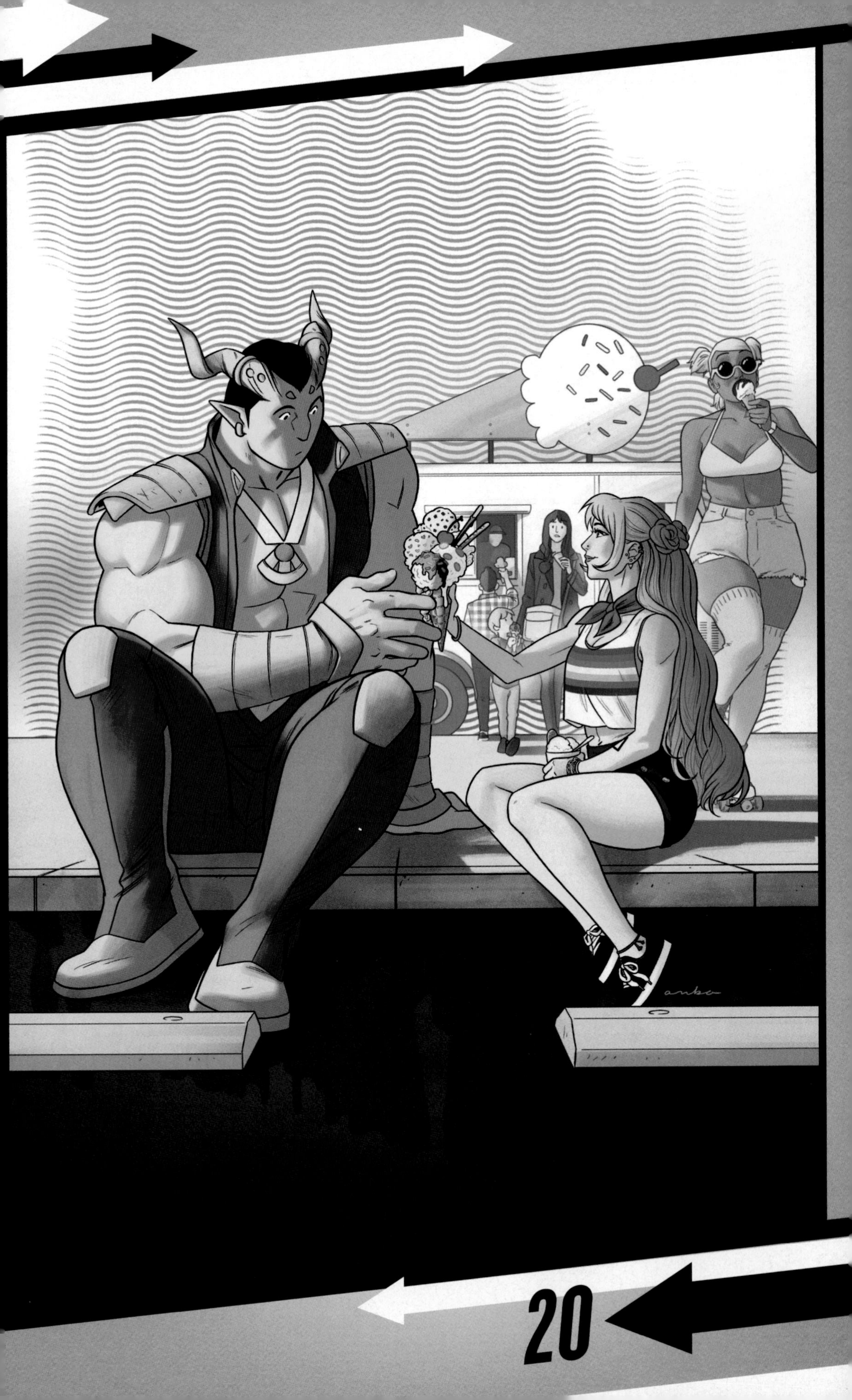
20

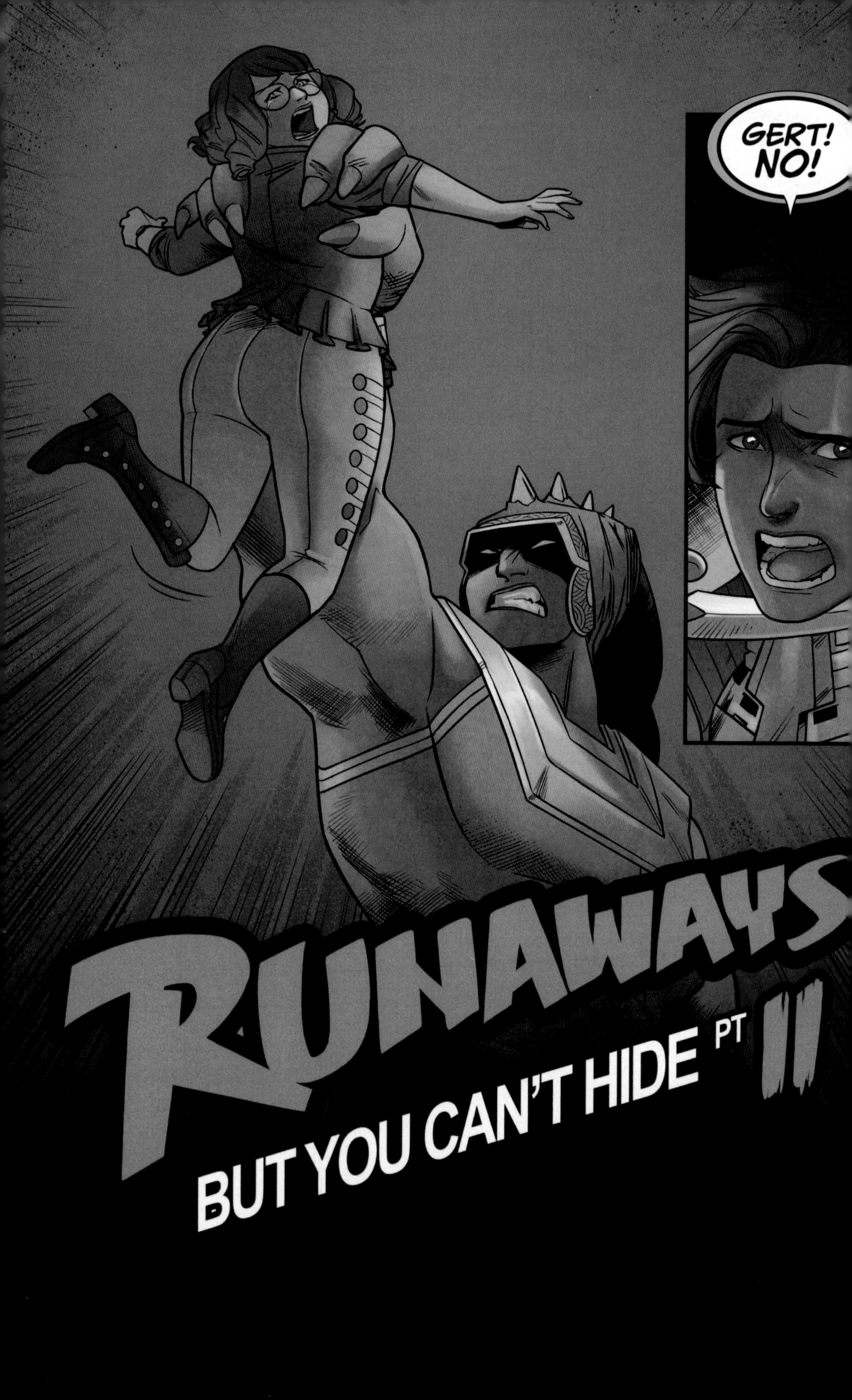
GERT! NO!
RUNAWAYS
BUT YOU CAN'T HIDE PT II

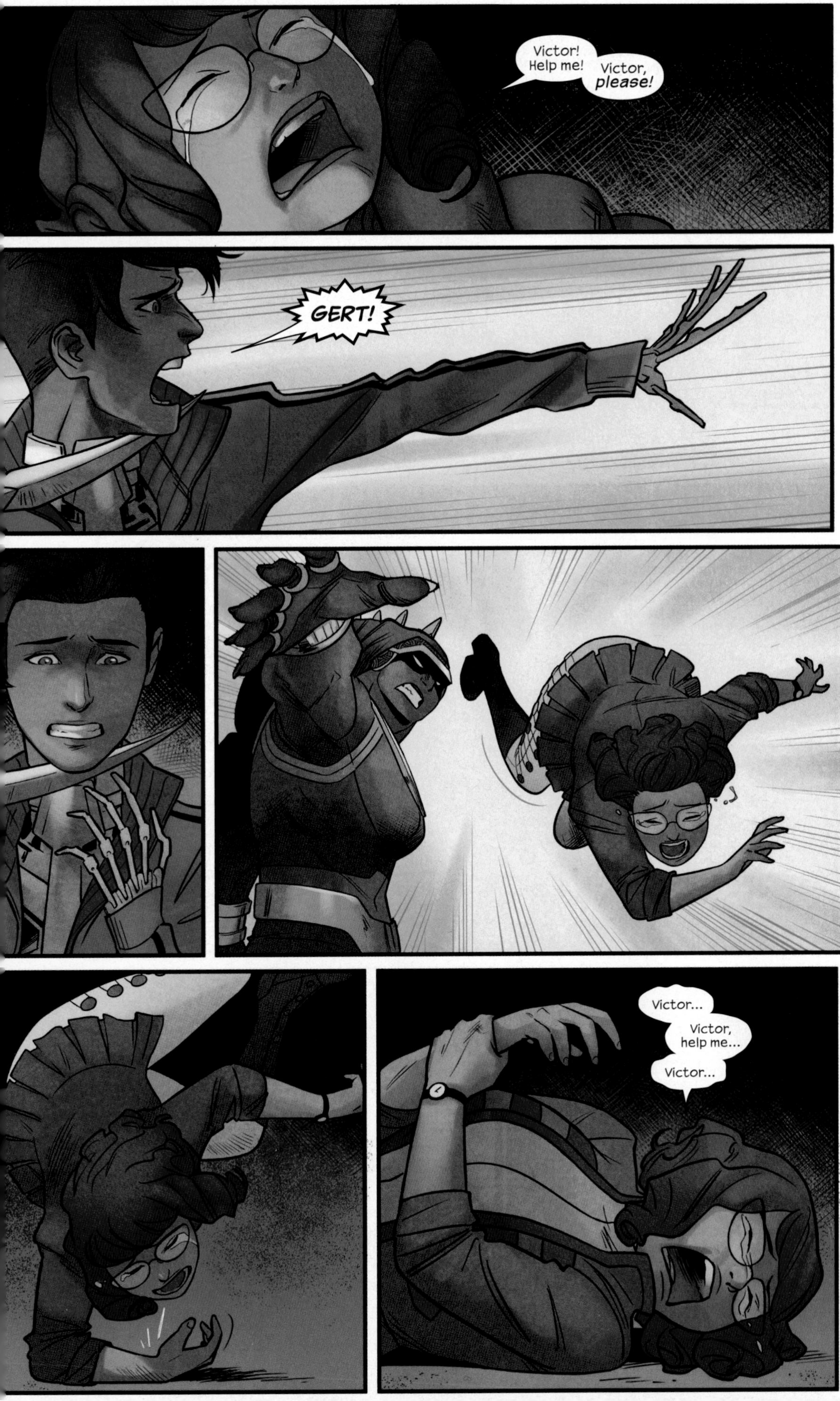

Victor! Help me!
Victor, please!
GERT!
Victor...
Victor, help me...
Victor...

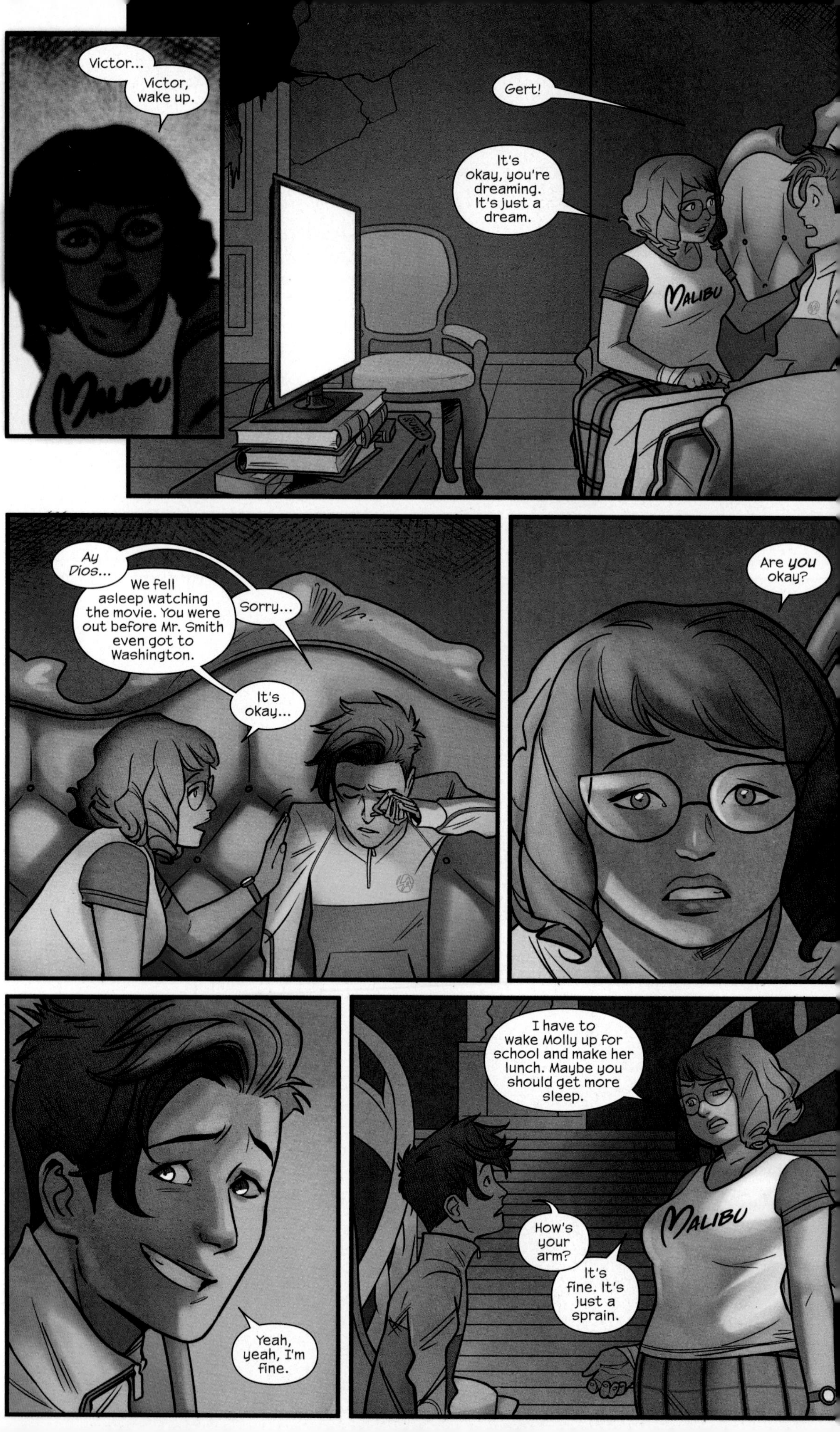

Victor...
Victor, wake up.
Gert!
It's okay, you're dreaming. It's just a dream.
Ay Dios...
We fell asleep watching the movie. You were out before Mr. Smith even got to Washington.
Sorry...
It's okay...
Are you okay?
Yeah, yeah, I'm fine.
I have to wake Molly up for school and make her lunch. Maybe you should get more sleep.
How's your arm?
It's fine. It's just a sprain.

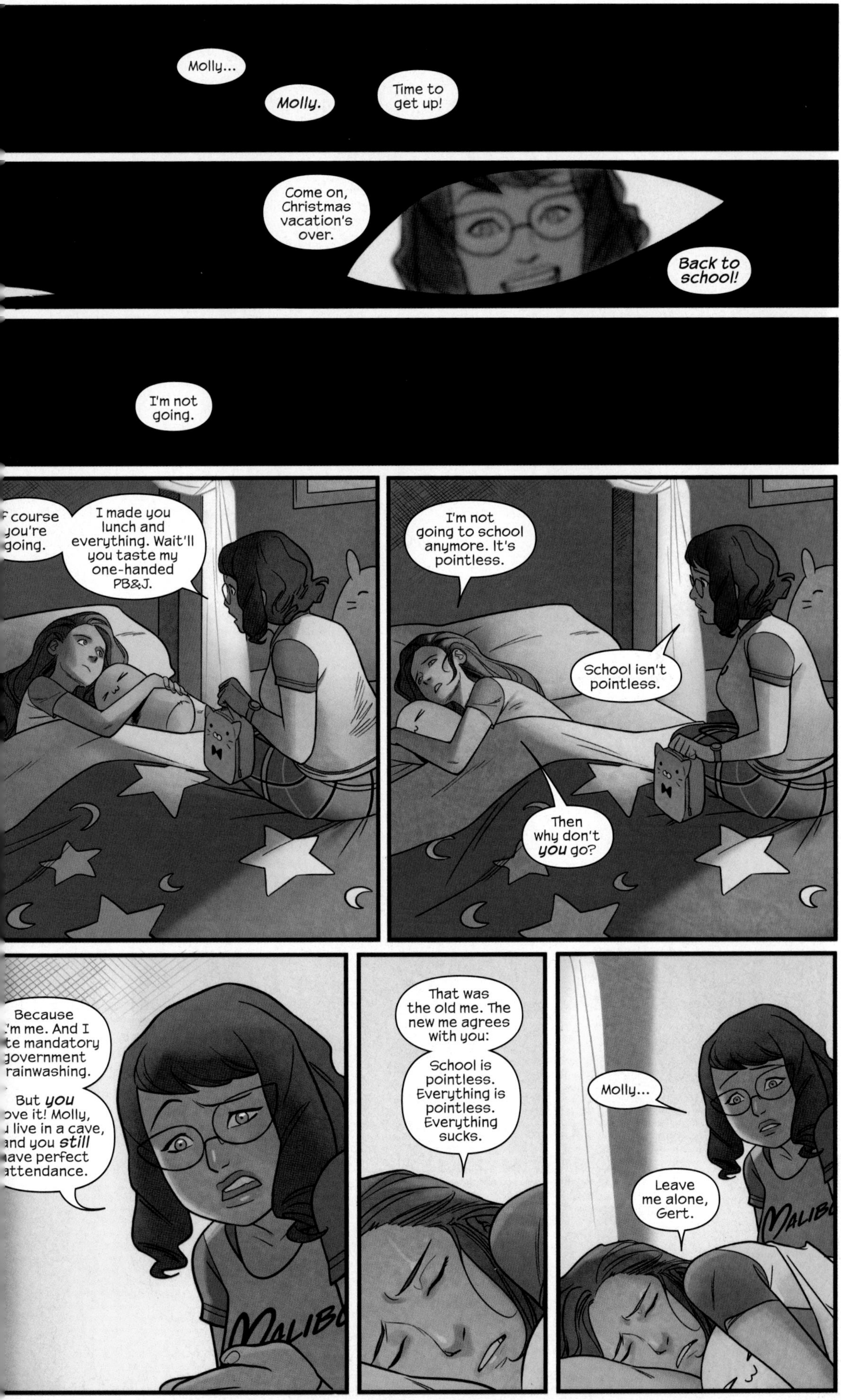

Molly...
Molly.
Time to get up!
Come on, Christmas vacation's over.
Back to school!
I'm not going.
f course you're going.
I made you lunch and everything. Wait'll you taste my one-handed PB&J.
I'm not going to school anymore. It's pointless.
School isn't pointless.
Then why don't you go?
Because 'm me. And I te mandatory government rainwashing.
But you ove it! Molly, u live in a cave, and you still ave perfect attendance.
That was the old me. The new me agrees with you:
School is pointless. Everything is pointless. Everything sucks.
Molly...
Leave me alone, Gert.

MOLLY

YOW.

Gert! I'm so sorry! I'm super la... sorr...

Hey, have you talked to Molly since... *everything?* With Alex?

Yep. She told me there was nothing to talk about.

But we still don't know how he talked her into leaving with him--or what he asked her to do.

She doesn't want to talk about it.

Well, now she doesn't want to go to school.

Sounds like a normal teenager.

Yeah, but Molly's *not* a normal teenager.

So you don't think we should talk to her?

You just d... righ

Yeah, but--

Gert, when you were her age, and you were feeling down, what did *you* want?

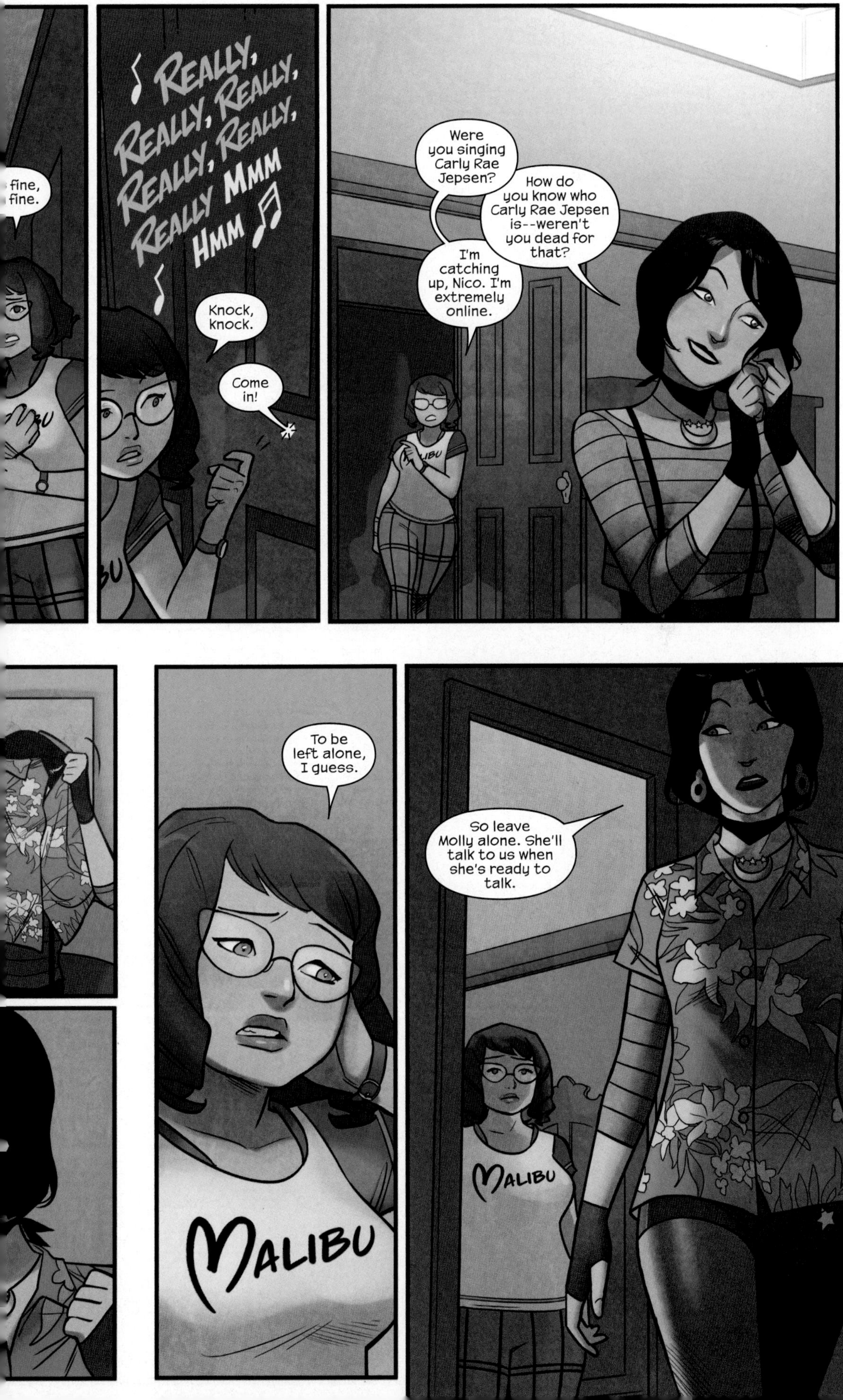
fine,
fine.
Really, Really, Really, Really, Really, Really Mmm Hmm
Knock, knock.
Come in!
Were you singing Carly Rae Jepsen?
How do you know who Carly Rae Jepsen is--weren't you dead for that?
I'm catching up, Nico. I'm extremely online.
Malibu
To be left alone, I guess.
So leave Molly alone. She'll talk to us when she's ready to talk.
Malibu
Malibu

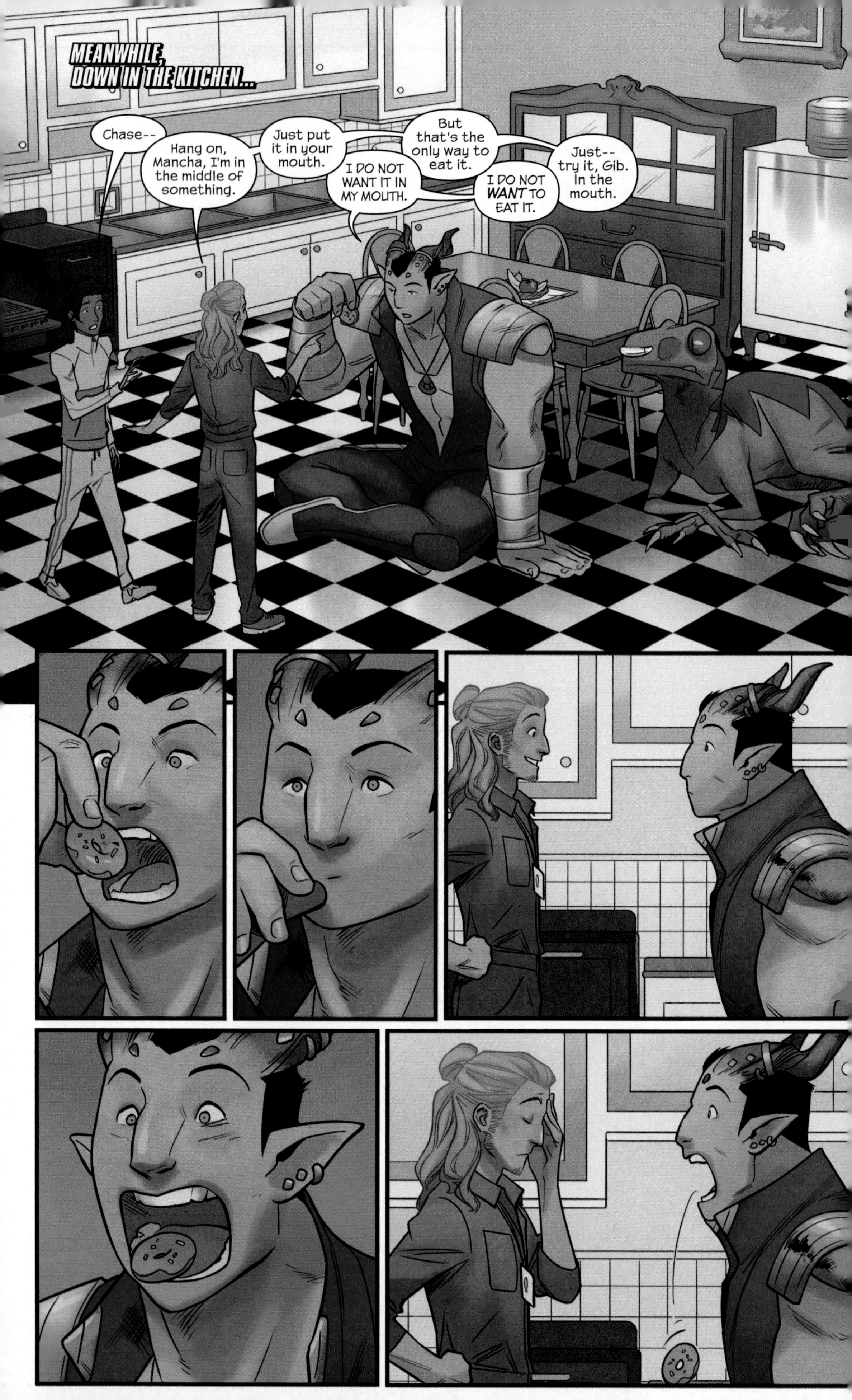
MEANWHILE, DOWN IN THE KITCHEN...
Chase--
Hang on, Mancha, I'm in the middle of something.
Just put it in your mouth.
I DO NOT WANT IT IN MY MOUTH.
But that's the only way to eat it.
I DO NOT WANT TO EAT IT.
Just-- try it, Gib. In the mouth.

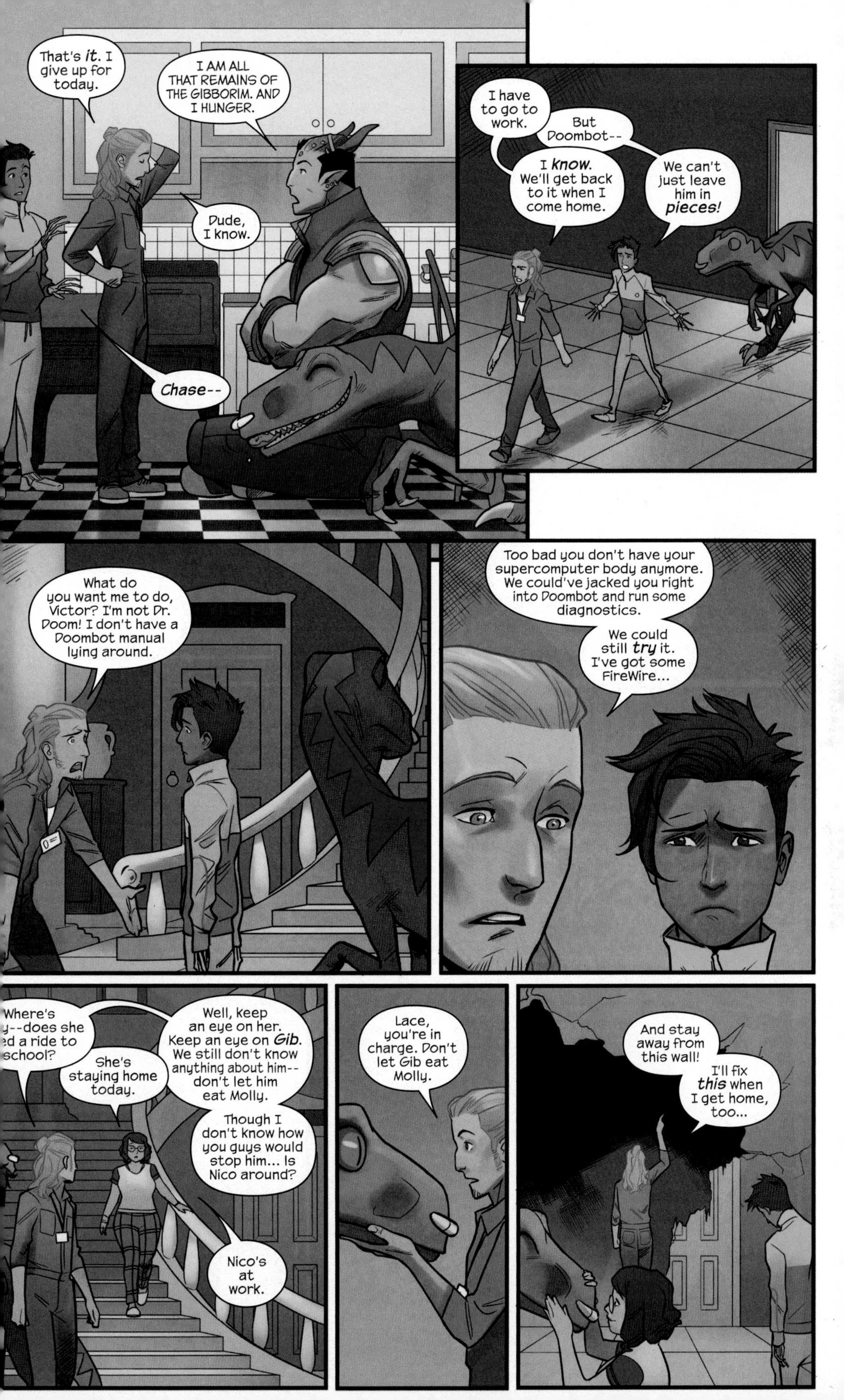
That's *it*. I give up for today.
I AM ALL THAT REMAINS OF THE GIBBORIM. AND I HUNGER.
Dude, I know.
Chase--
I have to go to work.
But Doombot--
I *know*. We'll get back to it when I come home.
We can't just leave him in *pieces!*
What do you want me to do, Victor? I'm not Dr. Doom! I don't have a Doombot manual lying around.
Too bad you don't have your supercomputer body anymore. We could've jacked you right into Doombot and run some diagnostics.
We could still *try* it. I've got some FireWire...
Where's
y--does she
ed a ride to
school?
She's staying home today.
Well, keep an eye on her. Keep an eye on *Gib*. We still don't know anything about him--don't let him eat Molly.
Though I don't know how you guys would stop him... Is Nico around?
Nico's at work.
Lace, you're in charge. Don't let Gib eat Molly.
And stay away from this wall!
I'll fix *this* when I get home, too...

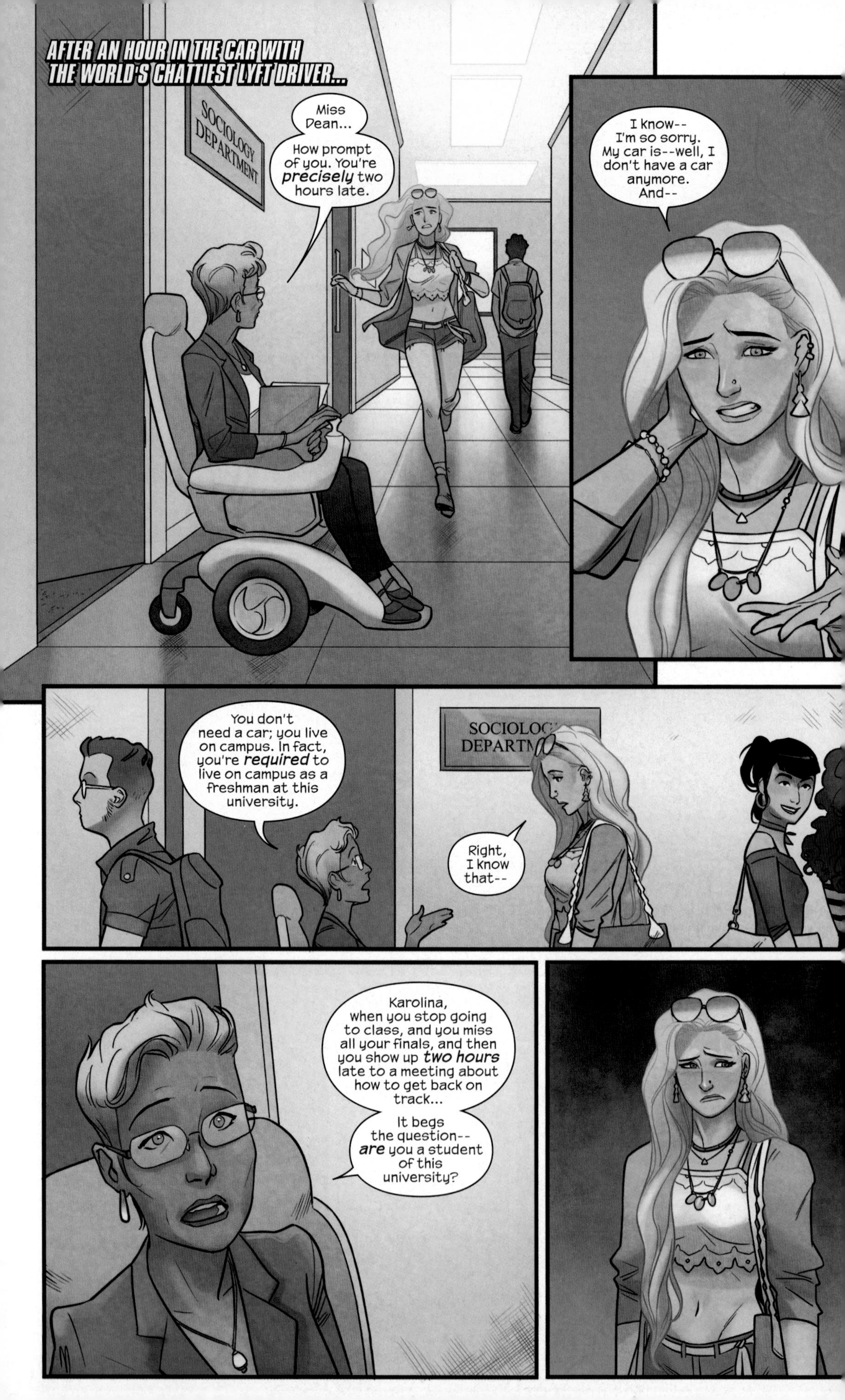
AFTER AN HOUR IN THE CAR WITH THE WORLD'S CHATTIEST LYFT DRIVER...
SOCIOLOGY DEPARTMENT
Miss Dean...
How prompt of you. You're precisely two hours late.
I know-- I'm so sorry. My car is--well, I don't have a car anymore. And--
You don't need a car; you live on campus. In fact, you're required to live on campus as a freshman at this university.
SOCIOLOGY DEPARTMENT
Right, I know that--
Karolina, when you stop going to class, and you miss all your finals, and then you show up two hours late to a meeting about how to get back on track...
It begs the question-- are you a student of this university?

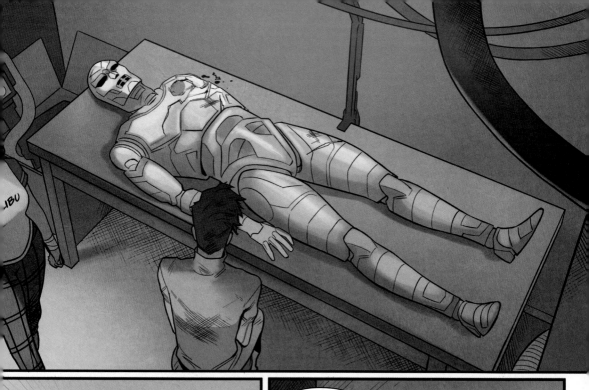

Whoa! Why Doombot naked?

I don't think Doombot cares. He's a robot.

Doombot *obviously* cares about clothes.

Maybe we should ask Gib to fix him. In the spirit of cleaning up one's own messes.

Gib can't even fix himself...

Hey, Victor, I was thinking--

Victor!

Victor, help me! Please!

Hey. *Victor.* Are you glitching or what? Where'd you go?

Gert... Are you okay?

Yeah, I'm fine. I'm fine!

You were right earlier. I should go back to bed.

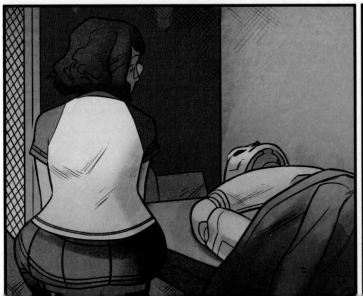

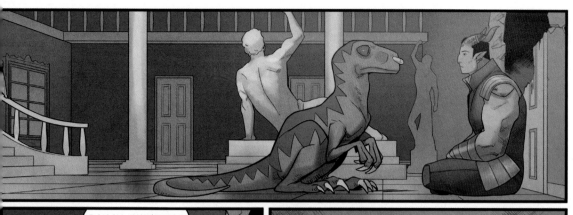

I AM ALL THAT IS LEFT OF THE GIBBORIM. I AM ALONE, AND I HUNGER.

I AM ALONE. AND I HUNGER.

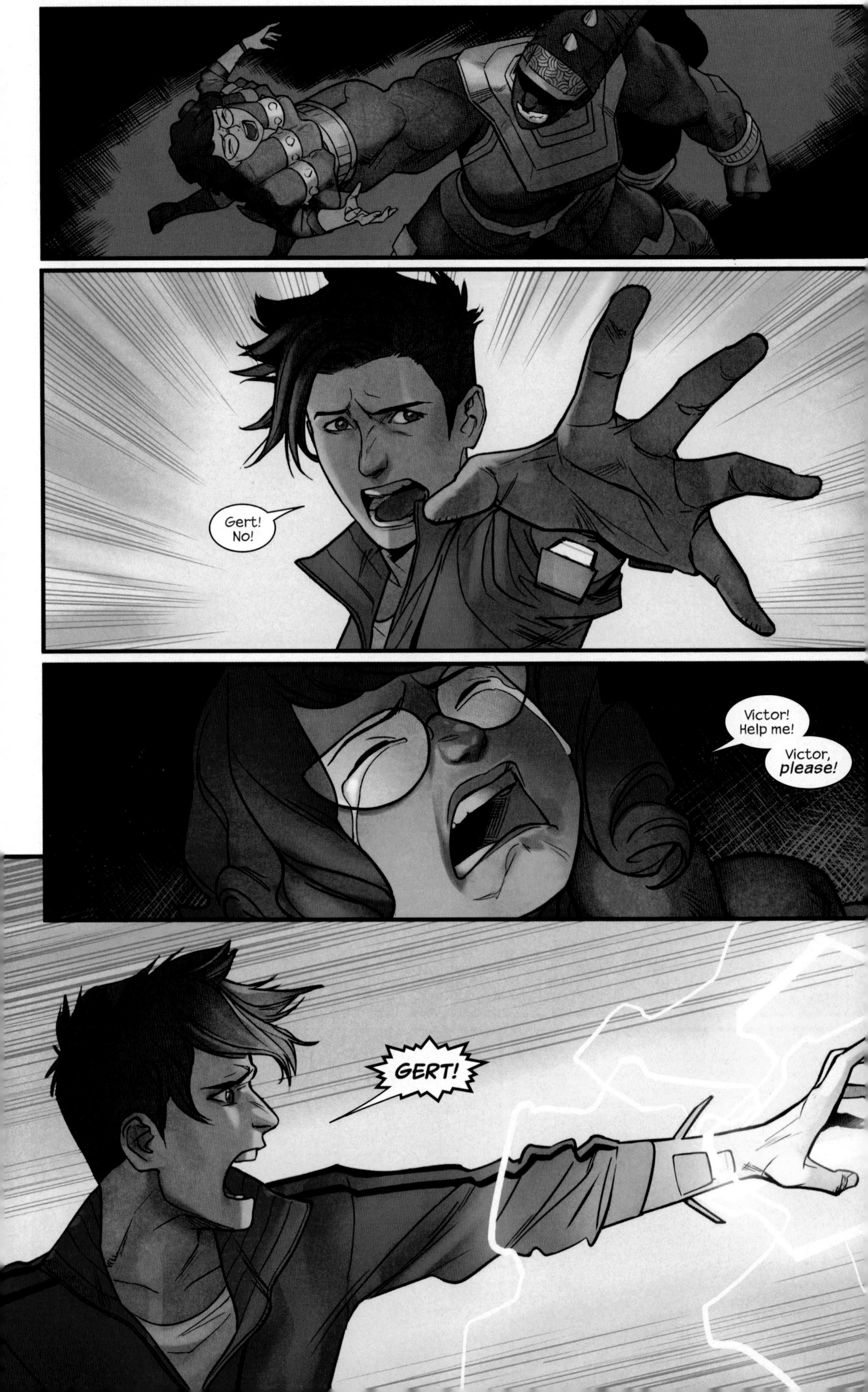
Gert! No!
Victor! Help me!
Victor, *please!*
GERT!

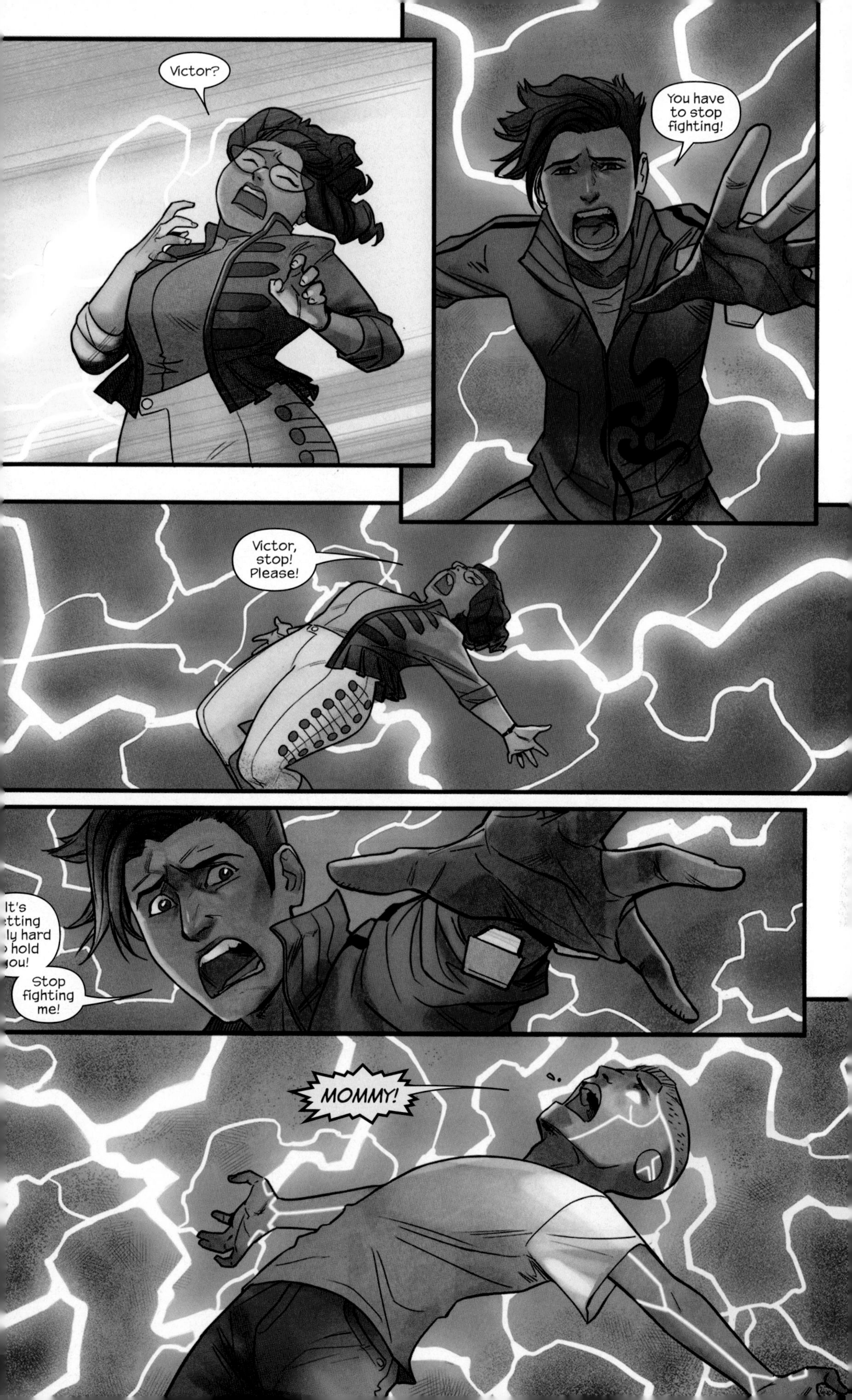
Victor?
You have to stop fighting!
Victor, stop! Please!
It's etting ly hard o hold ou!
Stop fighting me!
MOMMY!

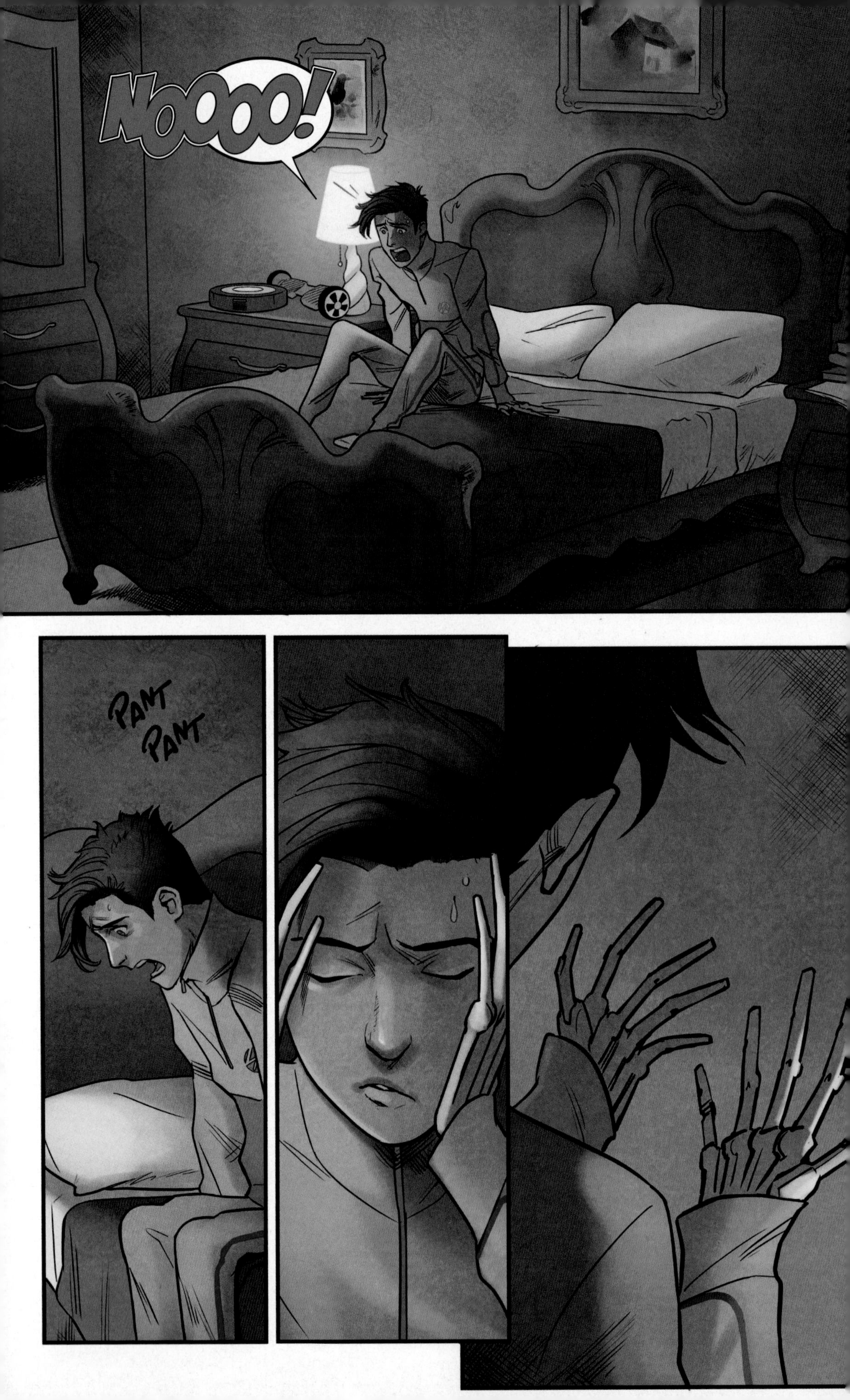
NOOOO!
PANT PANT

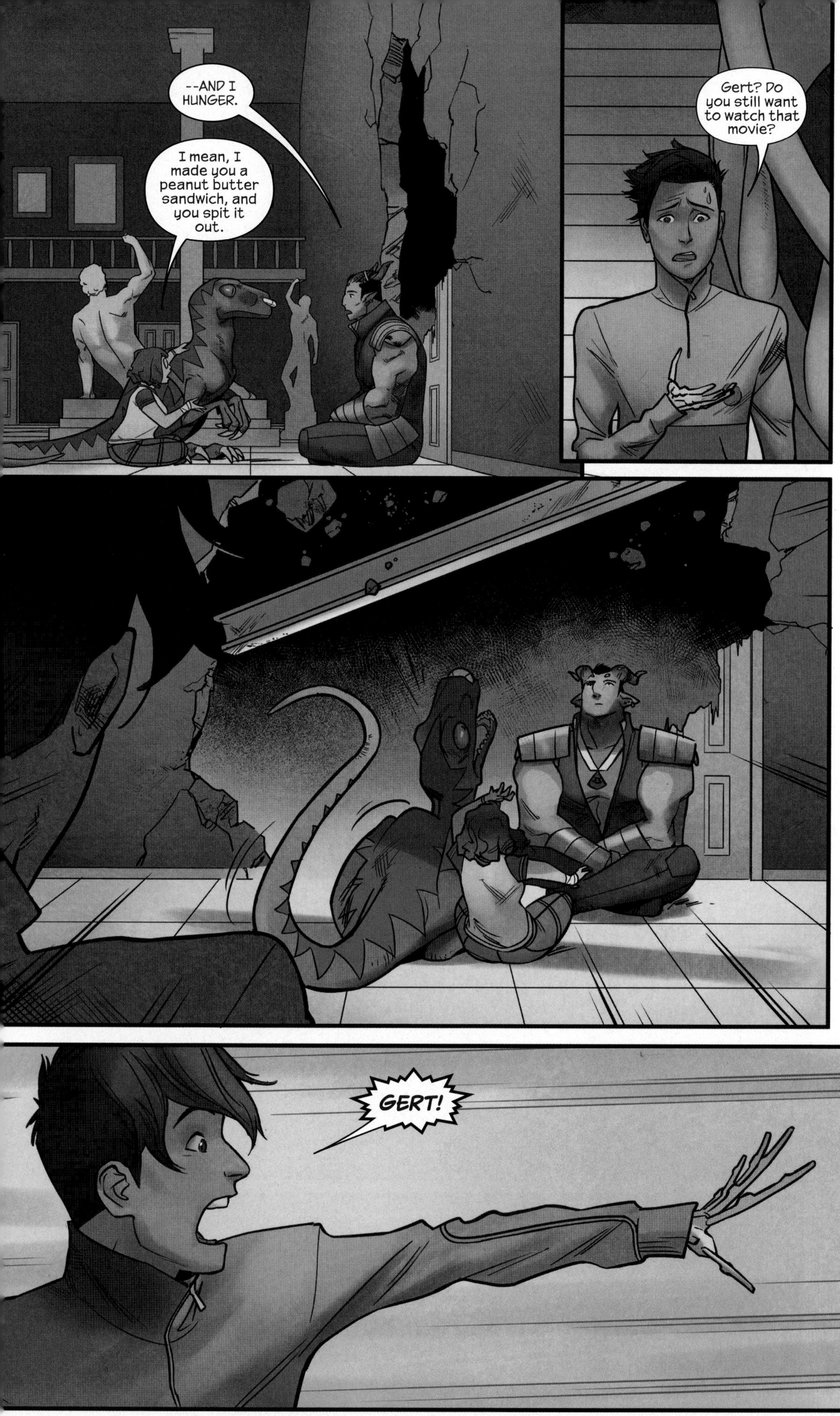
--AND I HUNGER.
I mean, I made you a peanut butter sandwich, and you spit it out.
Gert? Do you still want to watch that movie?
GERT!

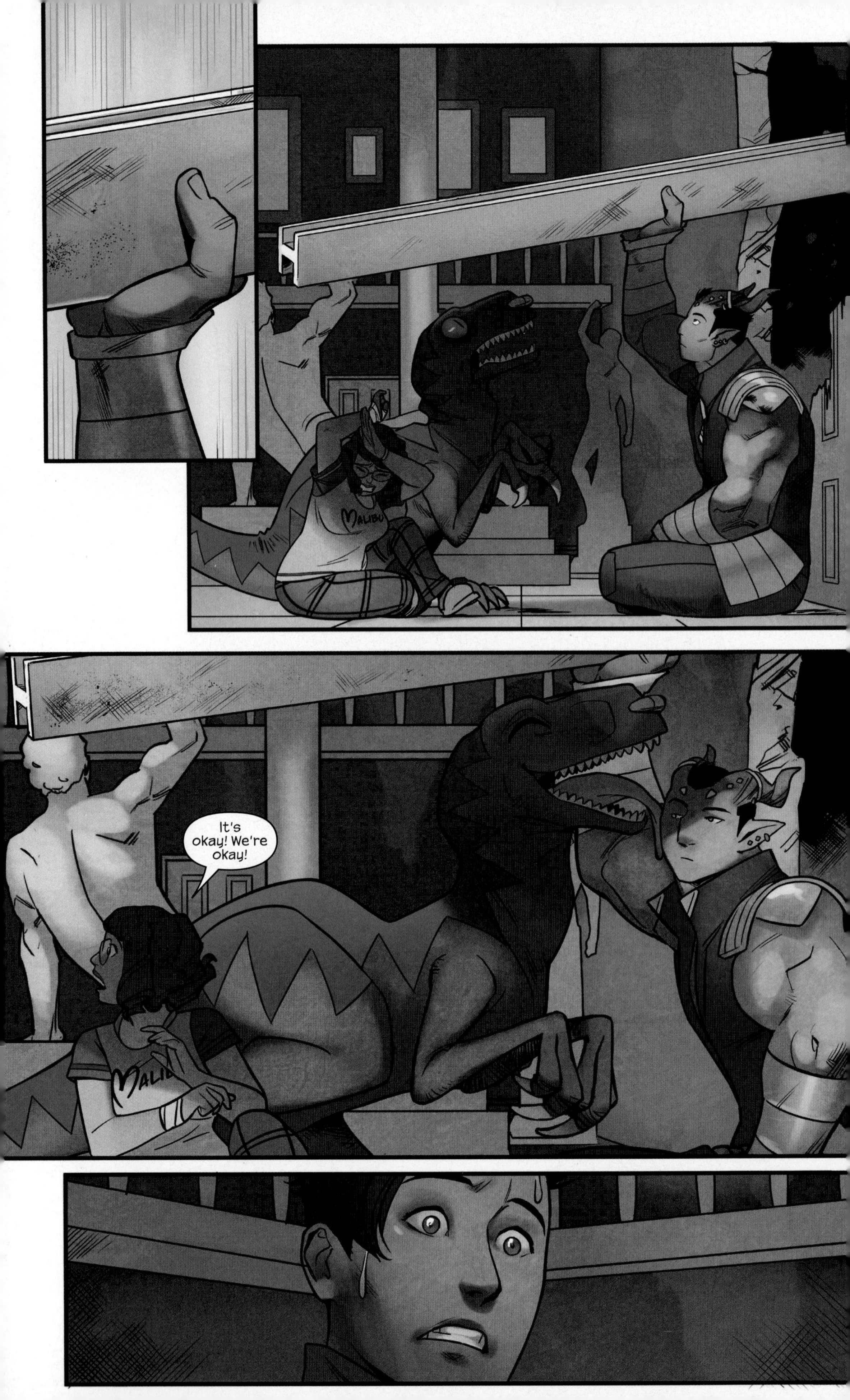
It's okay! We're okay!

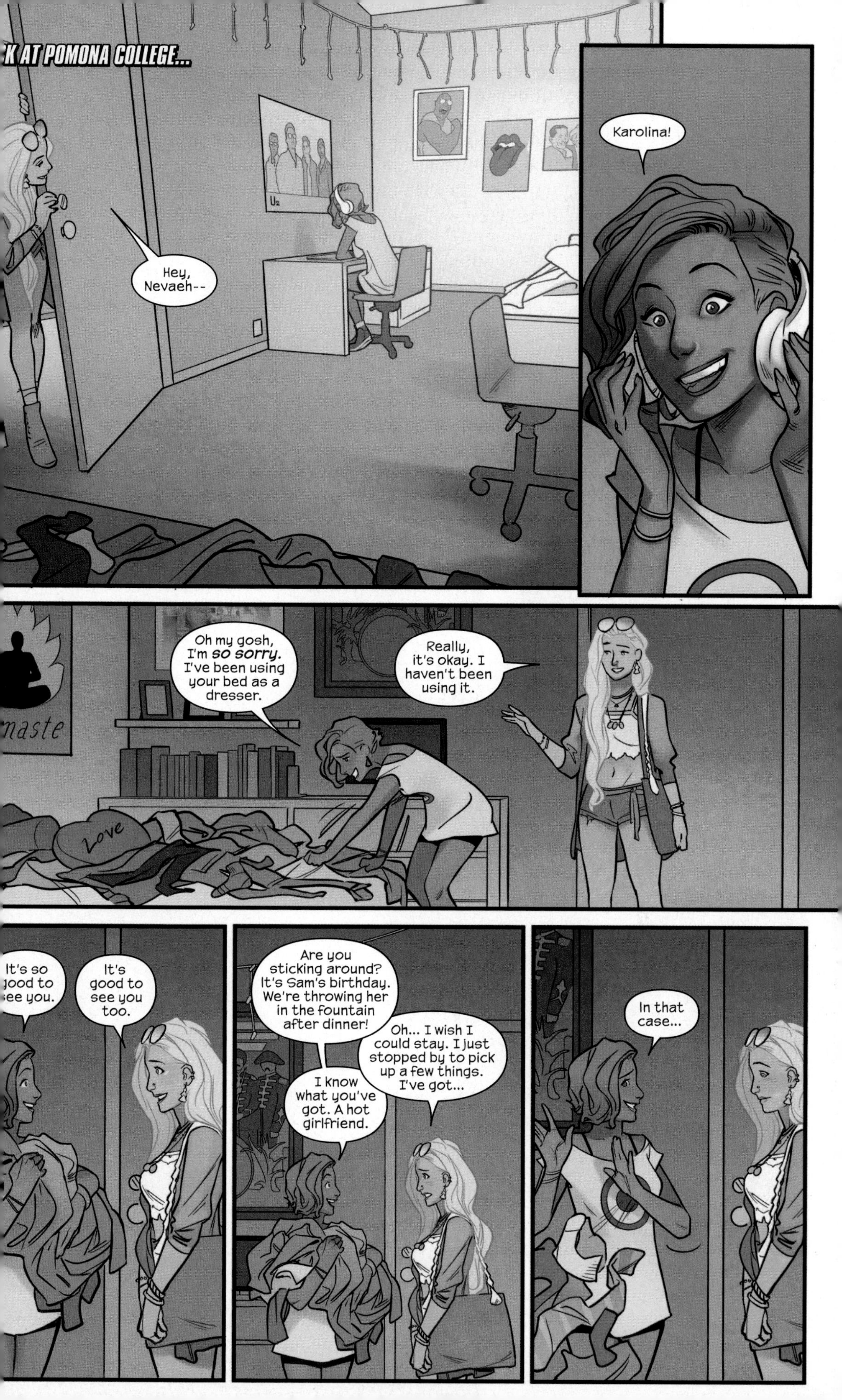
K AT POMONA COLLEGE...
Hey, Nevaeh--
U2
Karolina!
Oh my gosh, I'm *so sorry.* I've been using your bed as a dresser.
Really, it's okay. I haven't been using it.
maste
Love
It's so good to see you.
It's good to see you too.
Are you sticking around? It's Sam's birthday. We're throwing her in the fountain after dinner!
Oh... I wish I could stay. I just stopped by to pick up a few things. I've got...
I know what you've got. A hot girlfriend.
In that case...

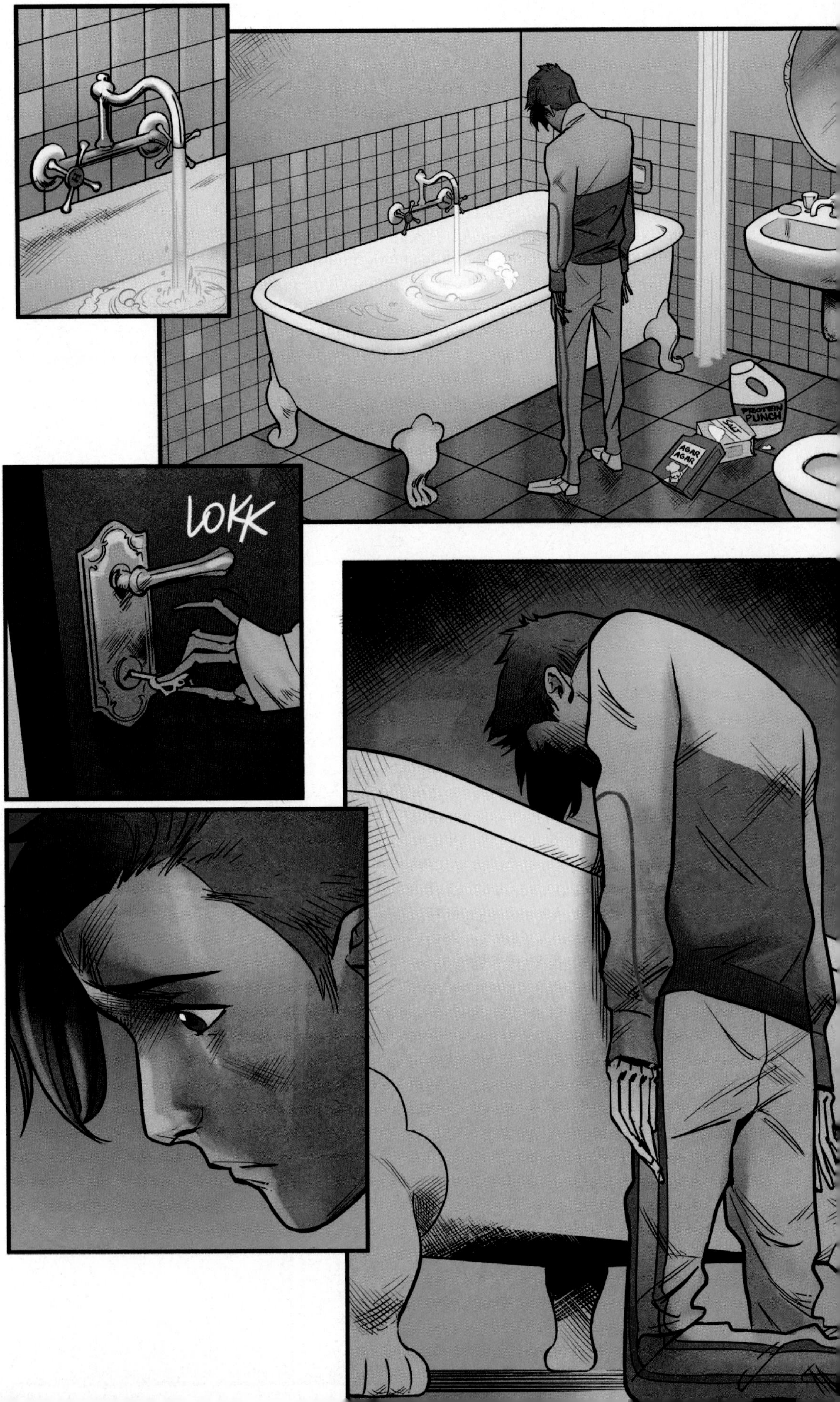
PROTEIN PUNCH
SALT
AGAR AGAR
LOKK

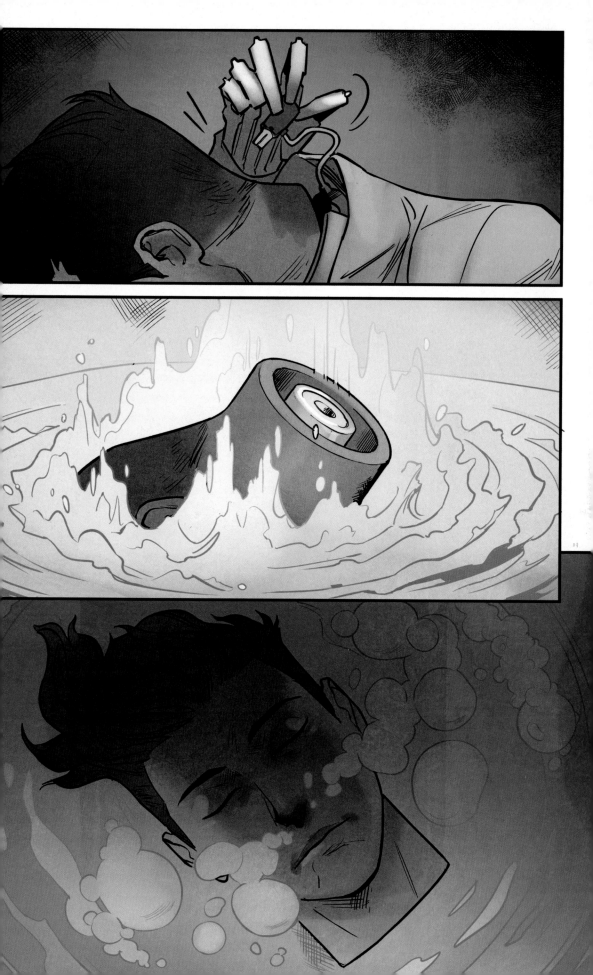

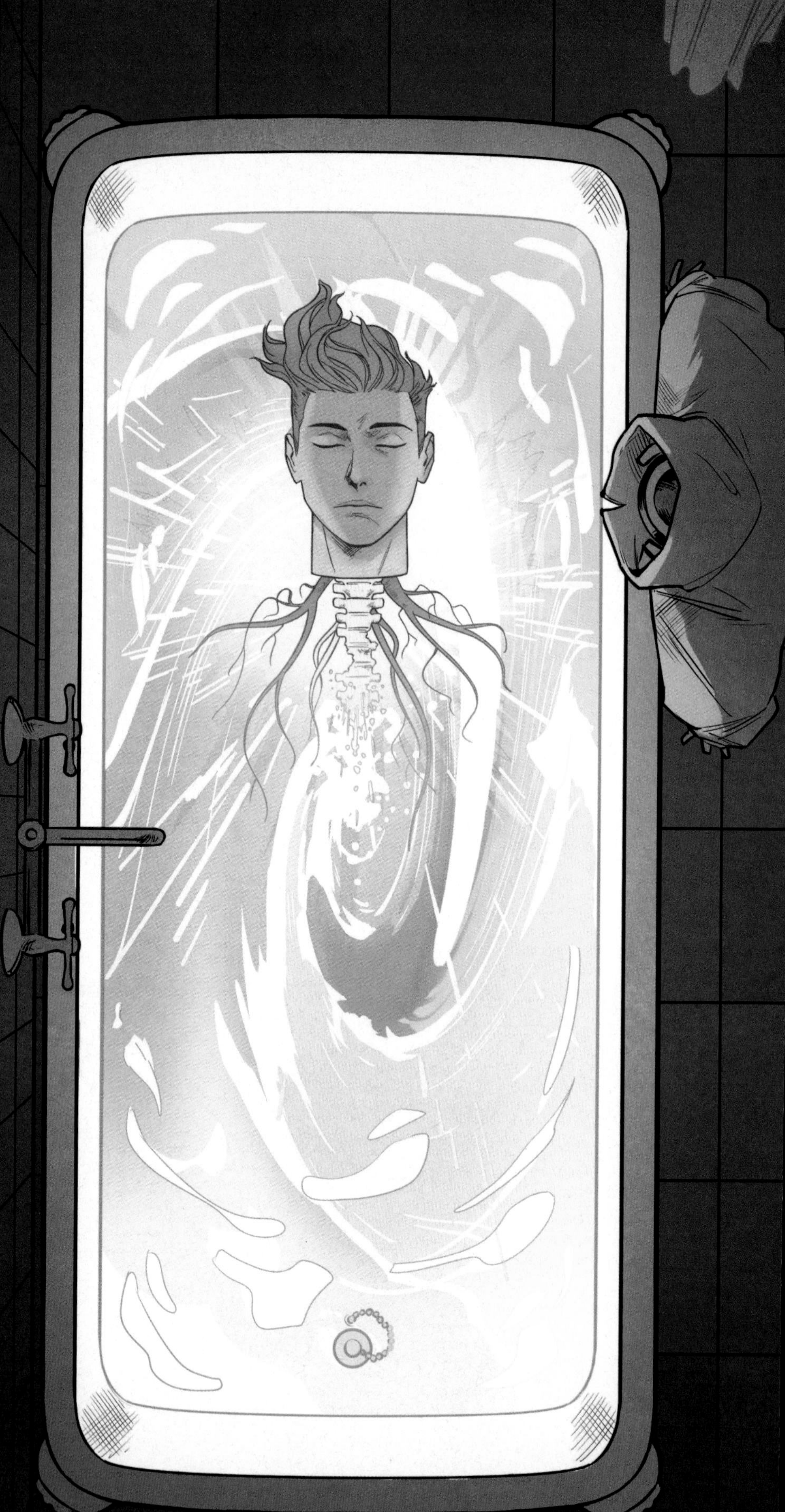

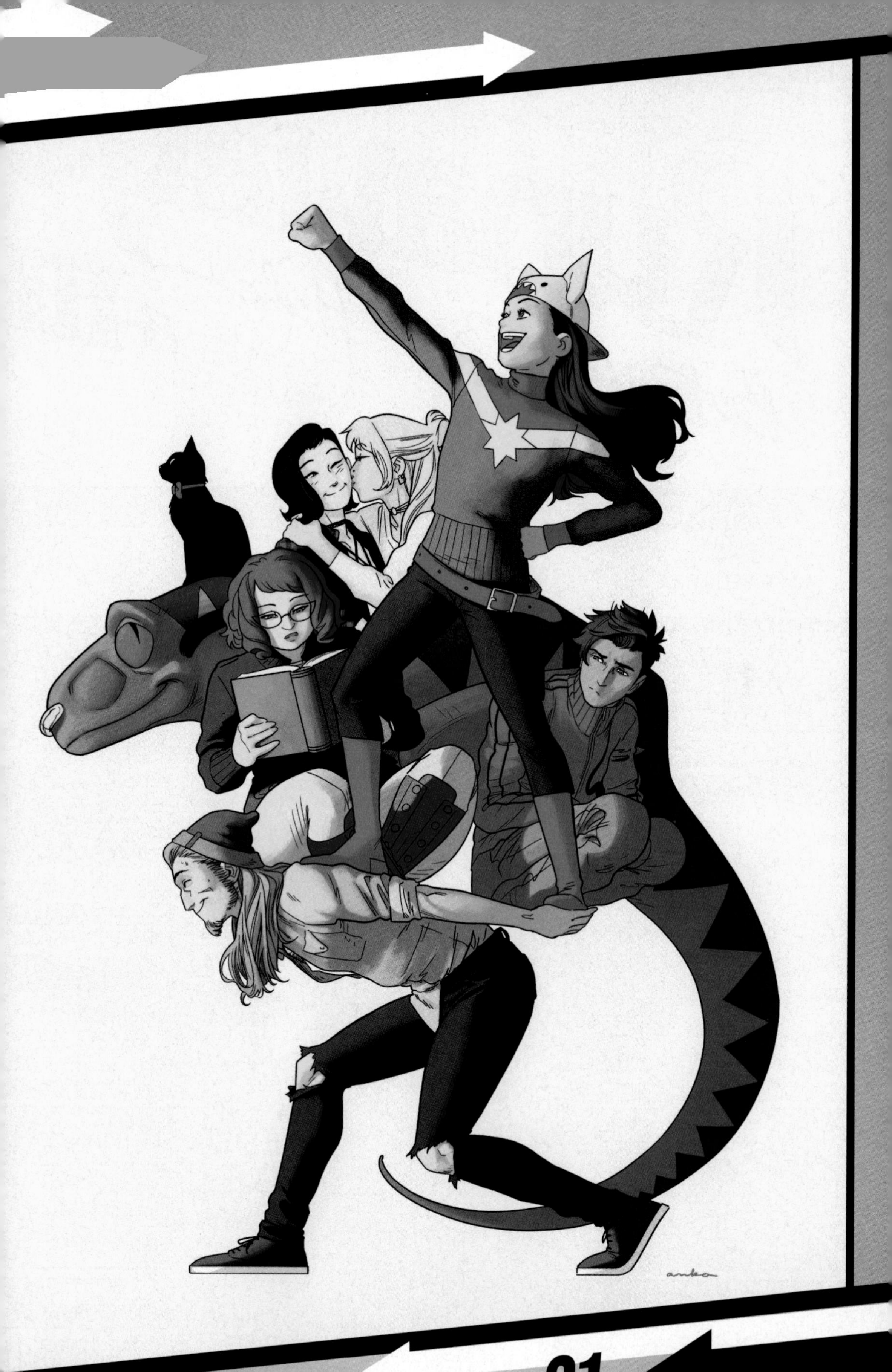
anka

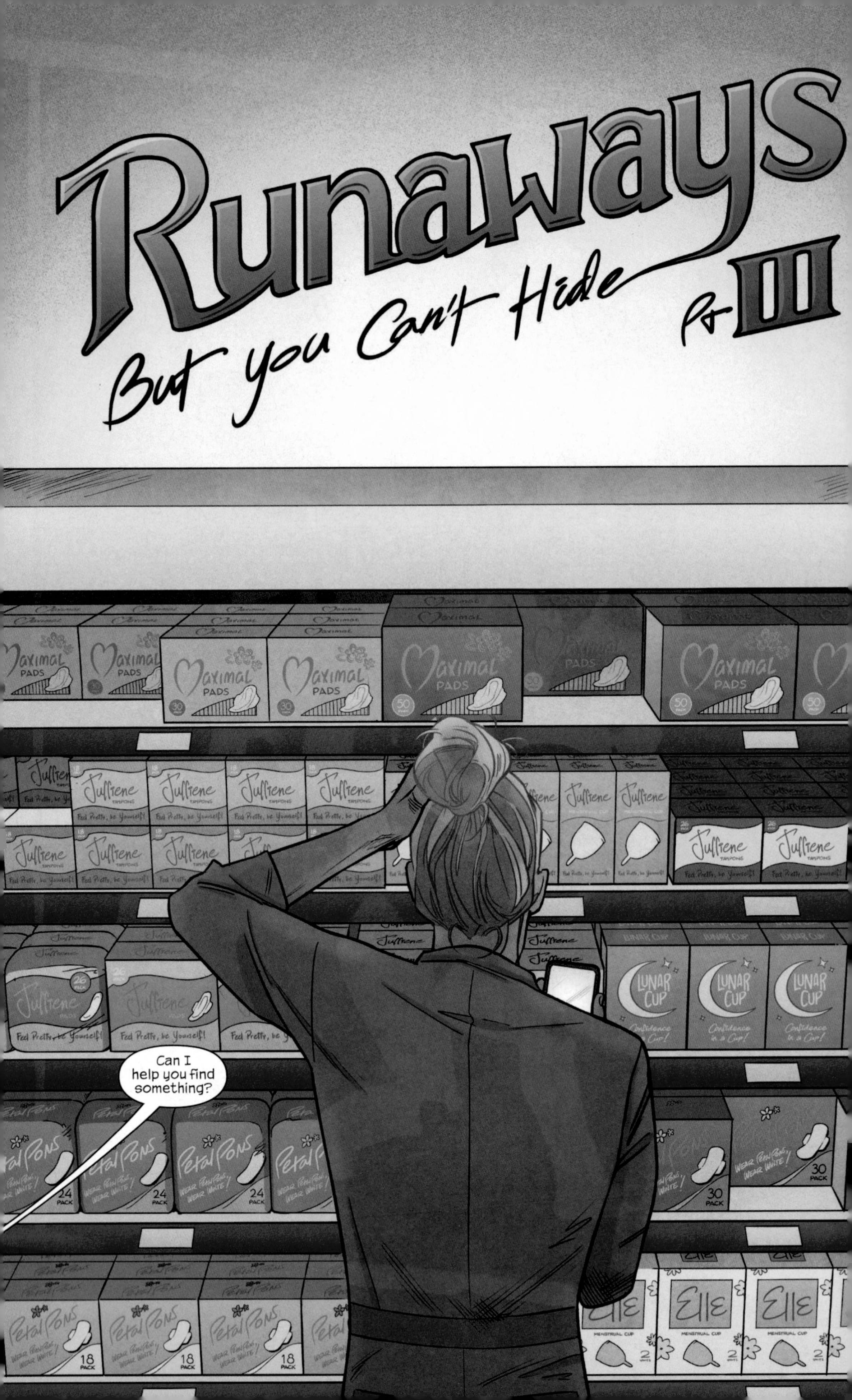
Runaways
But you Can't Hide
Pt III
Can I help you find something?

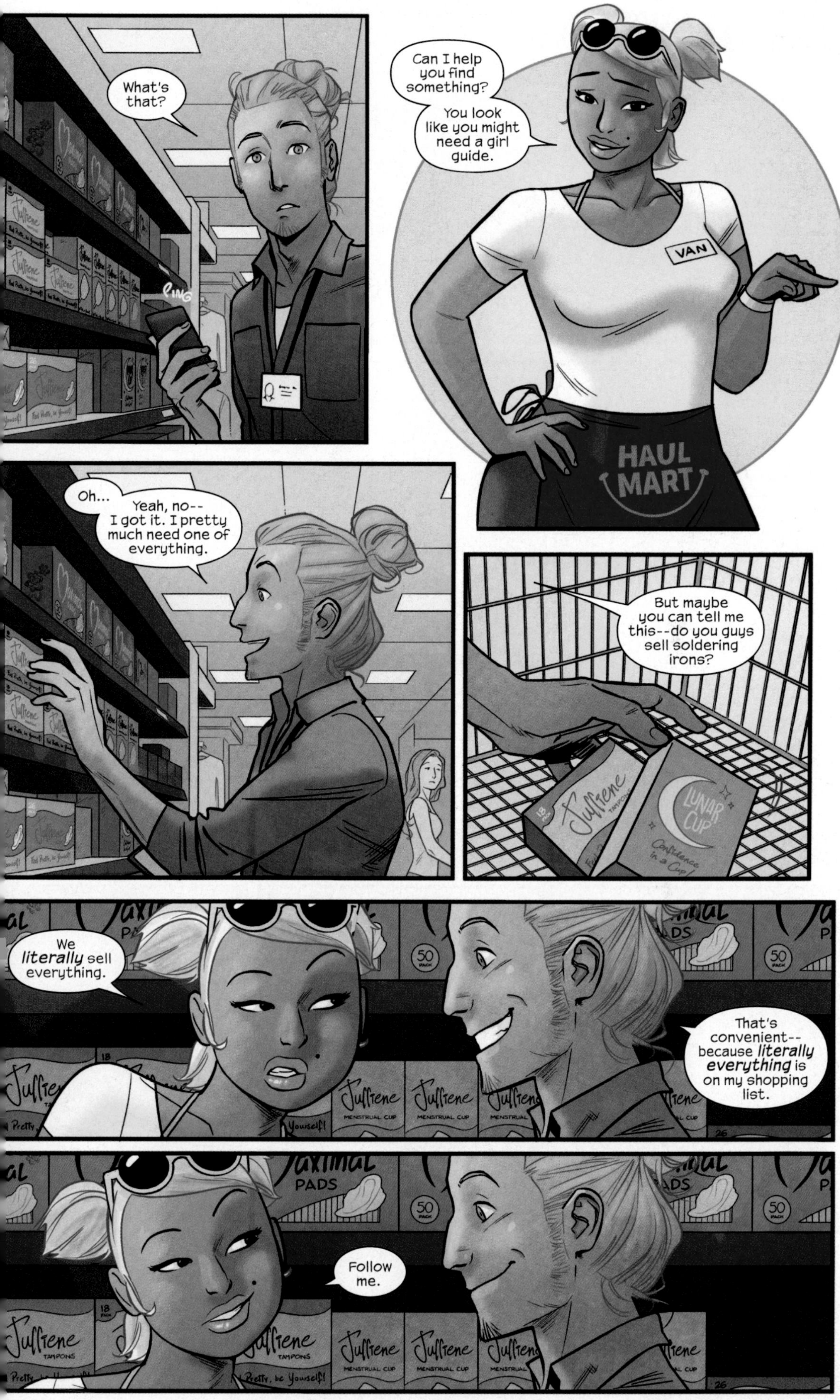
PING
What's that?
Can I help you find something?
You look like you might need a girl guide.
VAN
HAUL MART
Oh...
Yeah, no-- I got it. I pretty much need one of everything.
But maybe you can tell me this--do you guys sell soldering irons?
LUNAR CUP
Confidence in a Cup!
We *literally* sell everything.
That's convenient-- because *literally everything* is on my shopping list.
Follow me.

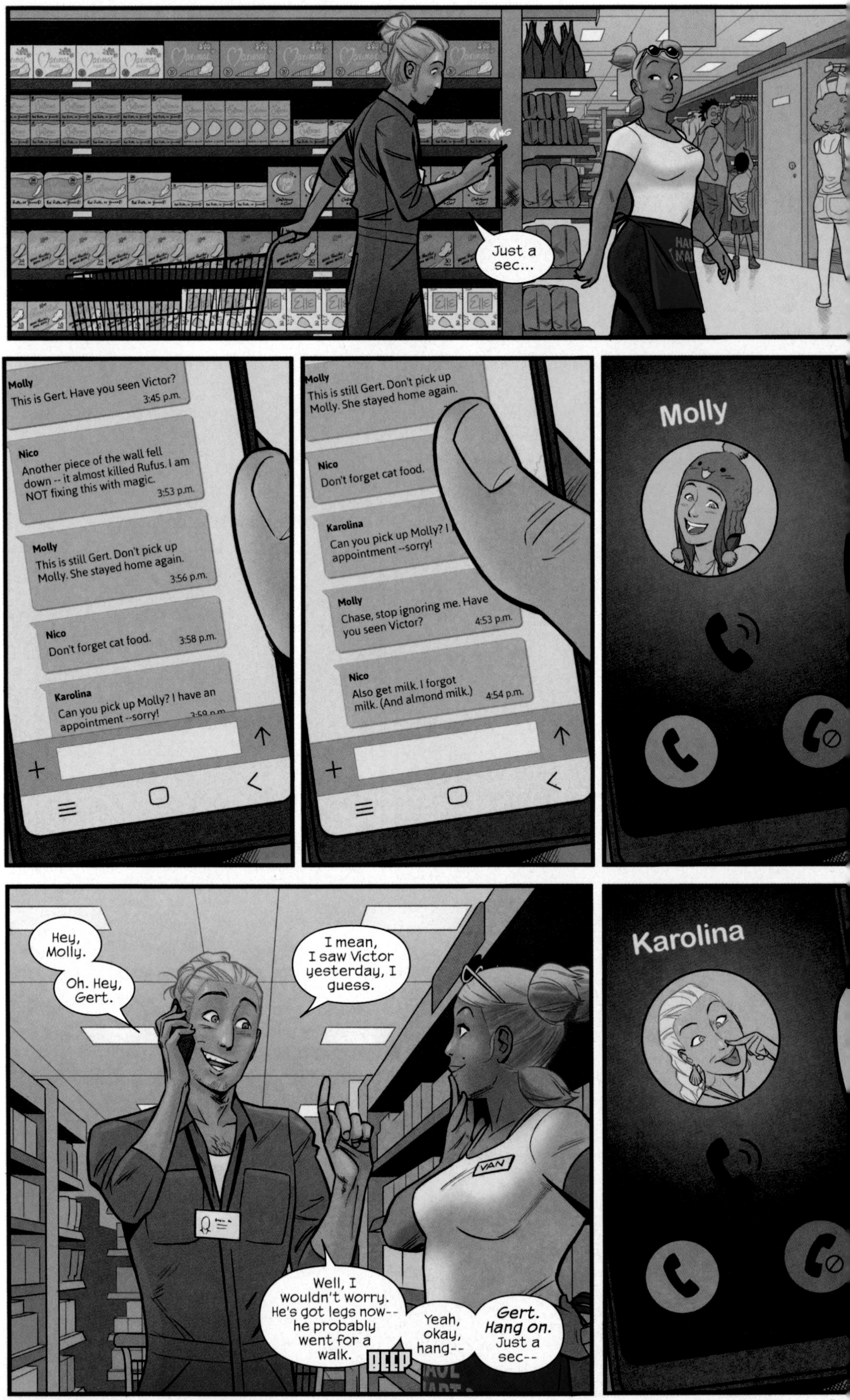
PING
Just a sec...
Molly
This is Gert. Have you seen Victor?
3:45 p.m.
Nico
Another piece of the wall fell down -- it almost killed Rufus. I am NOT fixing this with magic.
3:53 p.m.
Molly
This is still Gert. Don't pick up Molly. She stayed home again.
3:56 p.m.
Nico
Don't forget cat food.
3:58 p.m.
Karolina
Can you pick up Molly? I have an appointment --sorry!
Molly
This is still Gert. Don't pick up Molly. She stayed home again.
Nico
Don't forget cat food.
Karolina
Can you pick up Molly? I
appointment --sorry!
Molly
Chase, stop ignoring me. Have you seen Victor?
4:53 p.m.
Nico
Also get milk. I forgot milk. (And almond milk.)
4:54 p.m.
Molly
Hey, Molly.
Oh. Hey, Gert.
I mean, I saw Victor yesterday, I guess.
VAN
Well, I wouldn't worry. He's got legs now--he probably went for a walk.
BEEP
Yeah, okay, hang--
Gert. Hang on. Just a sec--
Karolina

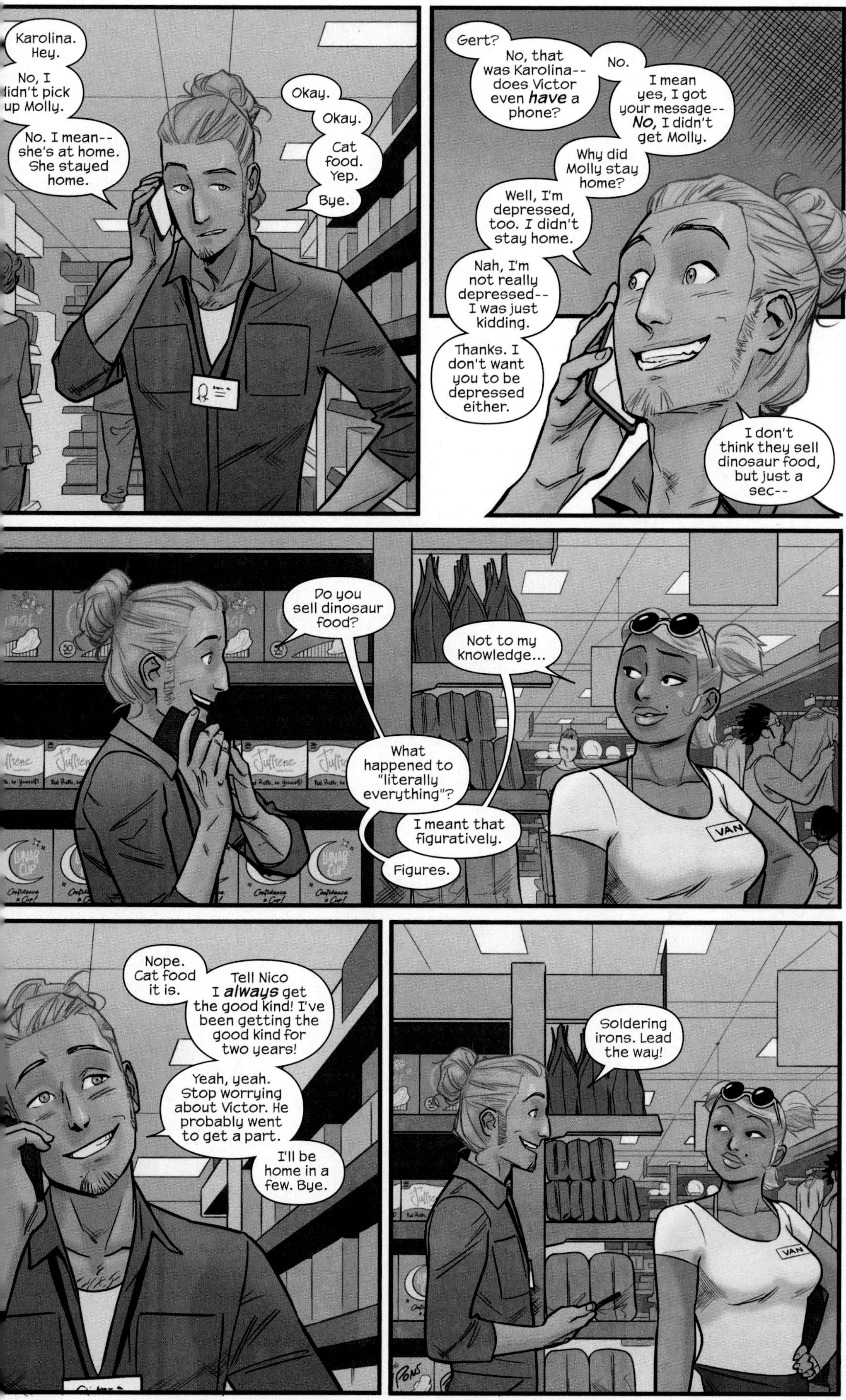
Karolina. Hey.
No, I didn't pick up Molly.
No. I mean--she's at home. She stayed home.
Okay.
Okay.
Cat food. Yep.
Bye.
Gert?
No, that was Karolina--does Victor even *have* a phone?
No.
I mean yes, I got your message--*No,* I didn't get Molly.
Why did Molly stay home?
Well, I'm depressed, too. I didn't stay home.
Nah, I'm not really depressed--I was just kidding.
Thanks. I don't want you to be depressed either.
I don't think they sell dinosaur food, but just a sec--
Do you sell dinosaur food?
Not to my knowledge...
What happened to "literally everything"?
I meant that figuratively.
Figures.
VAN
Nope. Cat food it is.
Tell Nico I *always* get the good kind! I've been getting the good kind for two years!
Yeah, yeah. Stop worrying about Victor. He probably went to get a part.
I'll be home in a few. Bye.
Soldering irons. Lead the way!
VAN

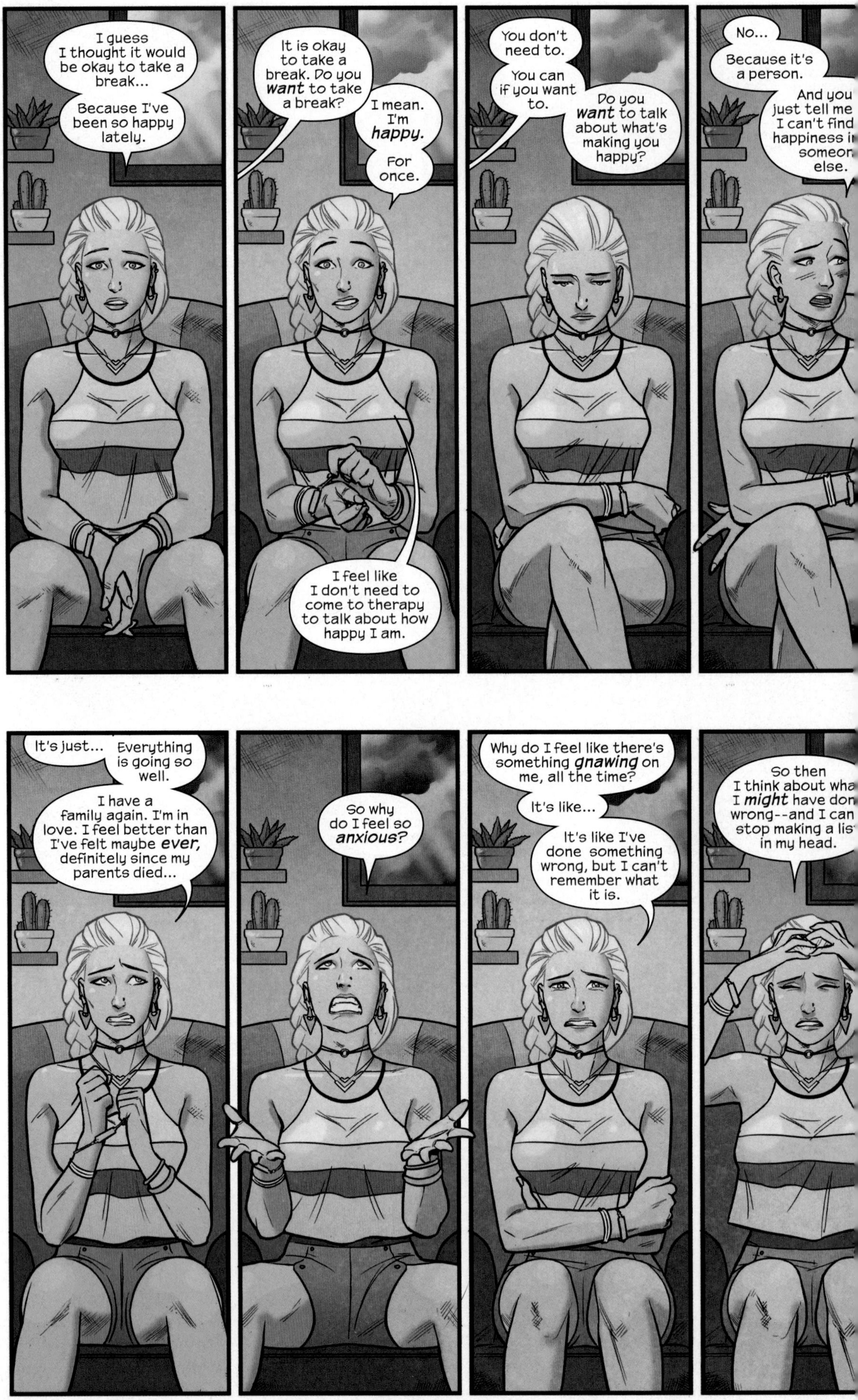

I guess I thought it would be okay to take a break...
Because I've been so happy lately.
It is okay to take a break. Do you *want* to take a break?
I mean. I'm *happy.*
For once.
I feel like I don't need to come to therapy to talk about how happy I am.
You don't need to.
You can if you want to.
Do you *want* to talk about what's making you happy?
No...
Because it's a person.
And you just tell me I can't find happiness i someon else.
It's just...
Everything is going so well.
I have a family again. I'm in love. I feel better than I've felt maybe *ever,* definitely since my parents died...
So why do I feel so *anxious?*
Why do I feel like there's something *gnawing* on me, all the time?
It's like...
It's like I've done something wrong, but I can't remember what it is.
So then I think about wha I *might* have don wrong--and I can stop making a lis in my head.

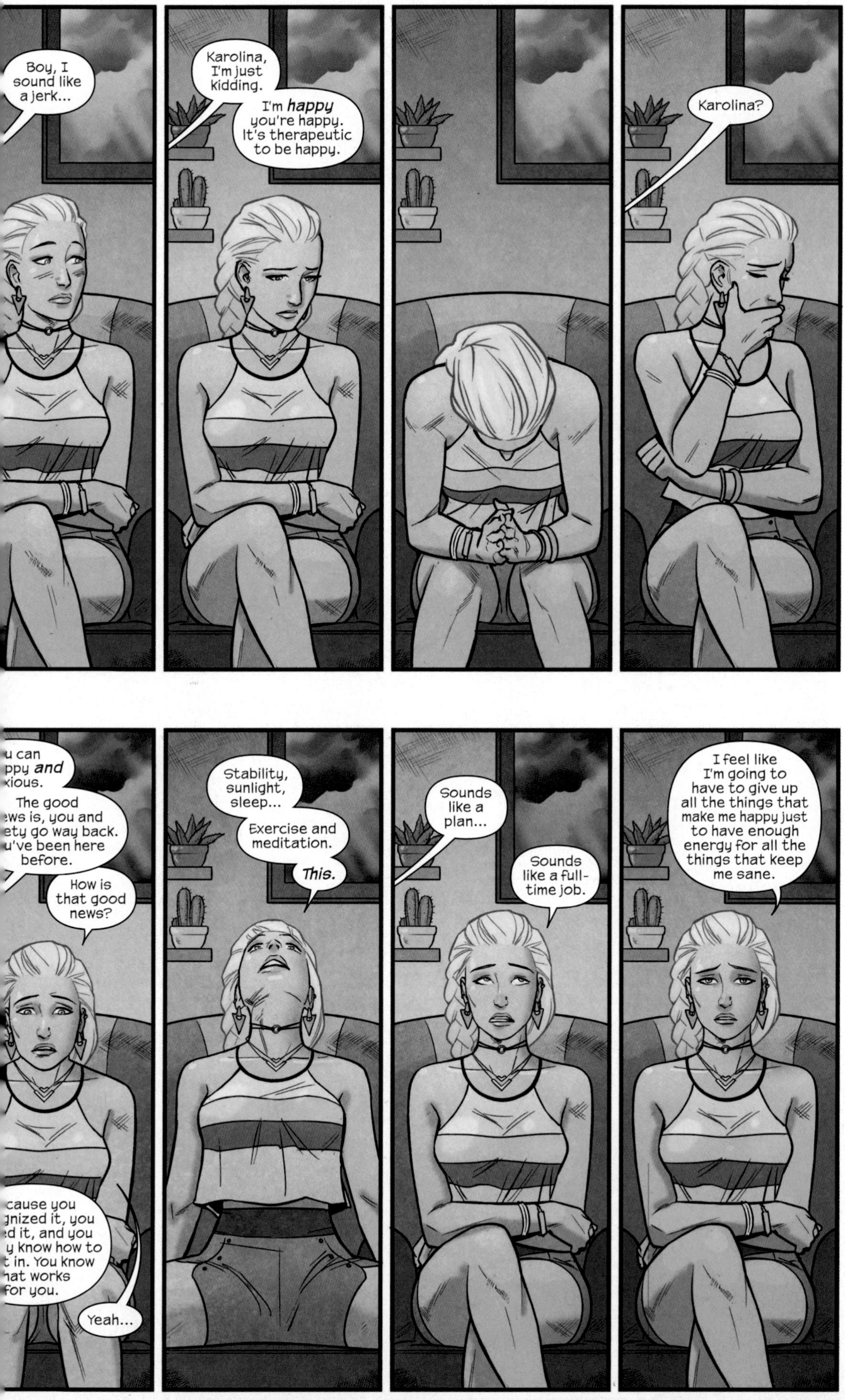
Boy, I sound like a jerk...
Karolina, I'm just kidding.
I'm *happy* you're happy. It's therapeutic to be happy.
Karolina?
u can ppy *and* xious.
The good ws is, you and ety go way back. u've been here before.
How is that good news?
cause you gnized it, you d it, and you y know how to t in. You know hat works for you.
Yeah...
Stability, sunlight, sleep...
Exercise and meditation.
This.
Sounds like a plan...
Sounds like a full-time job.
I feel like I'm going to have to give up all the things that make me happy just to have enough energy for all the things that keep me sane.

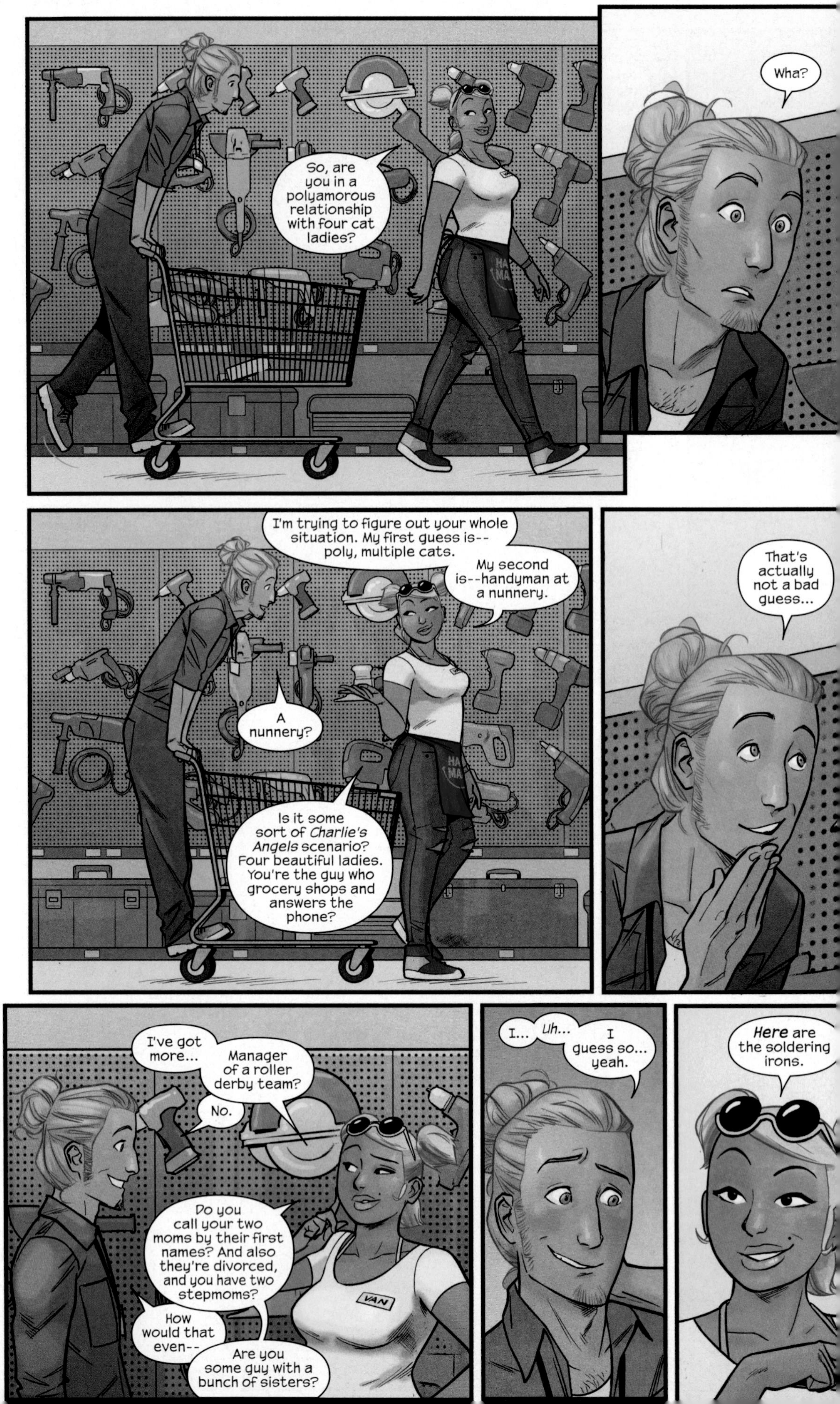
So, are you in a polyamorous relationship with four cat ladies?
Wha?
I'm trying to figure out your whole situation. My first guess is-- poly, multiple cats.
My second is--handyman at a nunnery.
A nunnery?
Is it some sort of *Charlie's Angels* scenario? Four beautiful ladies. You're the guy who grocery shops and answers the phone?
That's actually not a bad guess...
I've got more...
Manager of a roller derby team?
No.
Do you call your two moms by their first names? And also they're divorced, and you have two stepmoms?
How would that even--
Are you some guy with a bunch of sisters?
VAN
I...
Uh...
I guess so... yeah.
Here are the soldering irons.

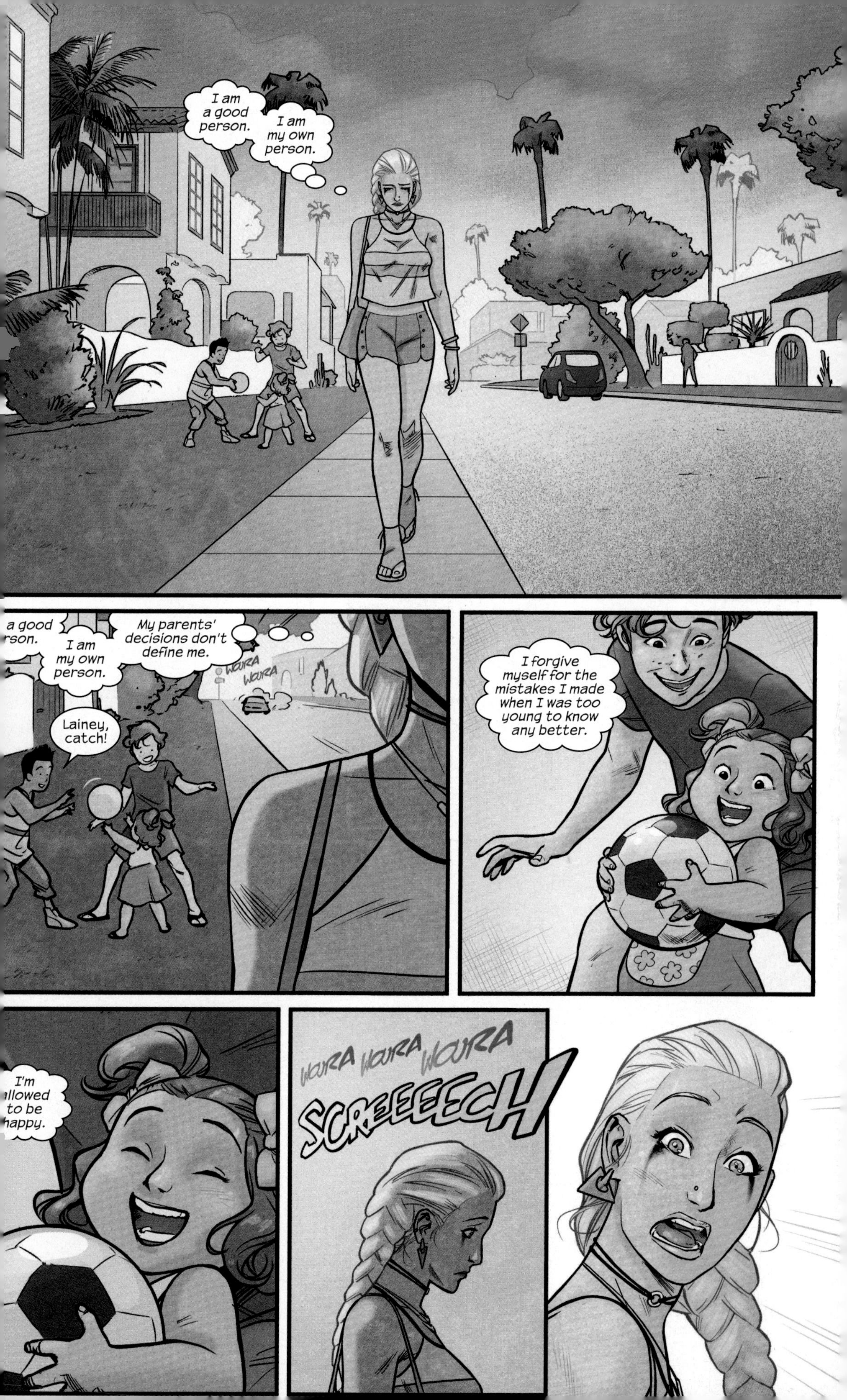
I am a good person.
I am my own person.
a good rson.
I am my own person.
My parents' decisions don't define me.
WOURA WOURA
Lainey, catch!
I forgive myself for the mistakes I made when I was too young to know any better.
I'm llowed to be appy.
WOURA WOURA WOURA
SCREEEECH

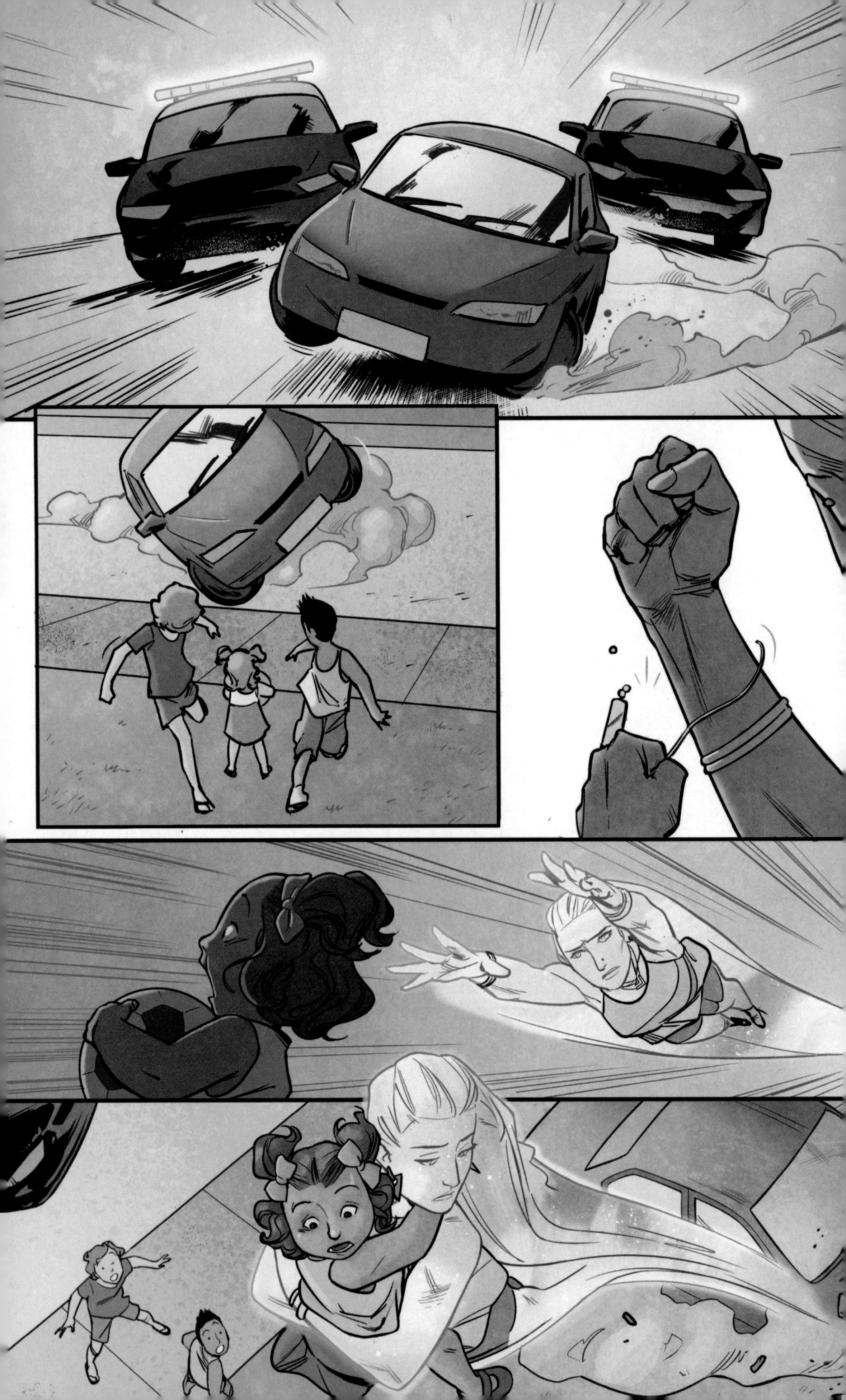

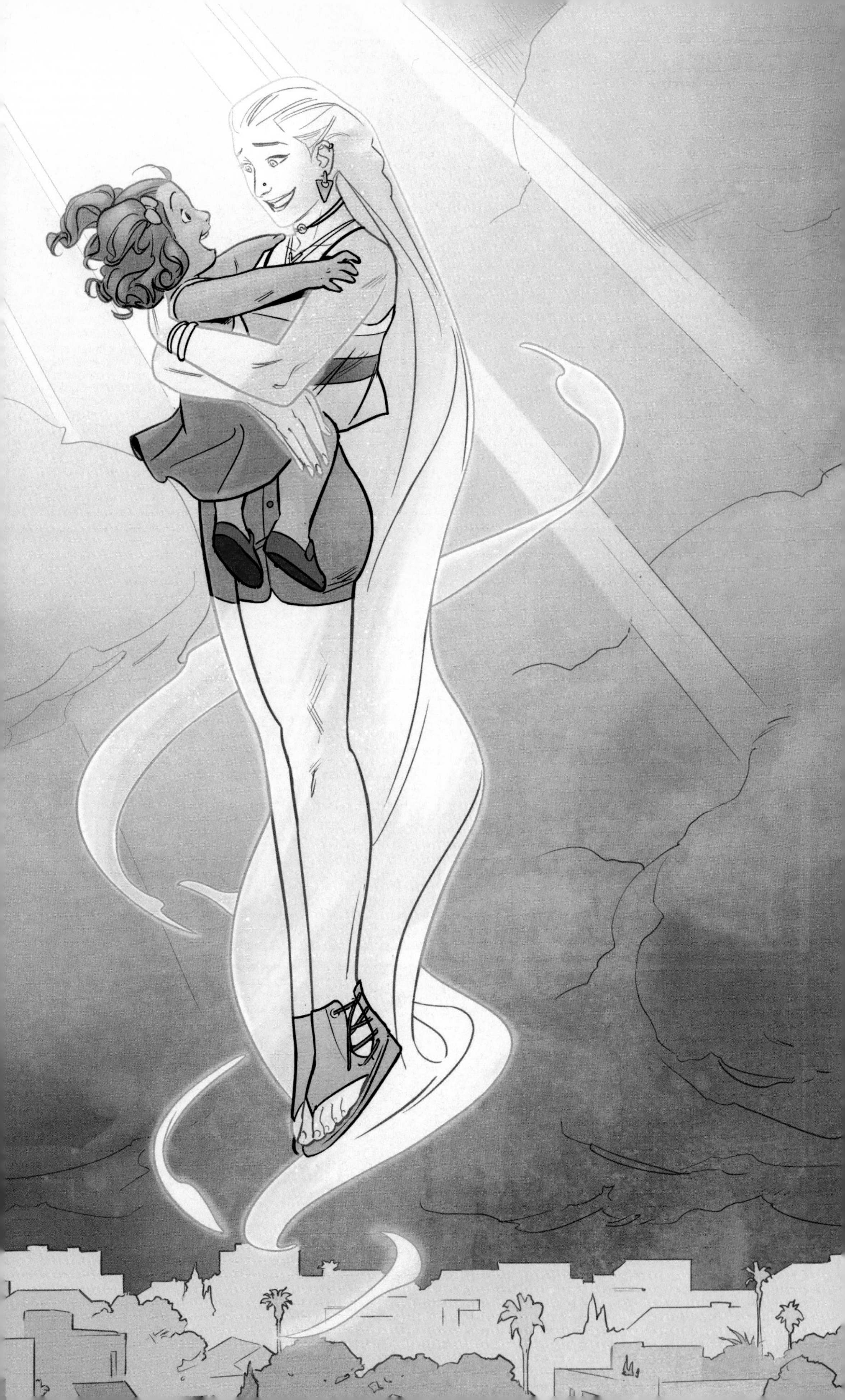

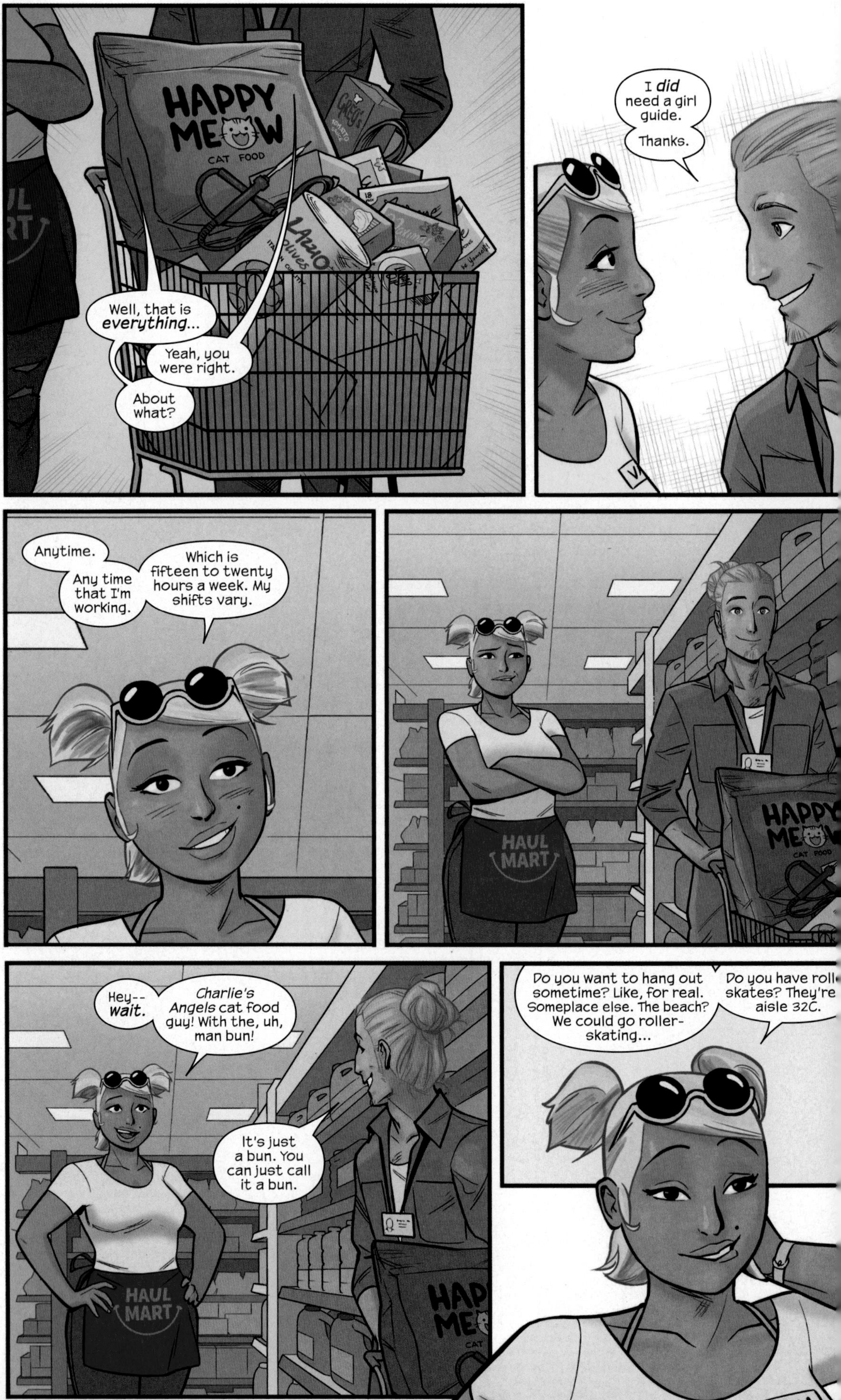
HAPPY MEOW
CAT FOOD
Well, that is *everything*...
Yeah, you were right.
About what?
I *did* need a girl guide.
Thanks.
Anytime.
Any time that I'm working.
Which is fifteen to twenty hours a week. My shifts vary.
HAUL MART
Hey-- *wait.*
Charlie's Angels cat food guy! With the, uh, man bun!
It's just a bun. You can just call it a bun.
Do you want to hang out sometime? Like, for real. Someplace else. The beach? We could go roller-skating...
Do you have roll
skates? They're
aisle 32C.

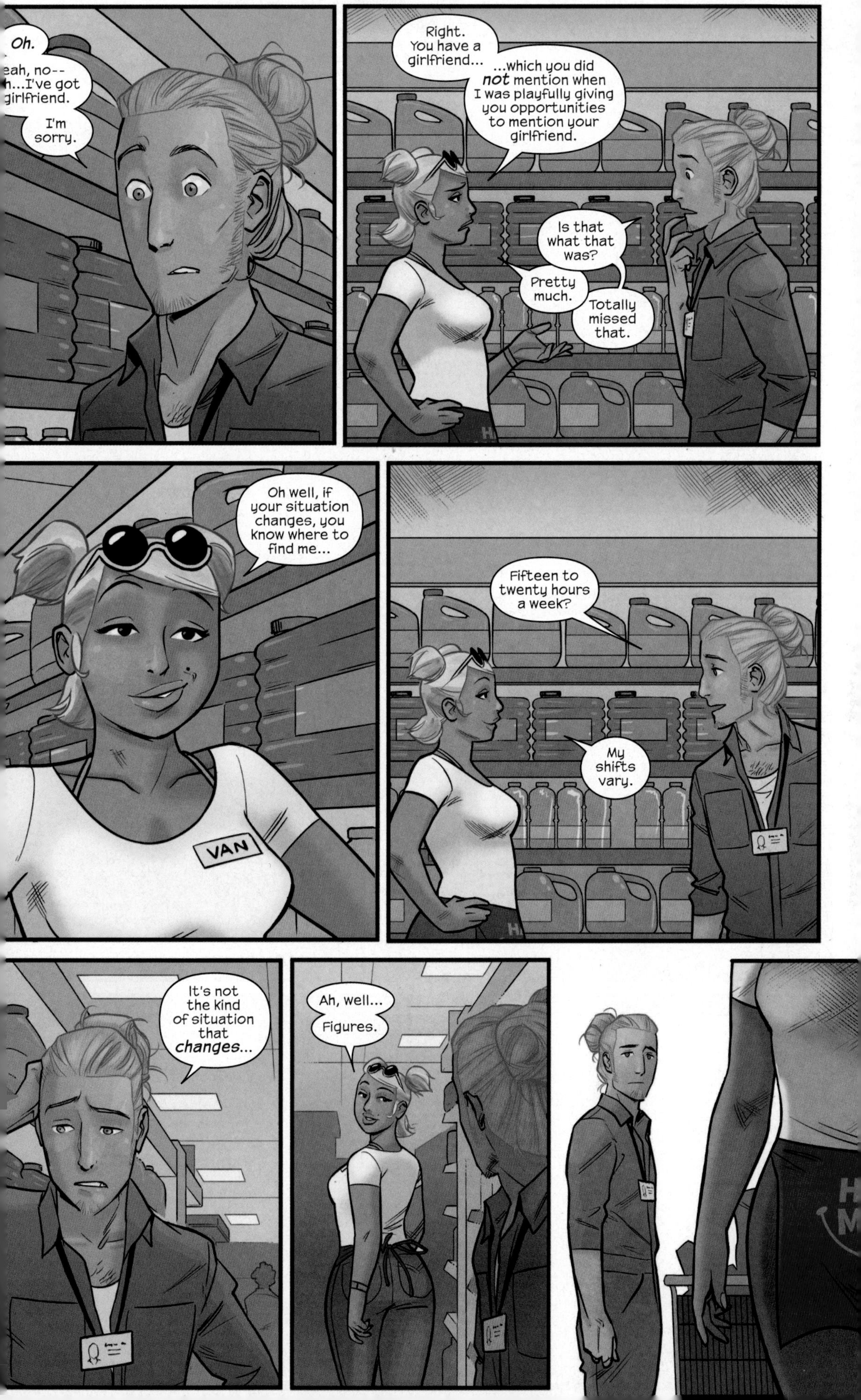
Oh.
eah, no-- h...I've got girlfriend.
I'm sorry.
Right. You have a girlfriend...
...which you did *not* mention when I was playfully giving you opportunities to mention your girlfriend.
Is that what that was?
Pretty much.
Totally missed that.
Oh well, if your situation changes, you know where to find me...
VAN
Fifteen to twenty hours a week?
My shifts vary.
It's not the kind of situation that *changes*...
Ah, well...
Figures.

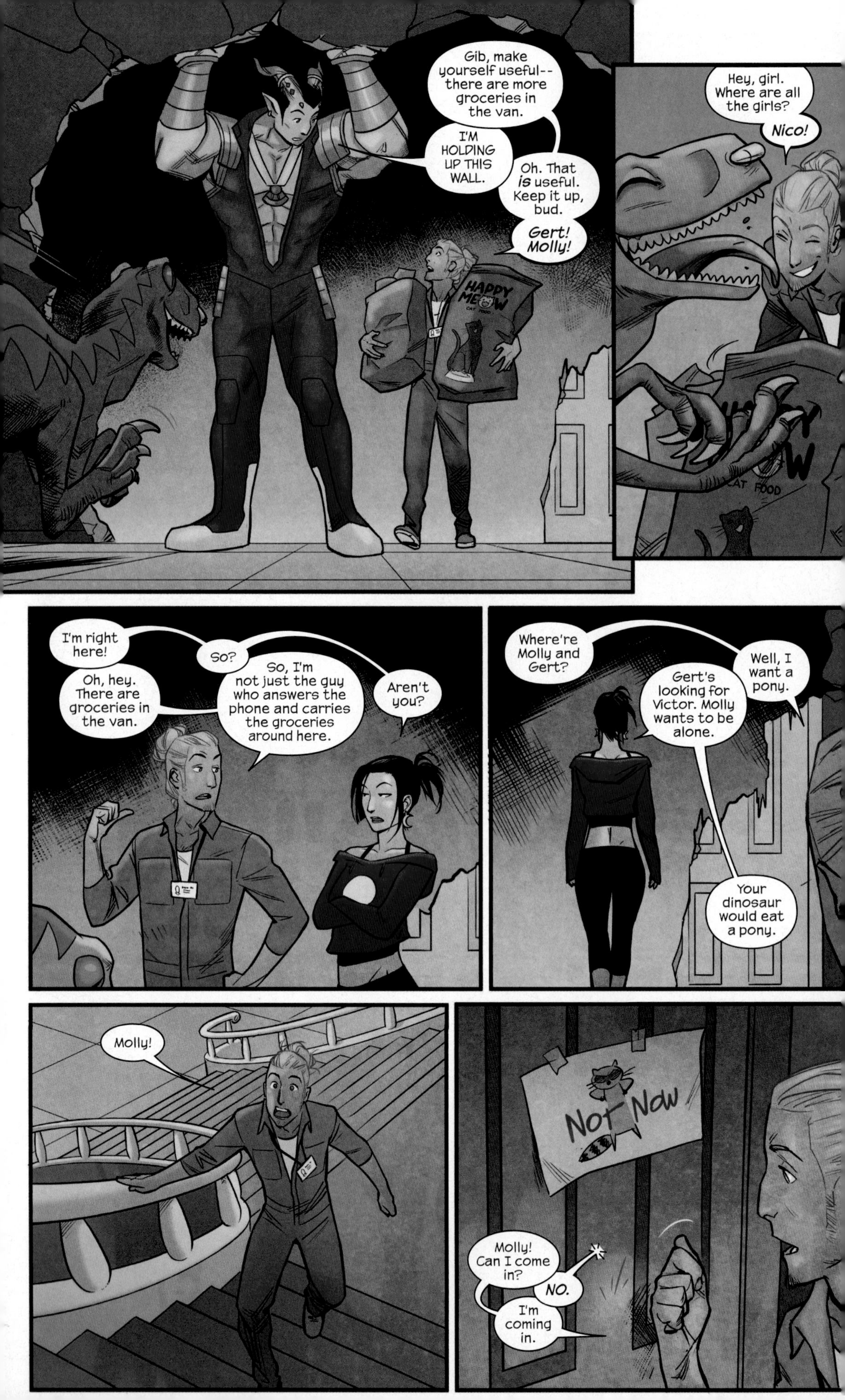

Gib, make yourself useful--there are more groceries in the van.
I'M HOLDING UP THIS WALL.
Oh. That *is* useful. Keep it up, bud.
Gert! Molly!
HAPPY MEOW CAT FOOD
Hey, girl. Where are all the girls?
Nico!
CAT FOOD
I'm right here!
So?
Oh, hey. There are groceries in the van.
So, I'm not just the guy who answers the phone and carries the groceries around here.
Aren't you?
Where're Molly and Gert?
Gert's looking for Victor. Molly wants to be alone.
Well, I want a pony.
Your dinosaur would eat a pony.
Molly!
NOT NOW
Molly! Can I come in?
NO.
I'm coming in.

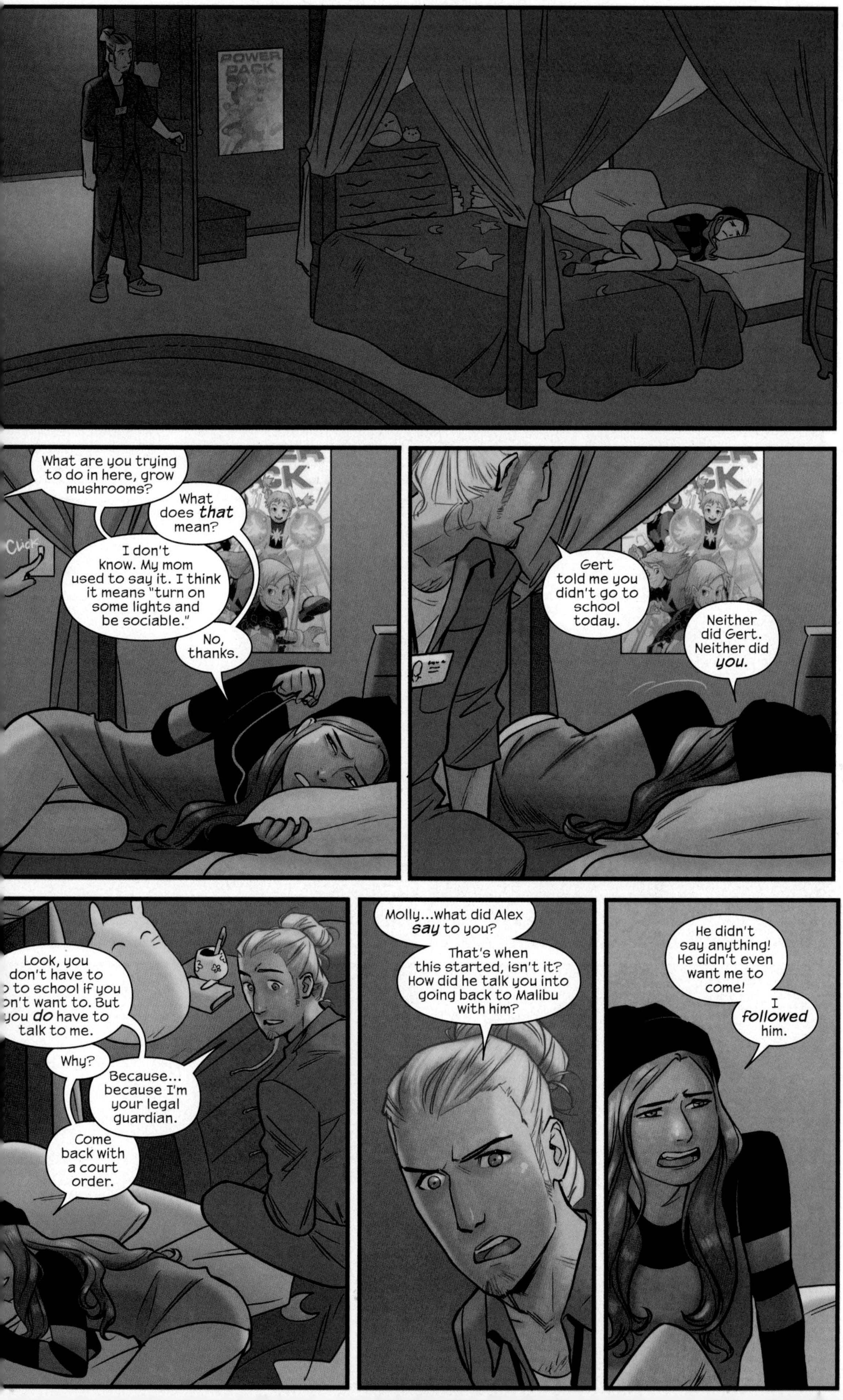
POWER PACK
What are you trying to do in here, grow mushrooms?
CLICK
What does that mean?
I don't know. My mom used to say it. I think it means "turn on some lights and be sociable."
No, thanks.
Gert told me you didn't go to school today.
Neither did Gert. Neither did you.
Look, you don't have to go to school if you don't want to. But you do have to talk to me.
Why?
Because... because I'm your legal guardian.
Come back with a court order.
Molly...what did Alex say to you?
That's when this started, isn't it? How did he talk you into going back to Malibu with him?
He didn't say anything! He didn't even want me to come!
I followed him.

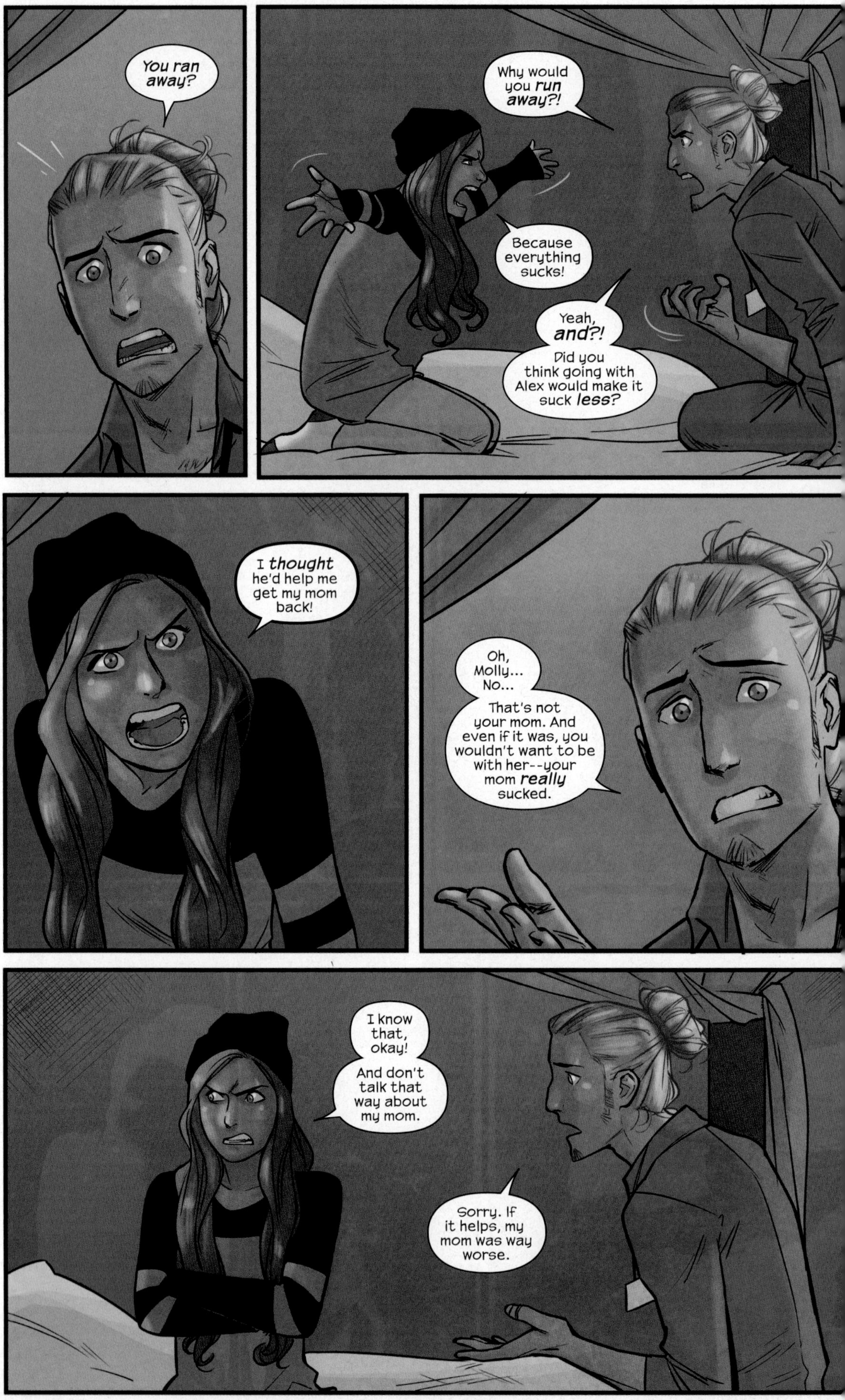
You ran away?
Why would you run away?!
Because everything sucks!
Yeah, and?!
Did you think going with Alex would make it suck less?
I thought he'd help me get my mom back!
Oh, Molly... No...
That's not your mom. And even if it was, you wouldn't want to be with her--your mom really sucked.
I know that, okay!
And don't talk that way about my mom.
Sorry. If it helps, my mom was way worse.

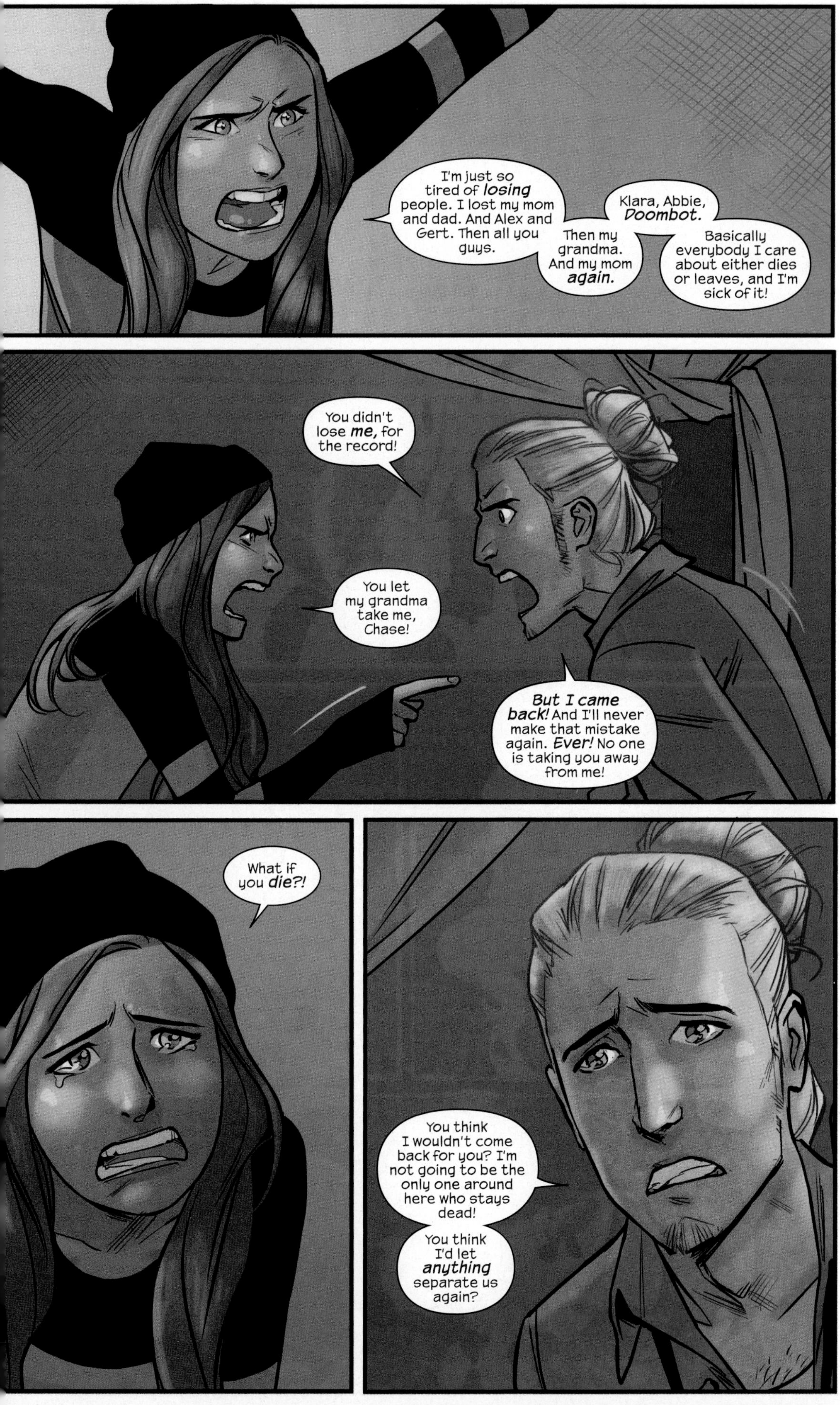
I'm just so tired of *losing* people. I lost my mom and dad. And Alex and Gert. Then all you guys.
Then my grandma. And my mom *again.*
Klara, Abbie, *Doombot.*
Basically everybody I care about either dies or leaves, and I'm sick of it!
You didn't lose *me,* for the record!
You let my grandma take me, Chase!
But I came back! And I'll never make that mistake again. *Ever!* No one is taking you away from me!
What if you *die?!*
You think I wouldn't come back for you? I'm not going to be the only one around here who stays dead!
You think I'd let *anything* separate us again?

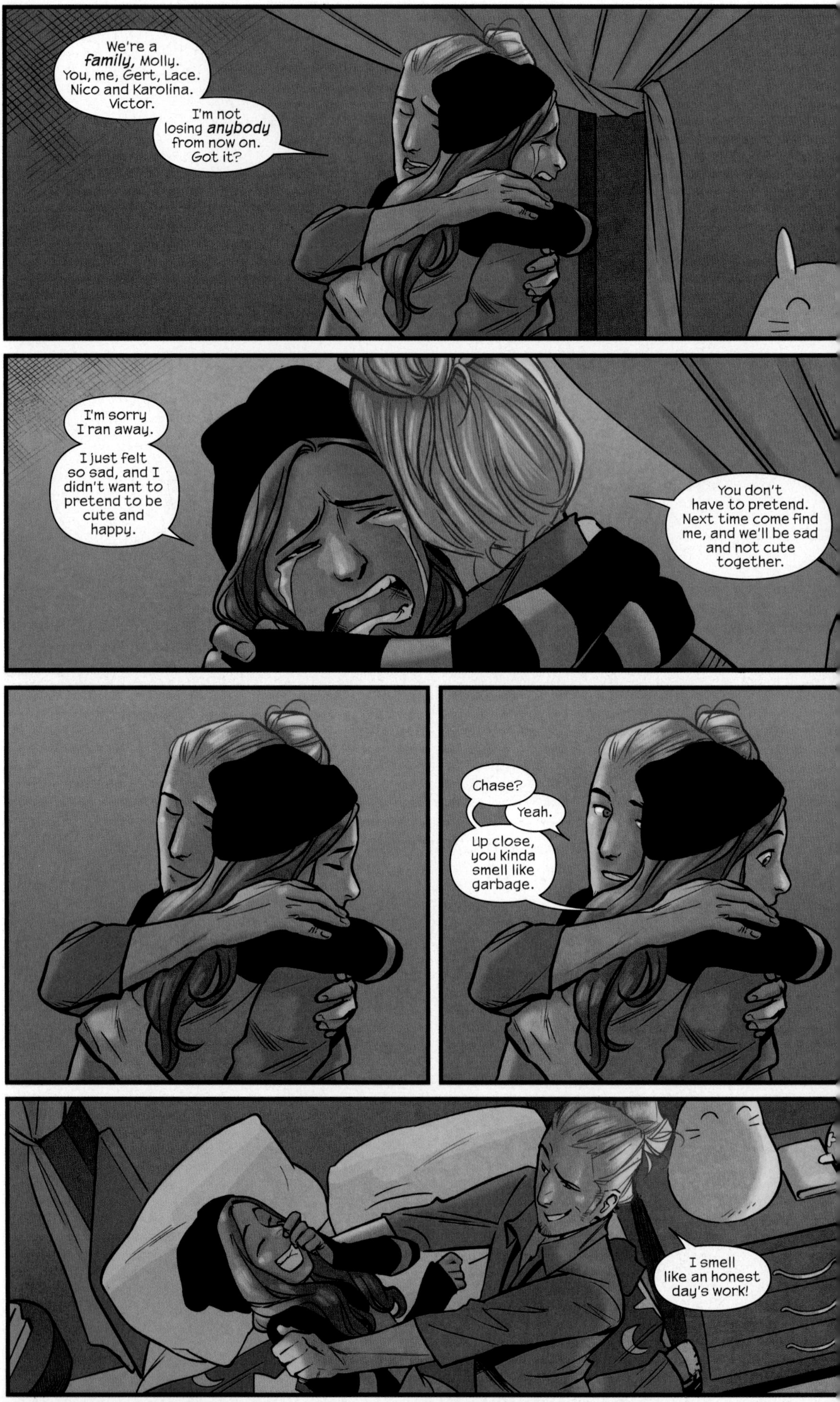

We're a *family,* Molly. You, me, Gert, Lace. Nico and Karolina. Victor.
I'm not losing *anybody* from now on. Got it?
I'm sorry I ran away.
I just felt so sad, and I didn't want to pretend to be cute and happy.
You don't have to pretend. Next time come find me, and we'll be sad and not cute together.
Chase?
Yeah.
Up close, you kinda smell like garbage.
I smell like an honest day's work!

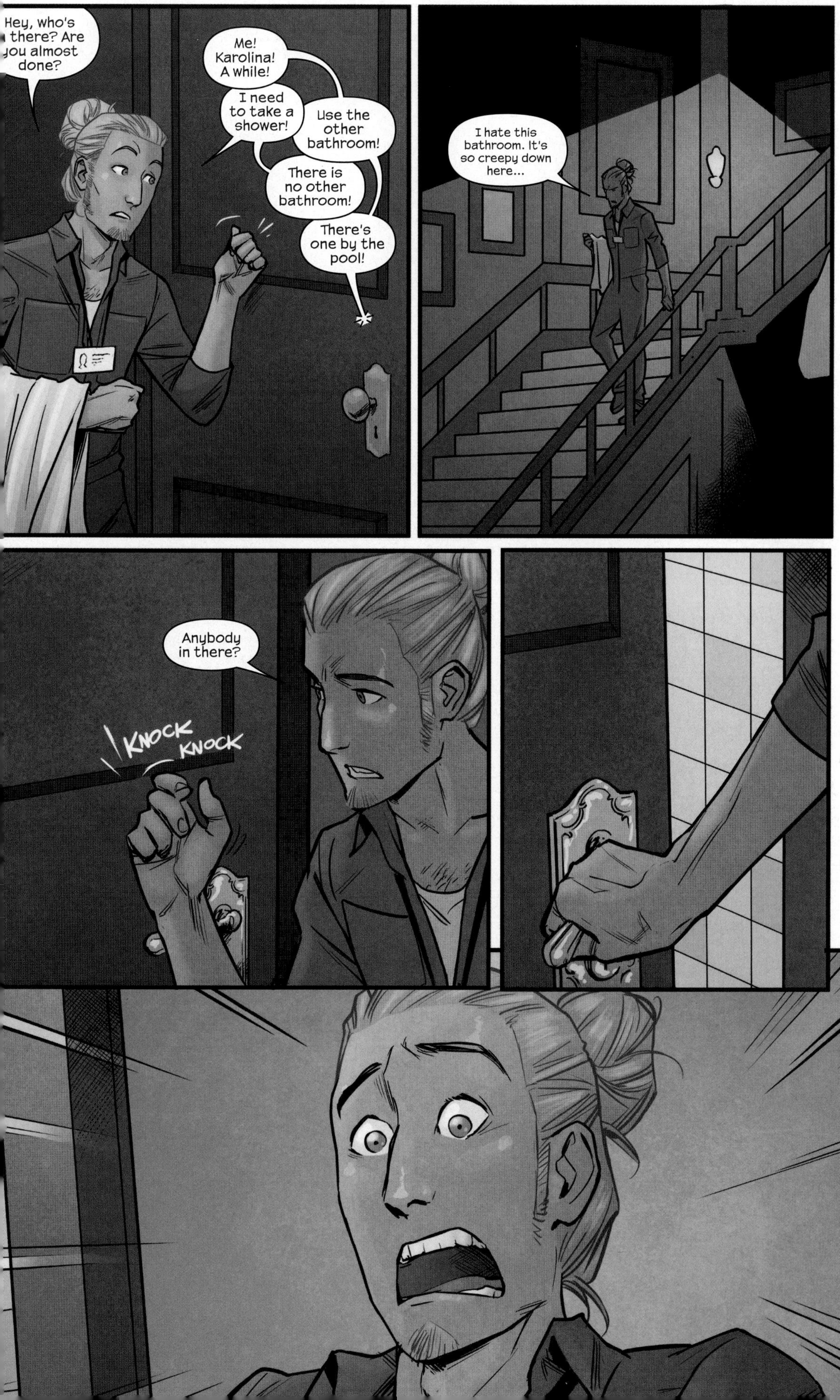
Hey, who's there? Are you almost done?
Me! Karolina! A while!
I need to take a shower!
Use the other bathroom!
There is no other bathroom!
There's one by the pool!
I hate this bathroom. It's so creepy down here...
Anybody in there?
KNOCK KNOCK

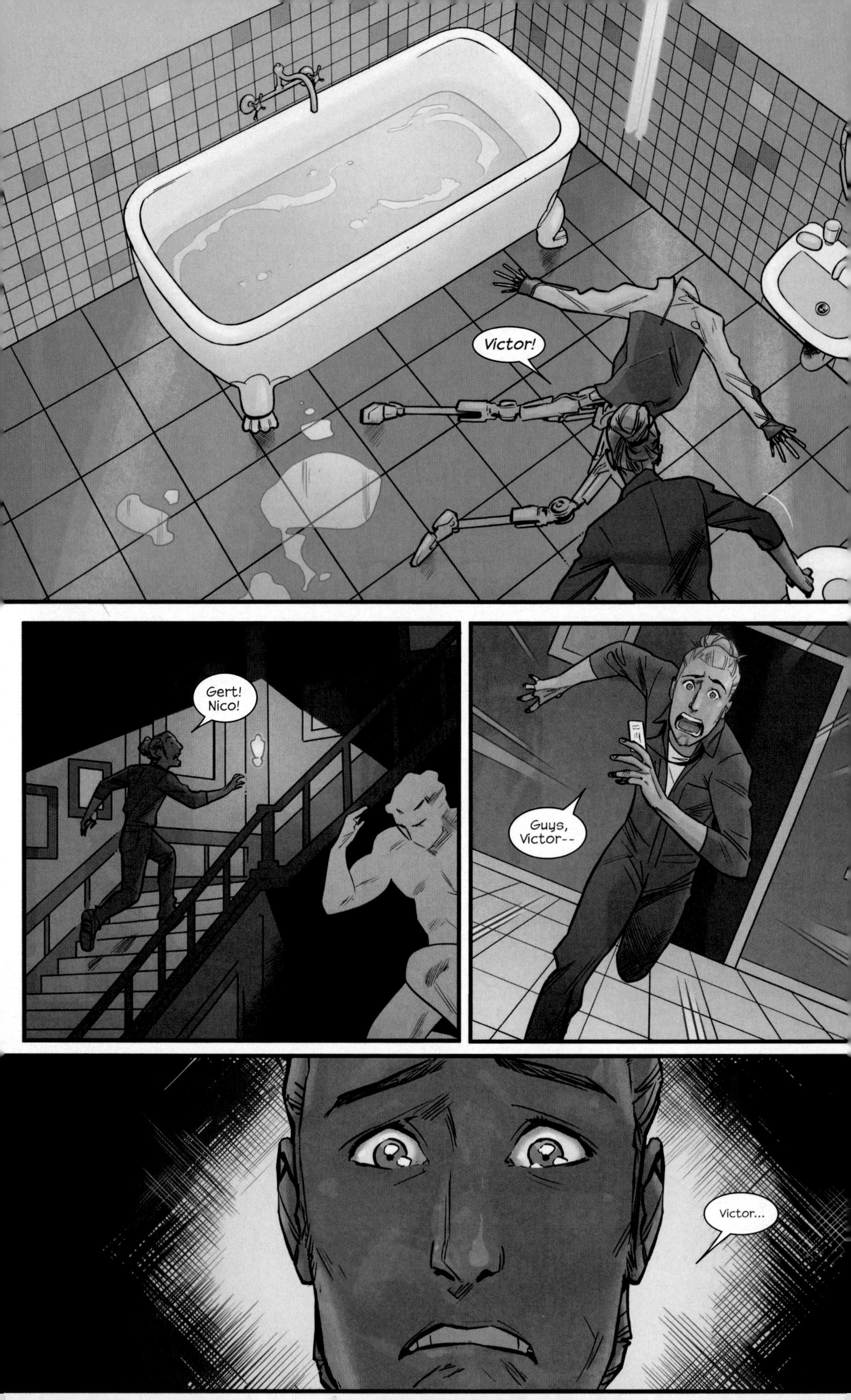
Victor!
Gert! Nico!
Guys, Victor--
Victor...

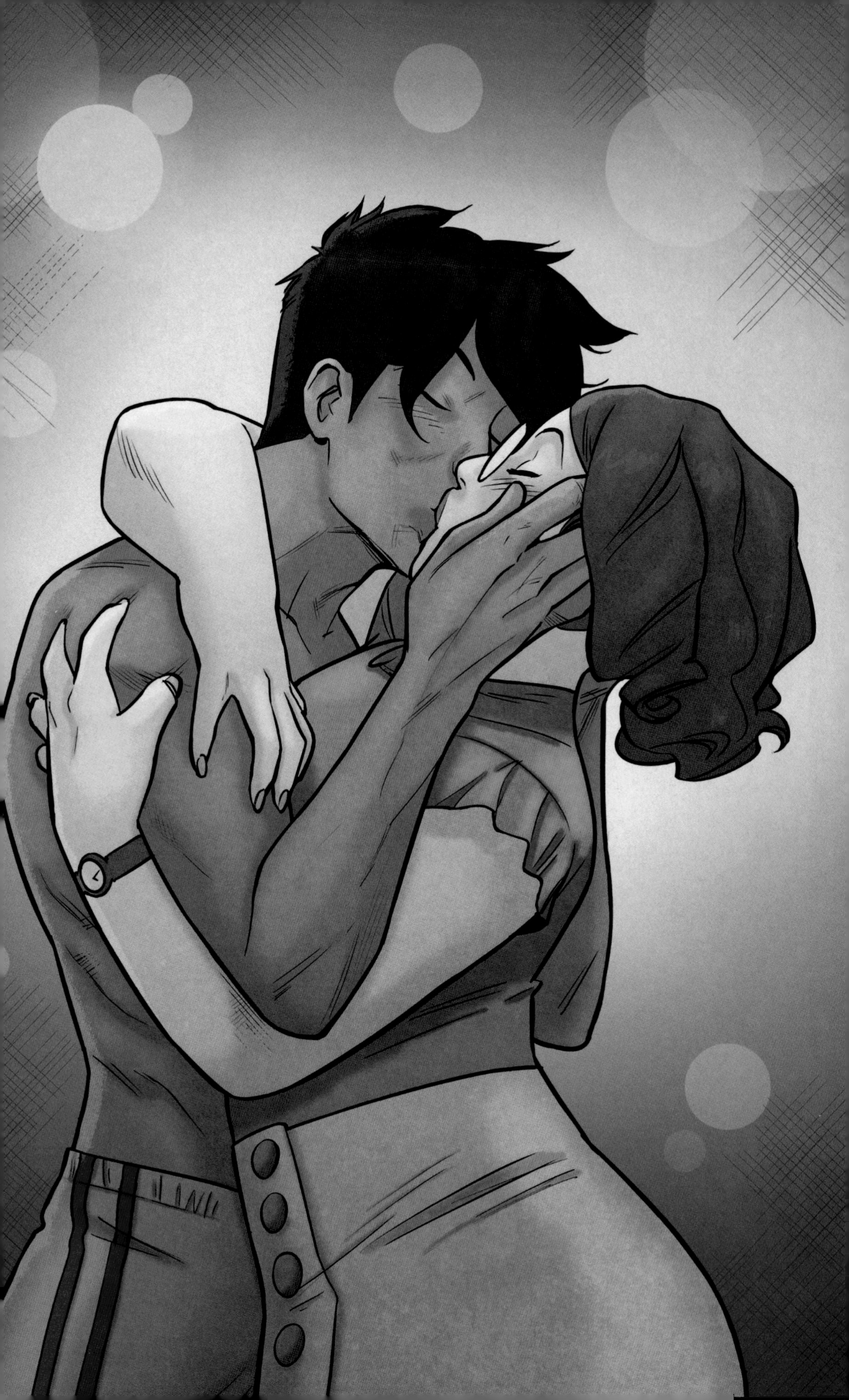

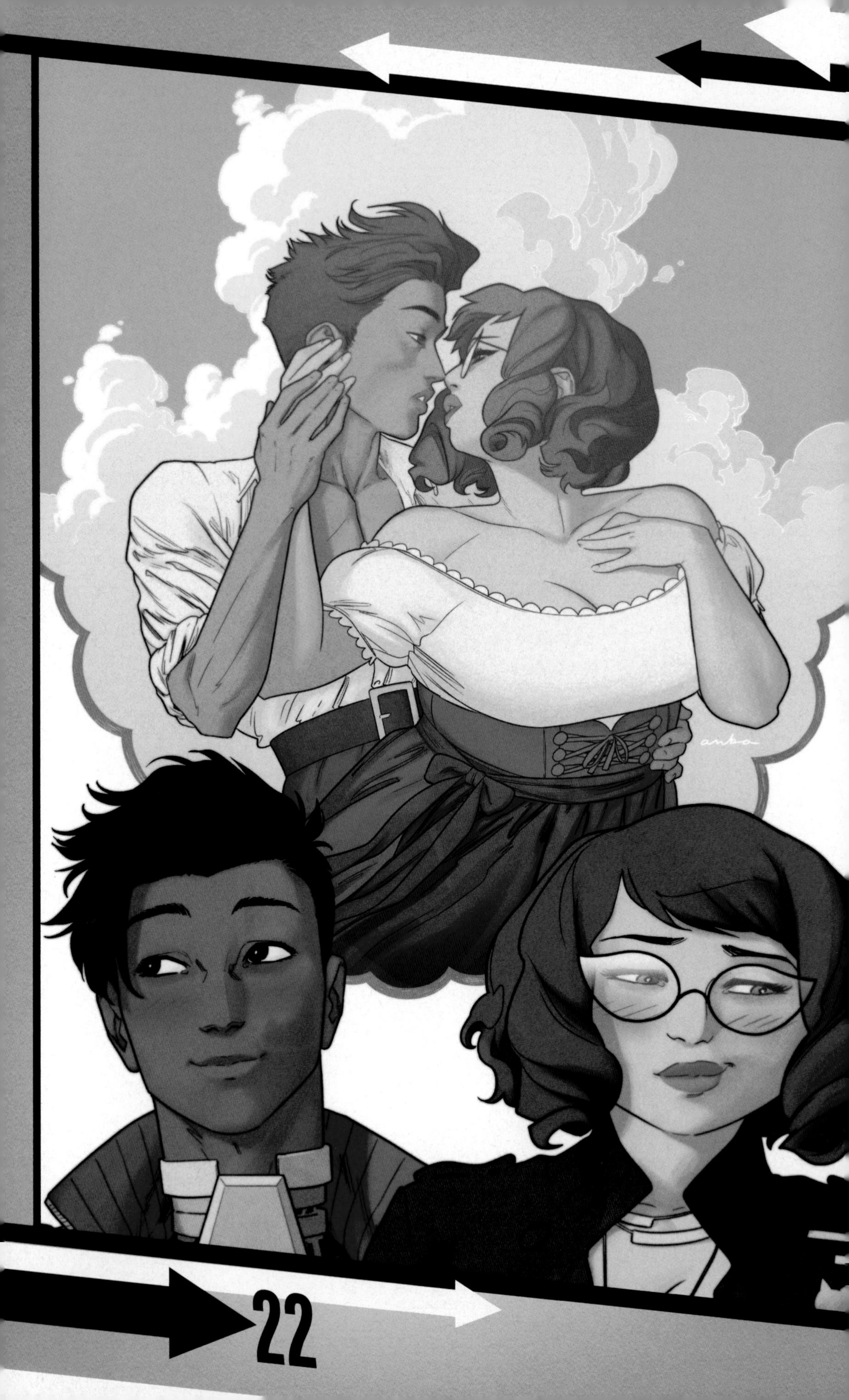
22

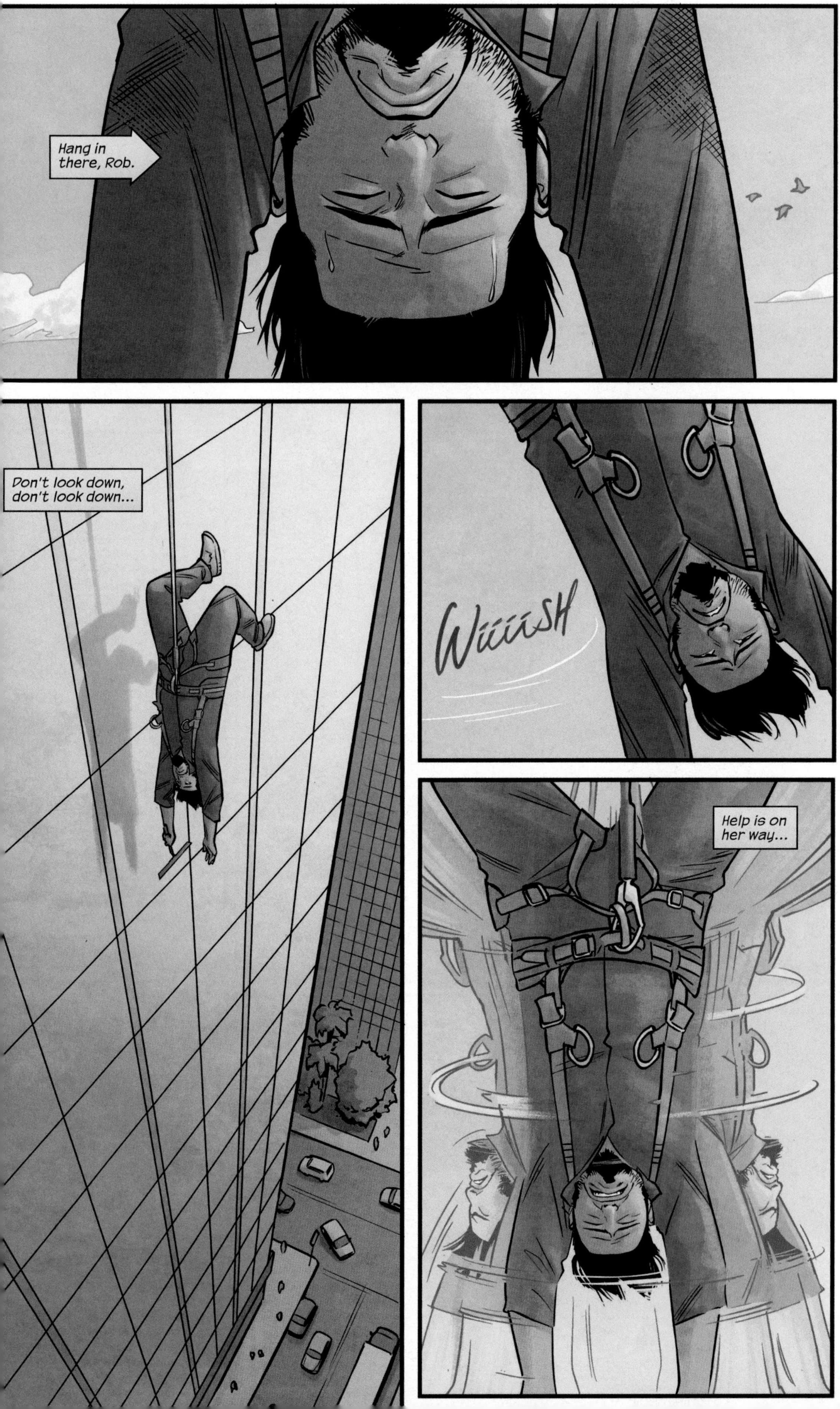
Hang in there, Rob.
Don't look down, don't look down...
WIIIISH
Help is on her way...

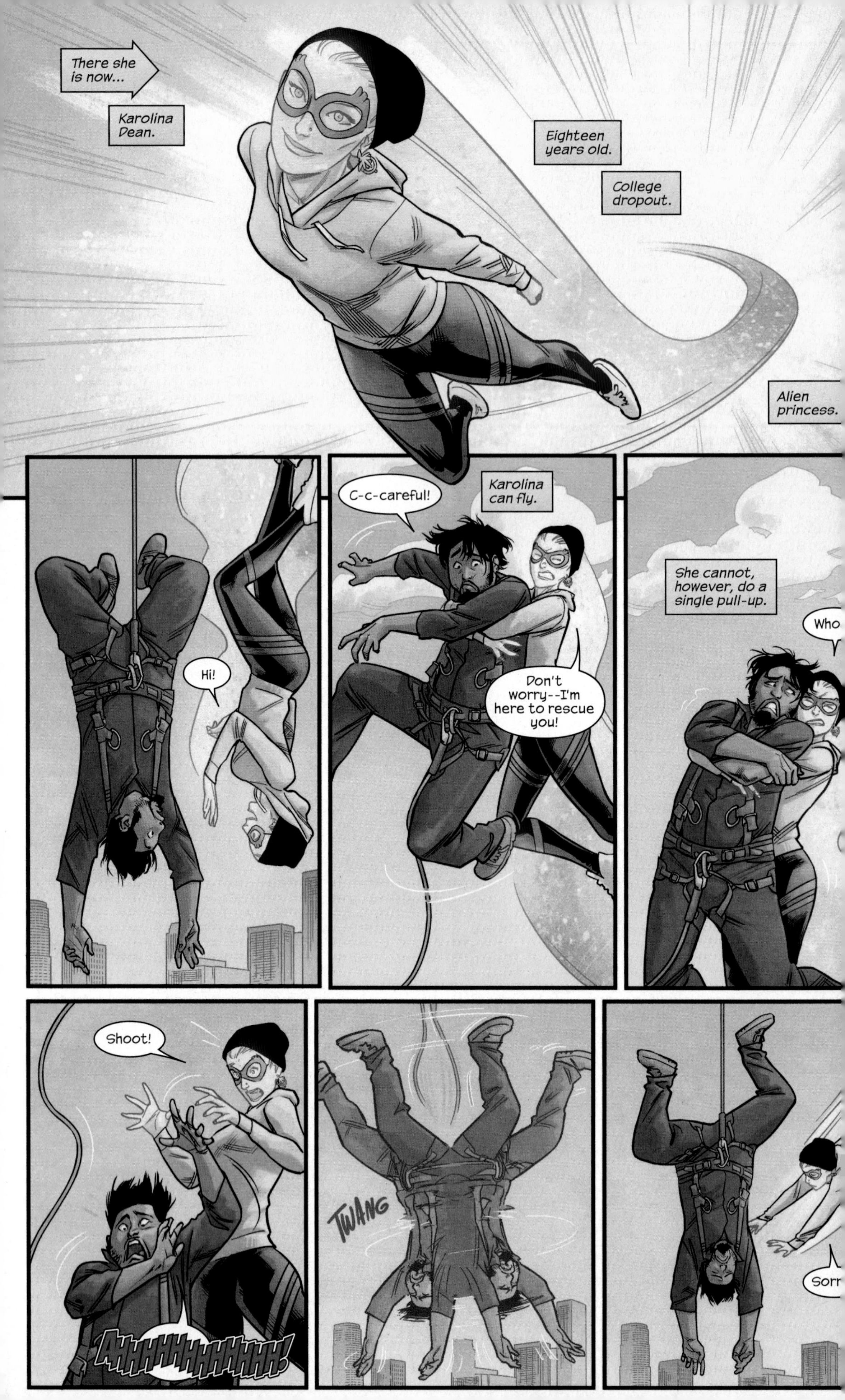
There she is now...
Karolina Dean.
Eighteen years old.
College dropout.
Alien princess.
Hi!
C-c-careful!
Karolina can fly.
Don't worry--I'm here to rescue you!
She cannot, however, do a single pull-up.
Shoot!
AHHHHHHHHHHH!
TWANG

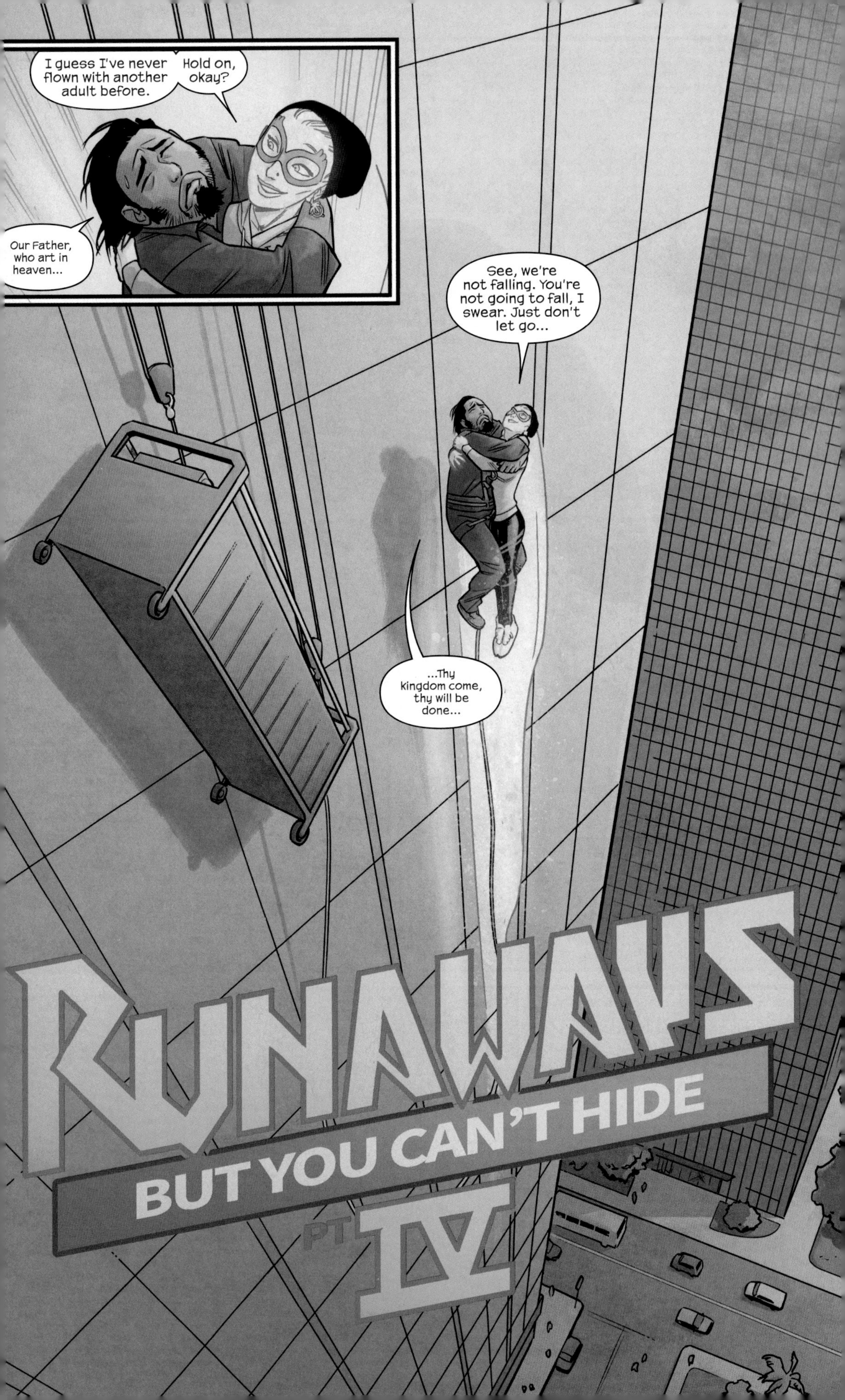

I guess I've never flown with another adult before.
Hold on, okay?
Our Father, who art in heaven...
See, we're not falling. You're not going to fall, I swear. Just don't let go...
...Thy kingdom come, thy will be done...
RUNAWAYS
BUT YOU CAN'T HIDE
PT IV

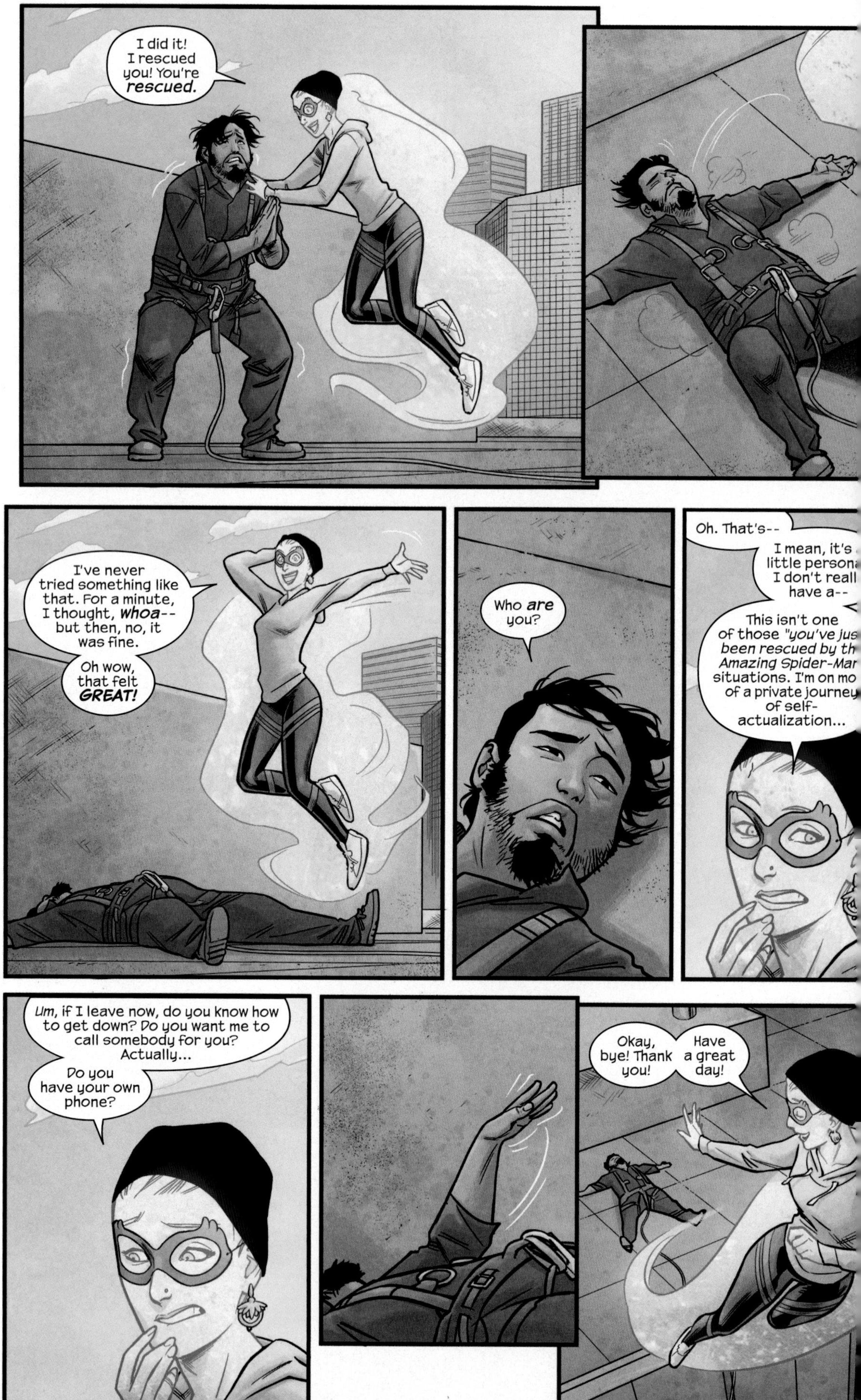
I did it! I rescued you! You're *rescued.*
I've never tried something like that. For a minute, I thought, *whoa*-- but then, no, it was fine.
Oh wow, that felt **GREAT!**
Who *are* you?
Oh. That's--
I mean, it's little persona I don't reall have a--
This isn't one of those *"you've jus been rescued by th Amazing Spider-Mar* situations. I'm on mo of a private journey of self-actualization...
Um, if I leave now, do you know how to get down? Do you want me to call somebody for you? Actually...
Do you have your own phone?
Okay, bye! Thank you!
Have a great day!

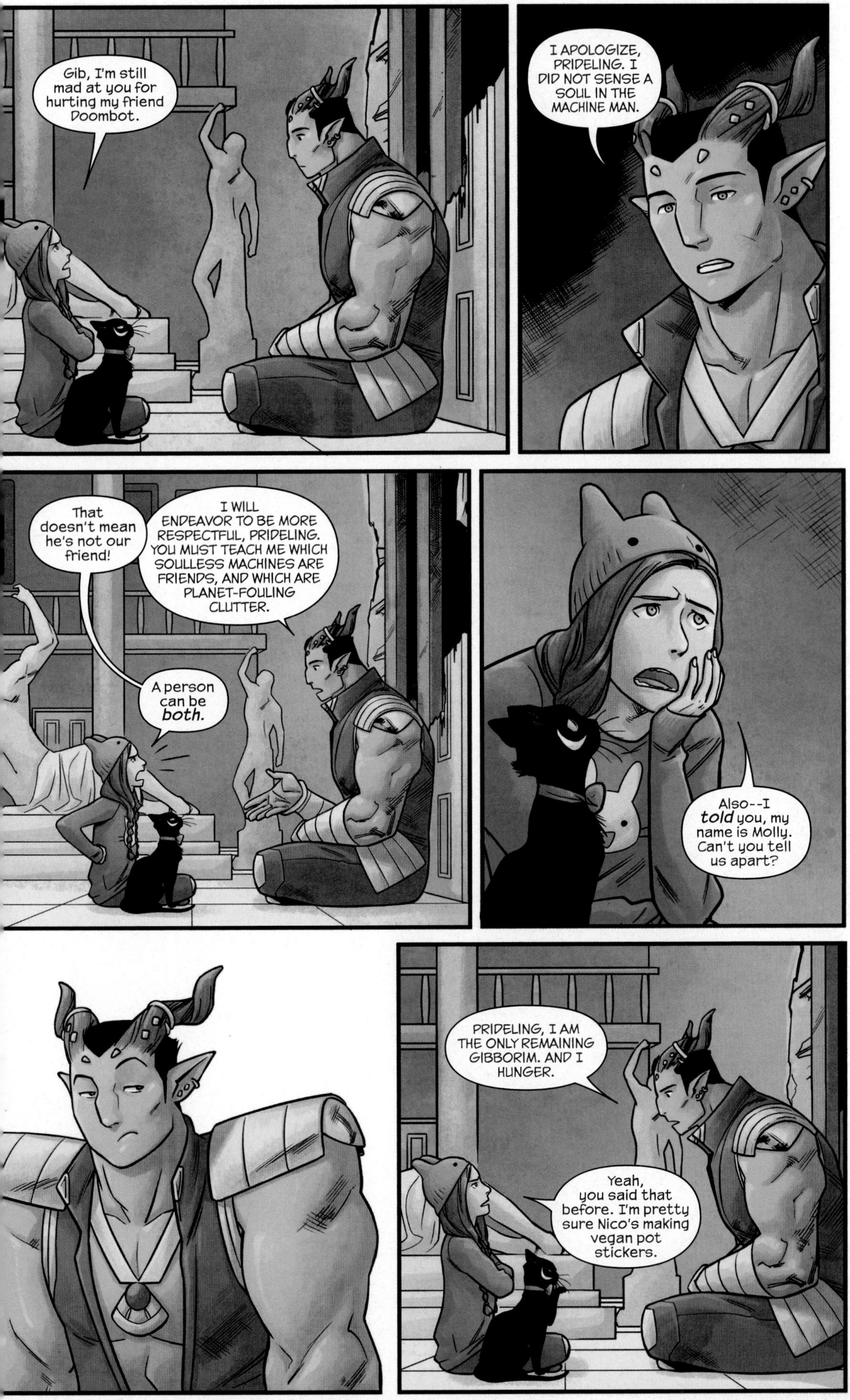
Gib, I'm still mad at you for hurting my friend Doombot.
I APOLOGIZE, PRIDELING. I DID NOT SENSE A SOUL IN THE MACHINE MAN.
That doesn't mean he's not our friend!
I WILL ENDEAVOR TO BE MORE RESPECTFUL, PRIDELING. YOU MUST TEACH ME WHICH SOULLESS MACHINES ARE FRIENDS, AND WHICH ARE PLANET-FOULING CLUTTER.
A person can be *both*.
Also--I *told* you, my name is Molly. Can't you tell us apart?
PRIDELING, I AM THE ONLY REMAINING GIBBORIM. AND I HUNGER.
Yeah, you said that before. I'm pretty sure Nico's making vegan pot stickers.

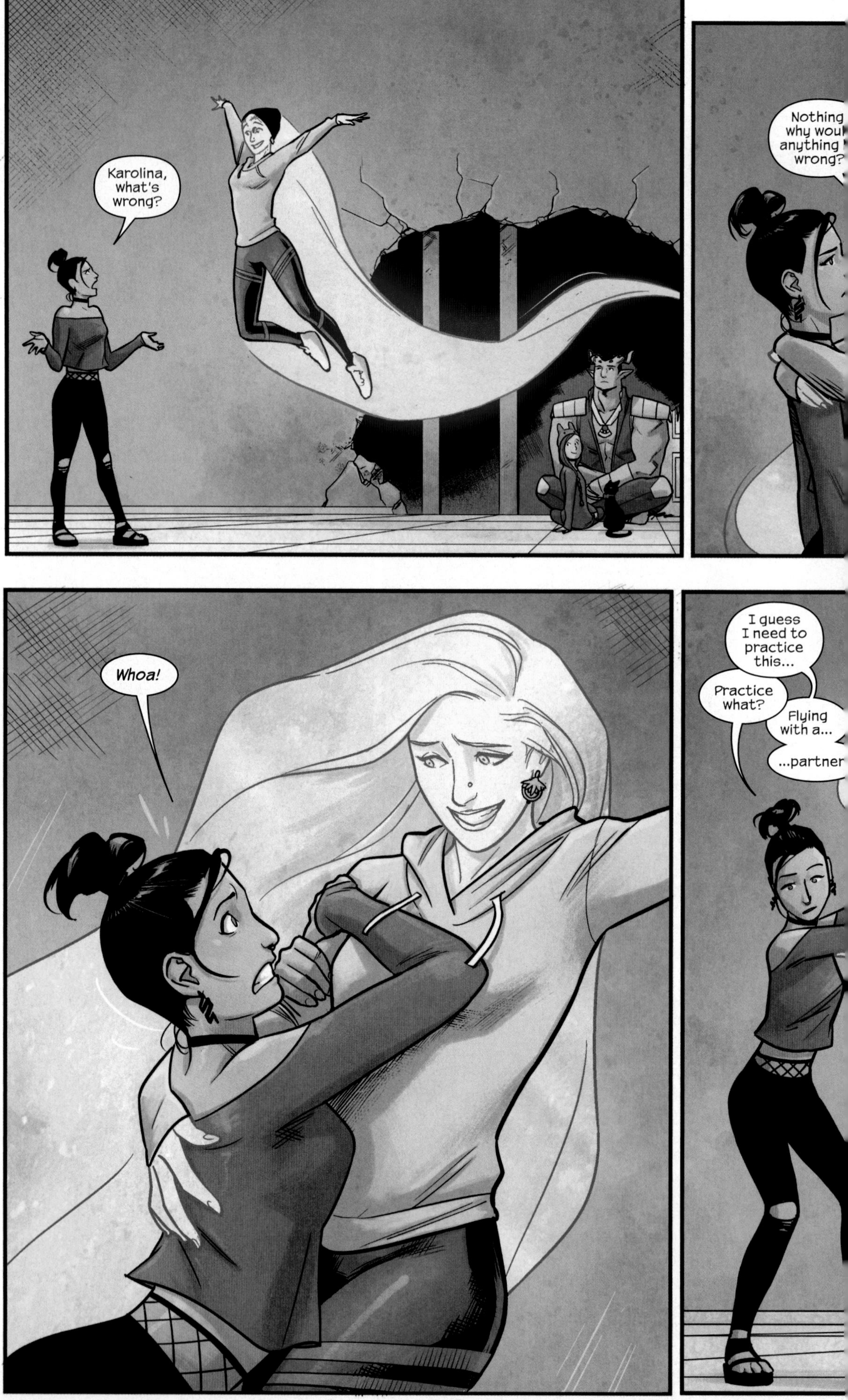
Karolina, what's wrong?
Nothing why woul anything wrong?
Whoa!
I guess I need to practice this...
Practice what?
Flying with a...
...partner

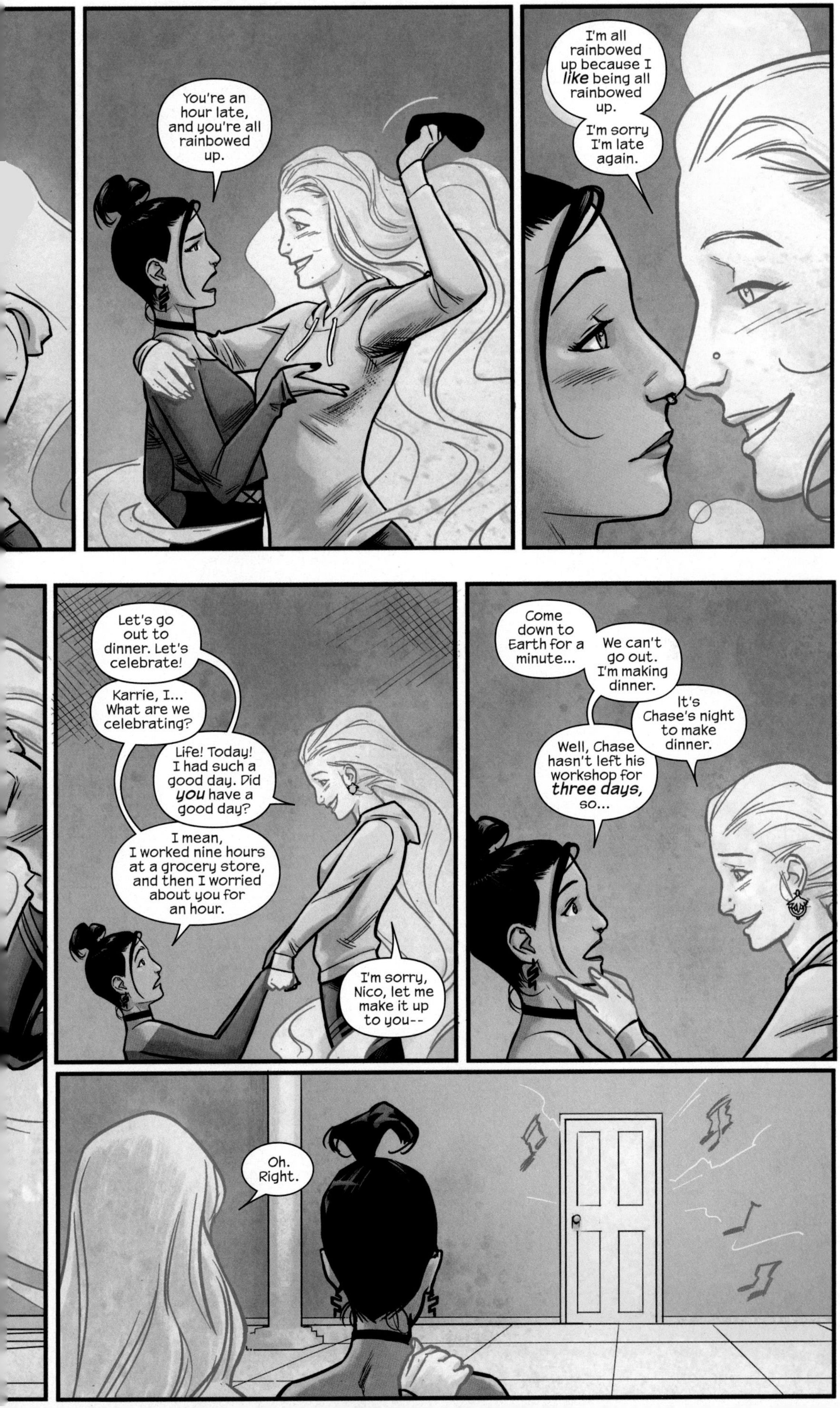

You're an hour late, and you're all rainbowed up.
I'm all rainbowed up because I *like* being all rainbowed up.
I'm sorry I'm late again.
Let's go out to dinner. Let's celebrate!
Karrie, I... What are we celebrating?
Life! Today! I had such a good day. Did *you* have a good day?
I mean, I worked nine hours at a grocery store, and then I worried about you for an hour.
I'm sorry, Nico, let me make it up to you--
Come down to Earth for a minute...
We can't go out. I'm making dinner.
It's Chase's night to make dinner.
Well, Chase hasn't left his workshop for *three days,* so...
Oh. Right.

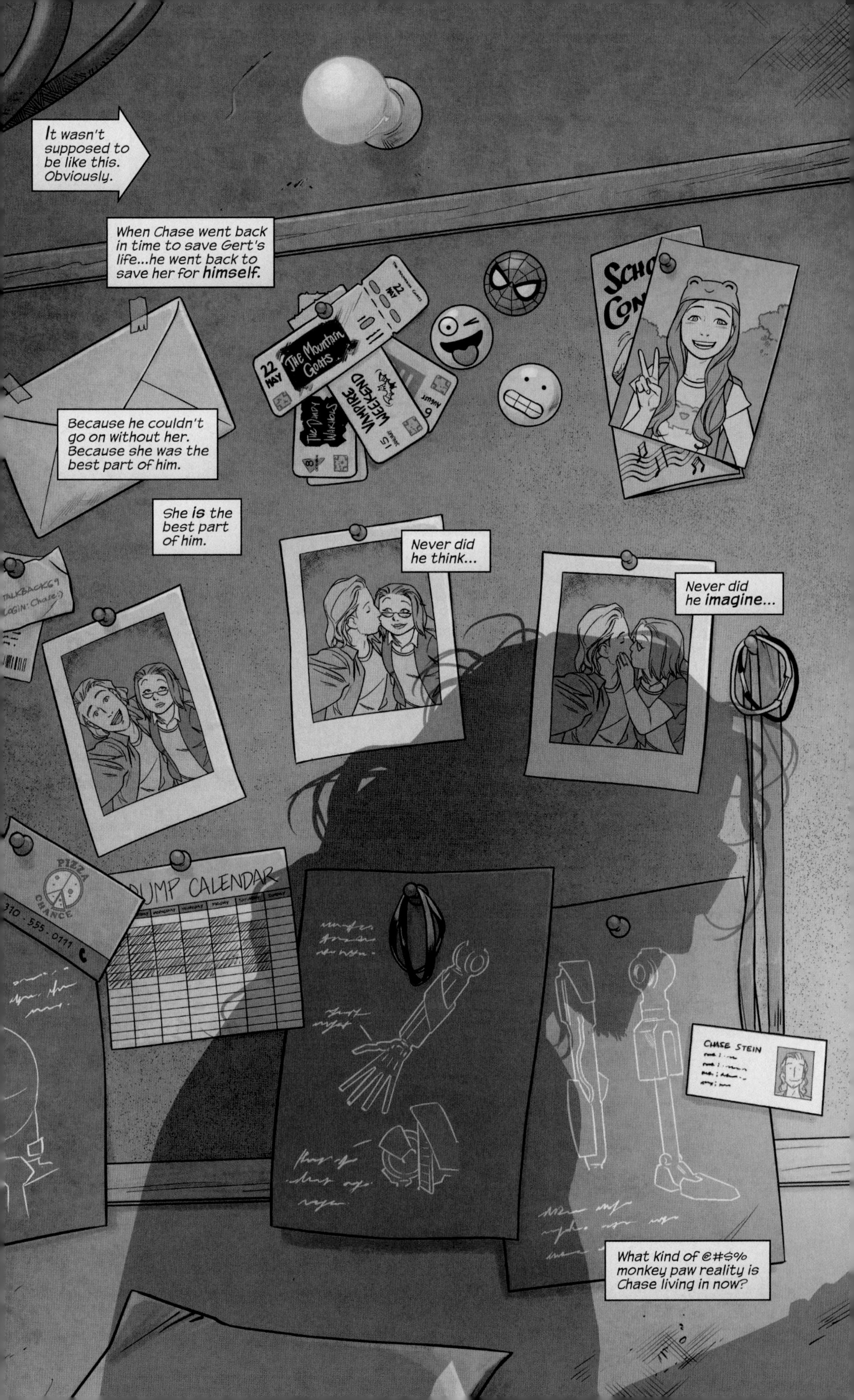
It wasn't supposed to be like this. Obviously.
When Chase went back in time to save Gert's life...he went back to save her for himself.
Because he couldn't go on without her. Because she was the best part of him.
She is the best part of him.
Never did he think...
Never did he imagine...
What kind of @#$% monkey paw reality is Chase living in now?
The Mountain Goats
22 May
Vampire Weekend
The Dandy Warhols
Pizza Chance
310 - 555 - 0111
DUMP CALENDAR
Chase Stein
TALKBACK69
LOGIN: Chase:)

He told himself that it was just a matter of **time**.

Everything is temporary.

This, too, shall pas[s]

But they won't always be 16 and 20...

It won't always matter the way it matters right now.

Chase isn't exac[tly] waiting for Ger[t] to grow up. Tha[t] sounds creepy.

He's ju[st]

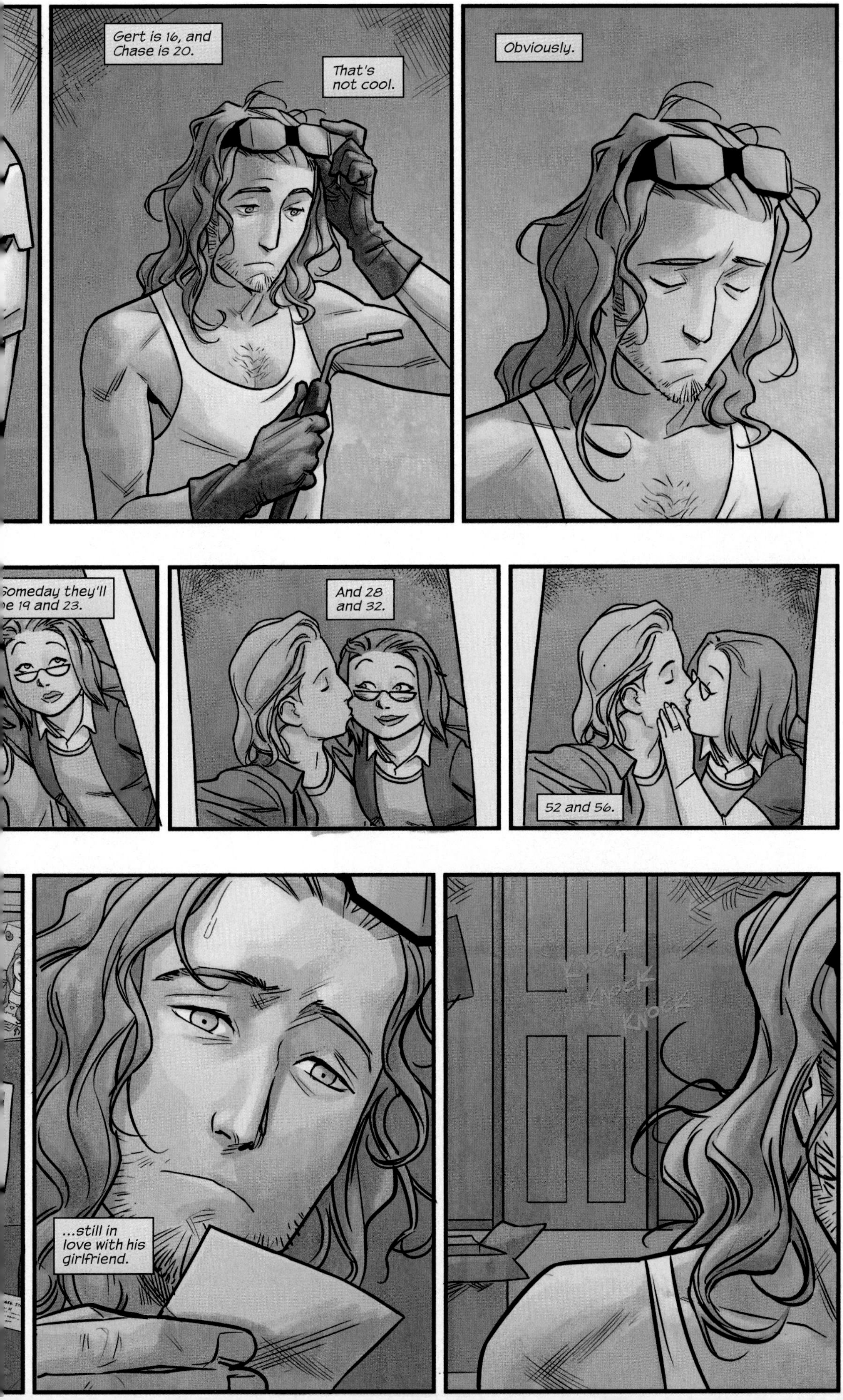

Gert is 16, and Chase is 20.
That's not cool.
Obviously.
Someday they'll
e 19 and 23.
And 28 and 32.
52 and 56.
...still in love with his girlfriend.
KNOCK
KNOCK
KNOCK

Chase! Come on! This is getting ridiculous. You have to let me--

--in.

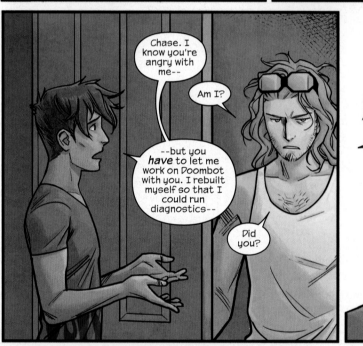

Chase. I know you're angry with me--

Am I?

--but you **have** to let me work on Doombot with you. I rebuilt myself so that I could run diagnostics--

Did you?

Chas
I'm so

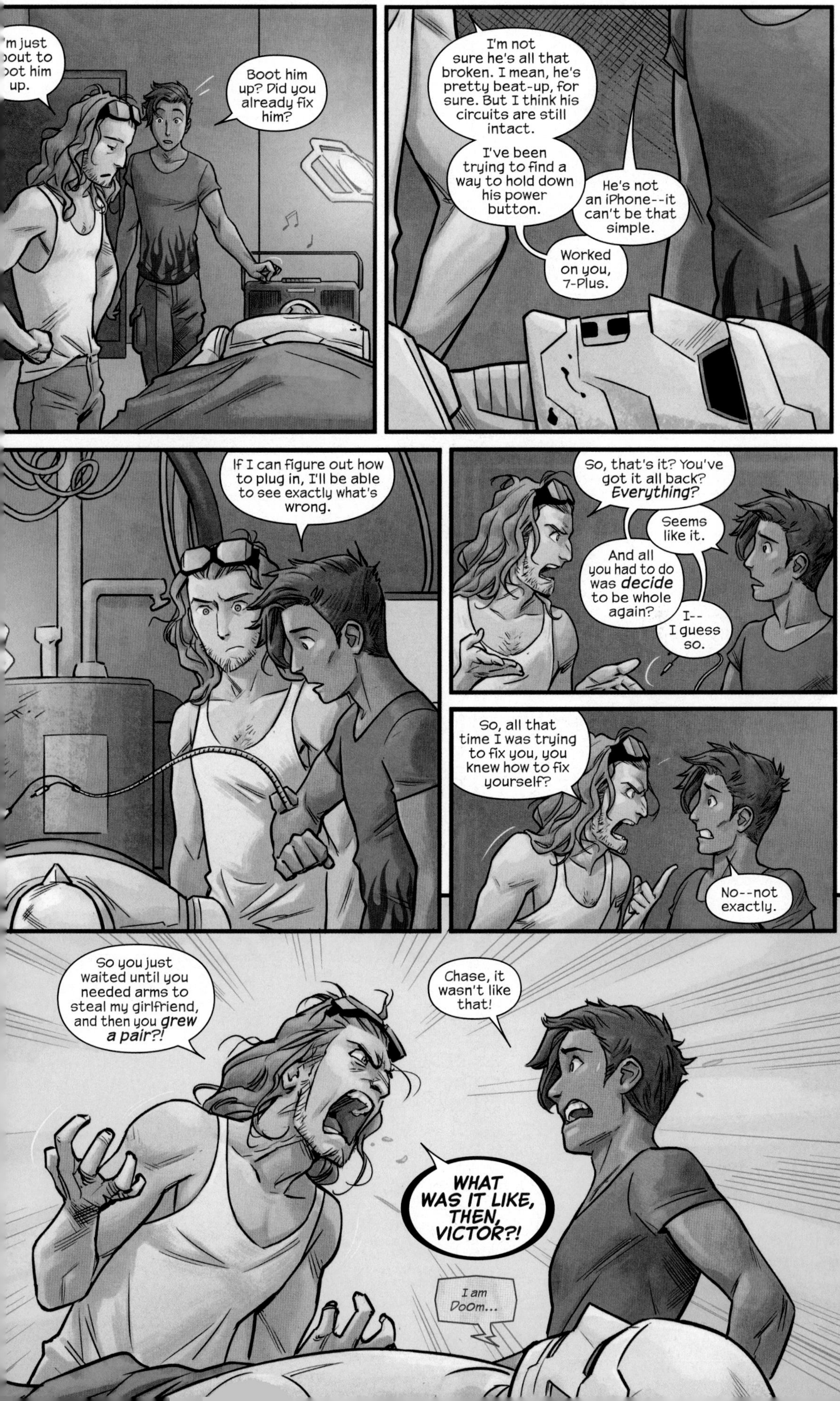
'm just
bout to
oot him
up.
Boot him up? Did you already fix him?
I'm not sure he's all that broken. I mean, he's pretty beat-up, for sure. But I think his circuits are still intact.
I've been trying to find a way to hold down his power button.
He's not an iPhone--it can't be that simple.
Worked on you, 7-Plus.
If I can figure out how to plug in, I'll be able to see exactly what's wrong.
So, that's it? You've got it all back? *Everything?*
Seems like it.
And all you had to do was *decide* to be whole again?
I-- I guess so.
So, all that time I was trying to fix you, you knew how to fix yourself?
No--not exactly.
So you just waited until you needed arms to steal my girlfriend, and then you *grew a pair?!*
Chase, it wasn't like that!
WHAT WAS IT LIKE, THEN, VICTOR?!
I am DoOm...

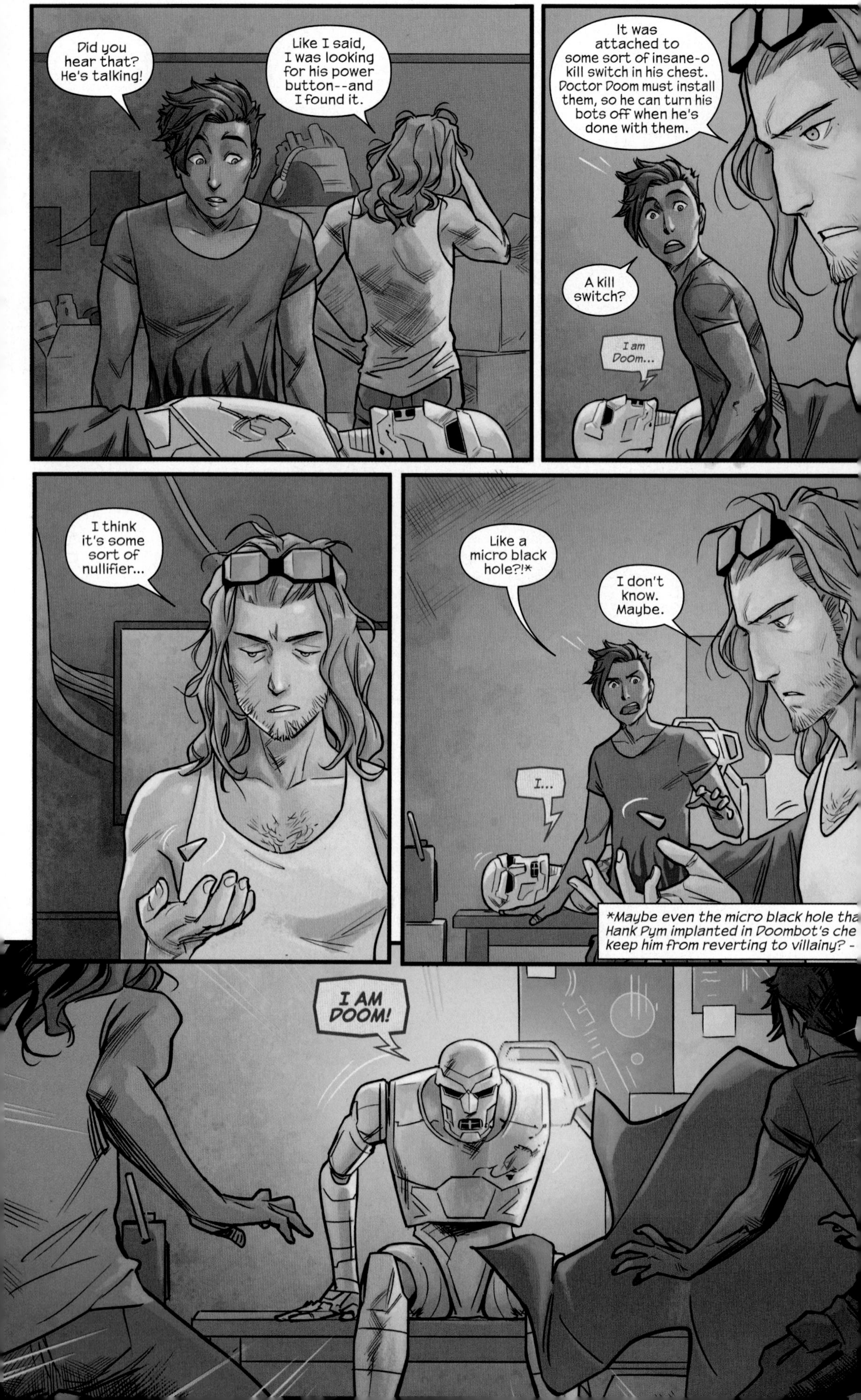
Did you hear that? He's talking!
Like I said, I was looking for his power button--and I found it.
It was attached to some sort of insane-o kill switch in his chest. Doctor Doom must install them, so he can turn his bots off when he's done with them.
A kill switch?
I am Doom...
I think it's some sort of nullifier...
Like a micro black hole?!*
I don't know. Maybe.
I...
*Maybe even the micro black hole tha Hank Pym implanted in Doombot's che keep him from reverting to villainy? -
I AM DOOM!

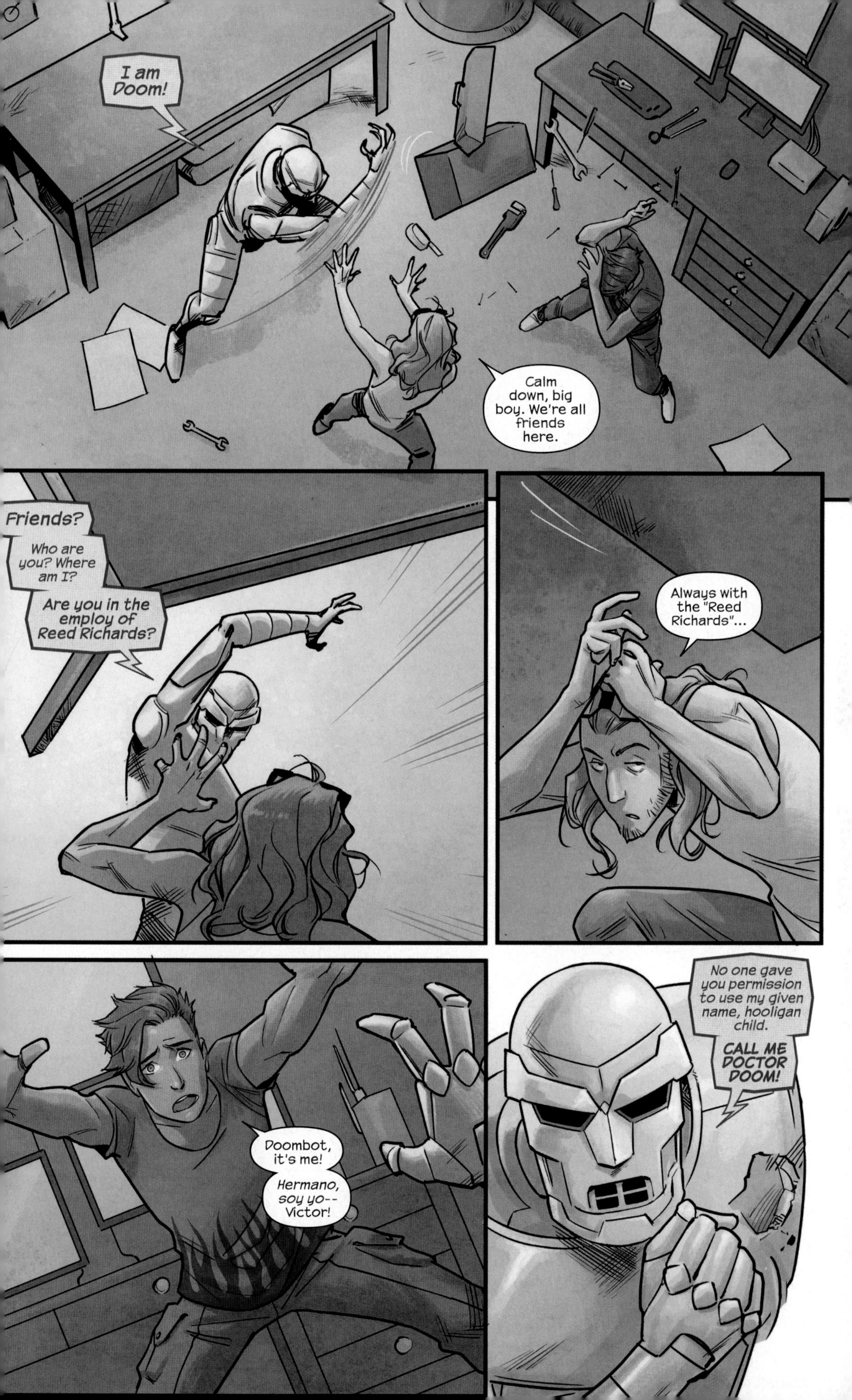
I am Doom!
Calm down, big boy. We're all friends here.
Friends?
Who are you? Where am I?
Are you in the employ of Reed Richards?
Always with the "Reed Richards"...
Doombot, it's me!
Hermano, soy yo-- Victor!
No one gave you permission to use my given name, hooligan child.
CALL ME DOCTOR DOOM!

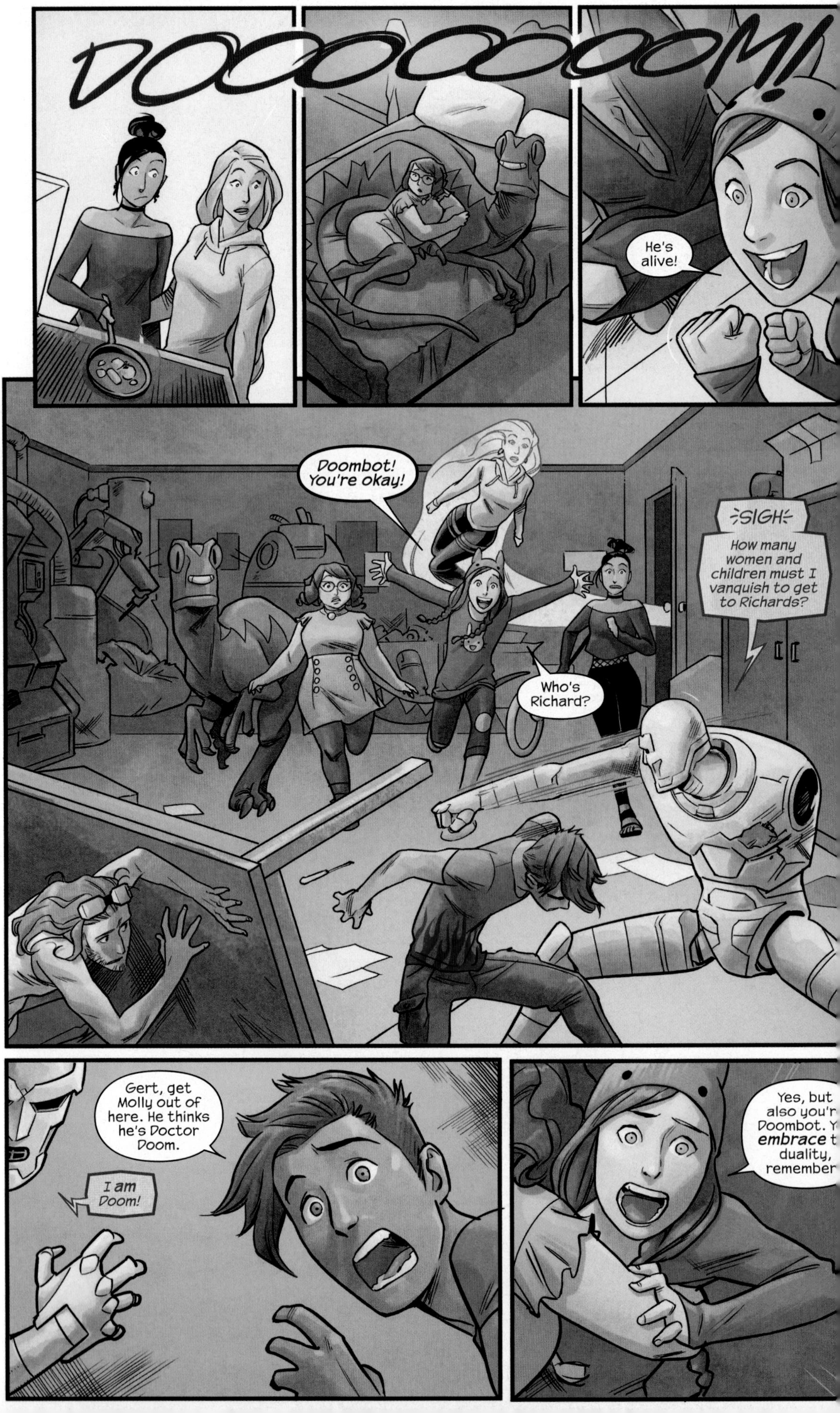
DOOOOOOOOM!
He's alive!
Doombot! You're okay!
SIGH
How many women and children must I vanquish to get to Richards?
Who's Richard?
Gert, get Molly out of here. He thinks he's Doctor Doom.
I am Doom!

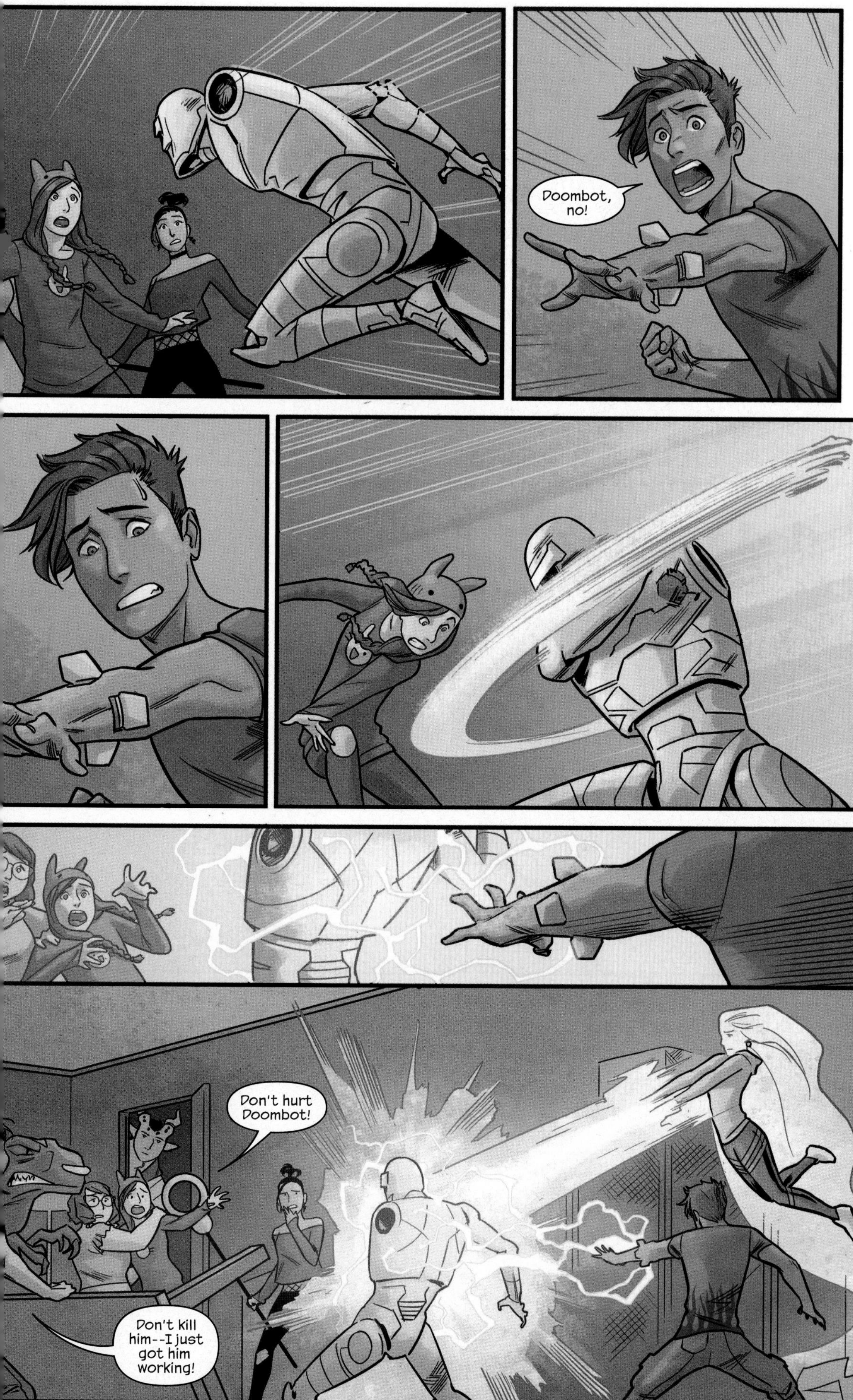
Doombot, no!
Don't hurt Doombot!
Don't kill him--I just got him working!

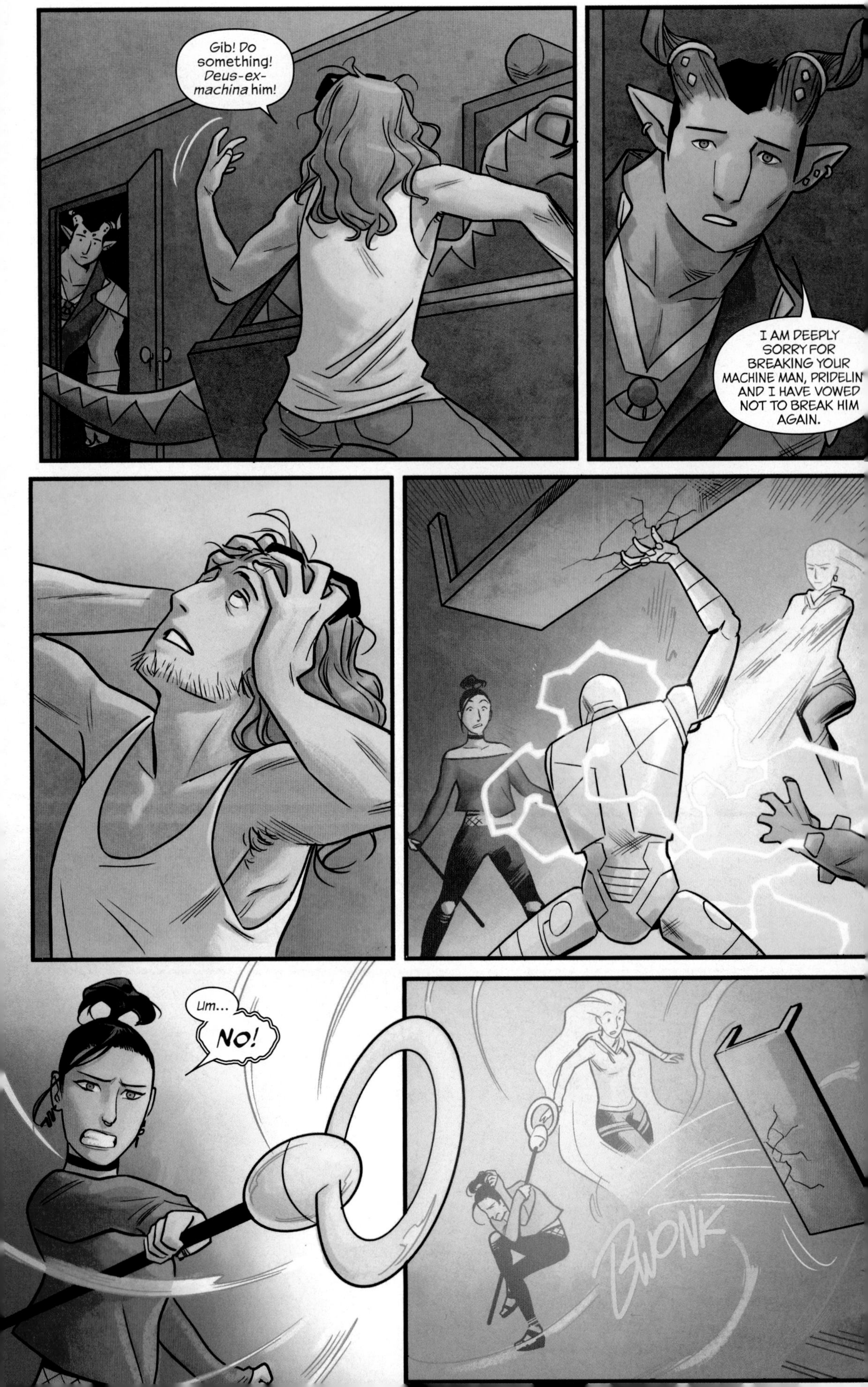
Gib! Do something! Deus-ex-machina him!
I AM DEEPLY SORRY FOR BREAKING YOUR MACHINE MAN, PRIDELIN AND I HAVE VOWED NOT TO BREAK HIM AGAIN.
Um...
NO!
BWONK

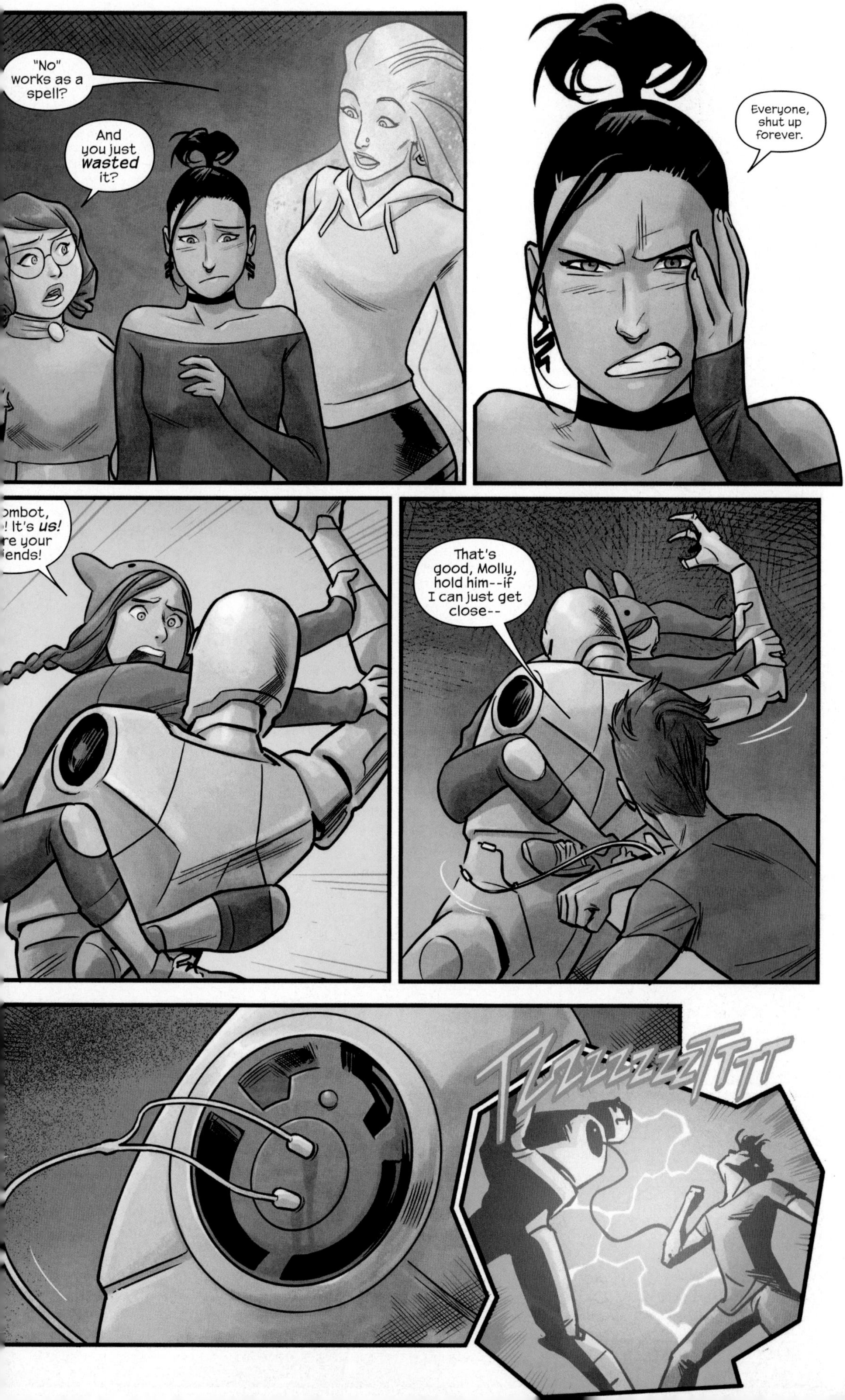

"No" works as a spell?
And you just *wasted* it?
Everyone, shut up forever.
...mbot, ...! It's *us!* ...re your ...iends!
That's good, Molly, hold him--if I can just get close--
TZzzzzzzTTTT

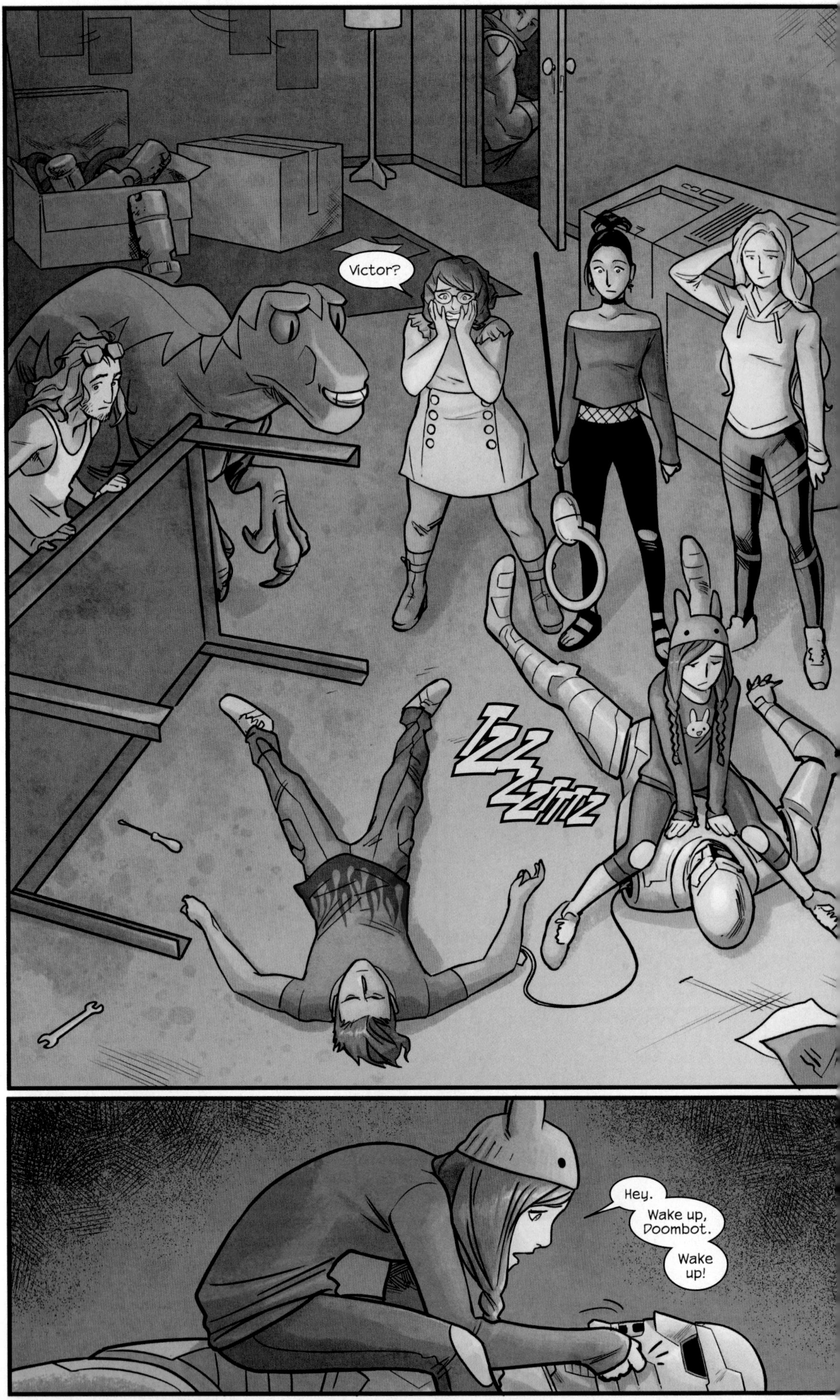
Victor?
ZZZZZTTZ
Hey.
Wake up, Doombot.
Wake up!

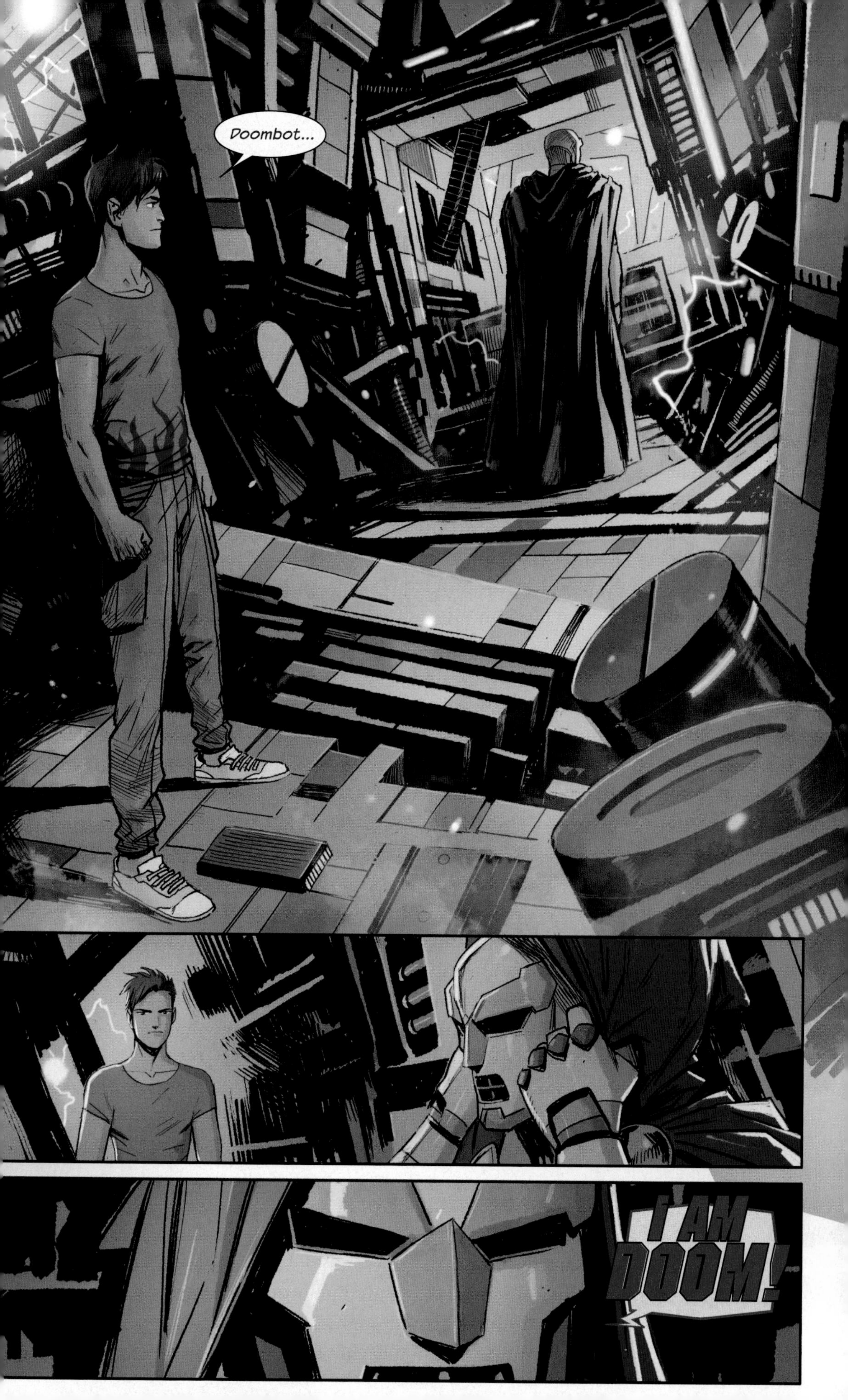
Doombot...
I AM DOOM!

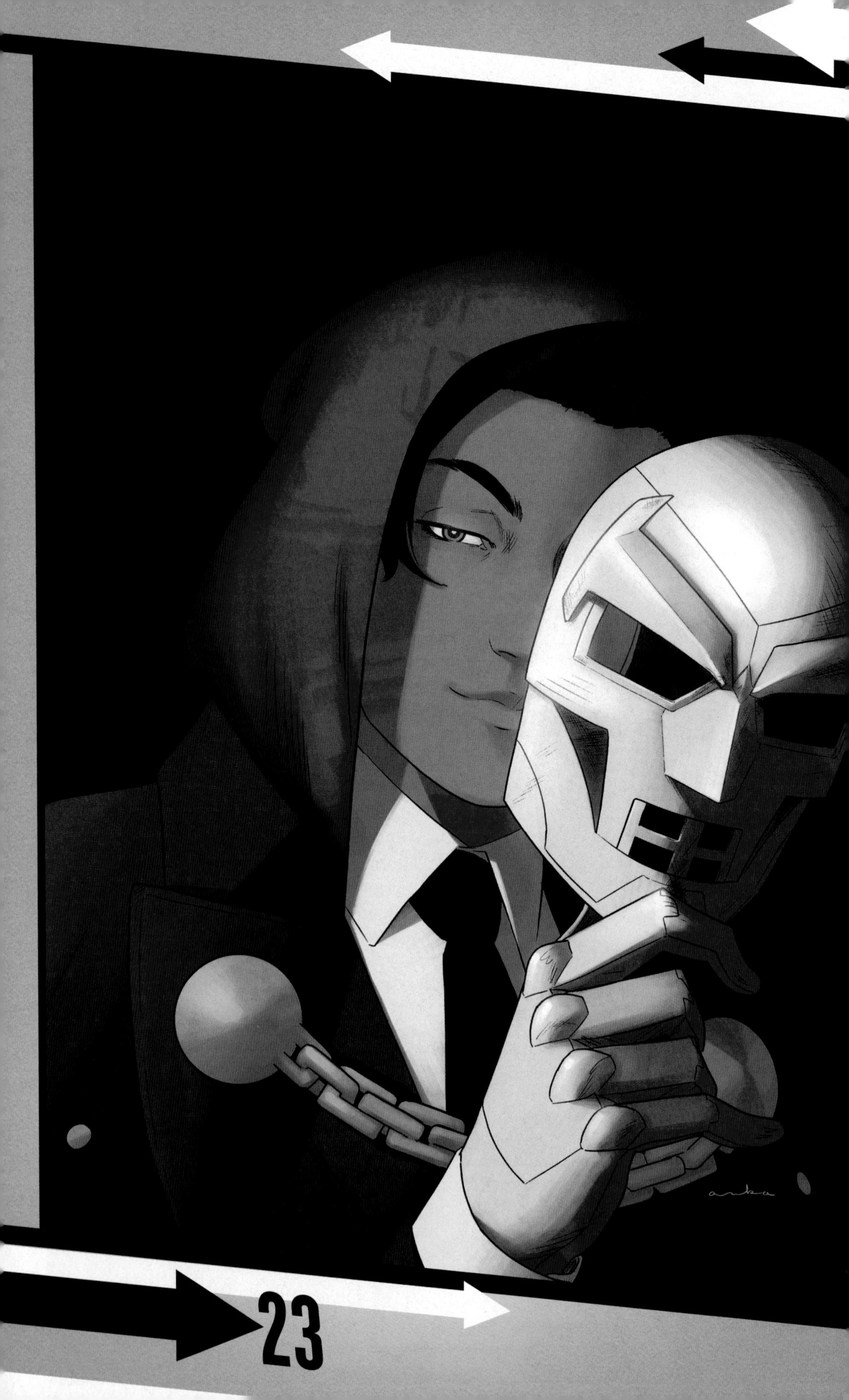
23

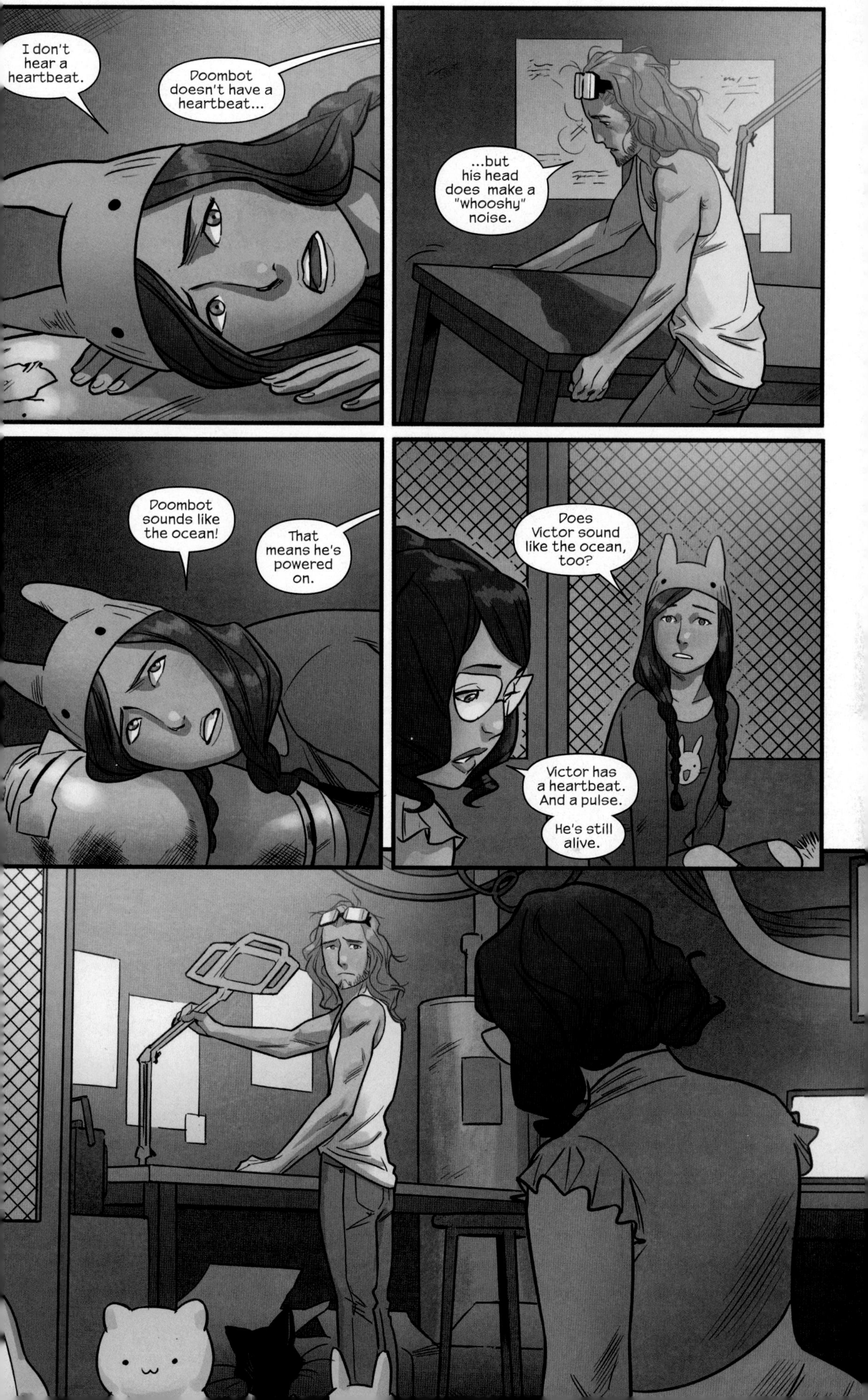
I don't hear a heartbeat.
Doombot doesn't have a heartbeat...
...but his head does make a "whooshy" noise.
Doombot sounds like the ocean!
That means he's powered on.
Does Victor sound like the ocean, too?
Victor has a heartbeat. And a pulse.
He's still alive.

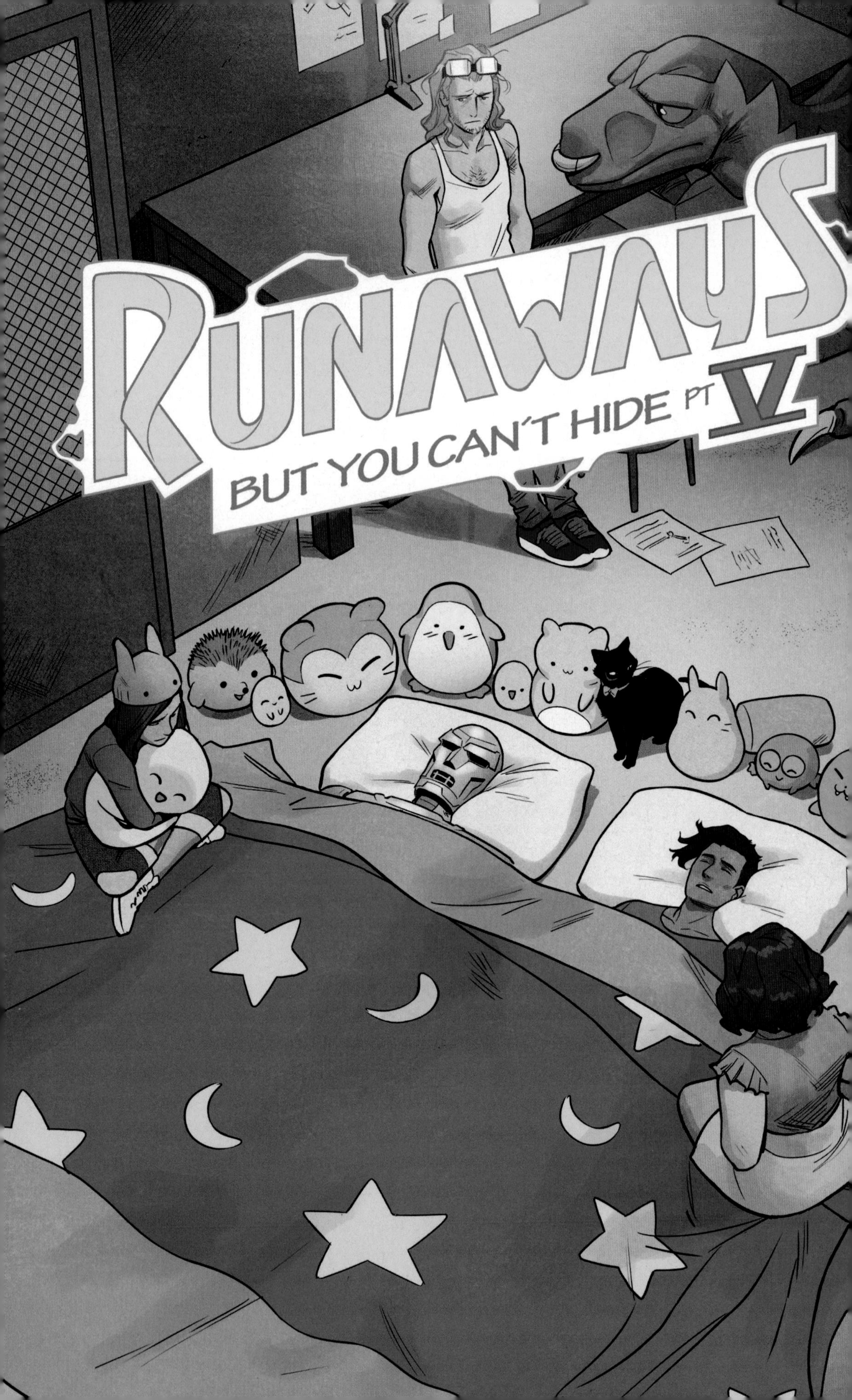
RUNAWAYS
BUT YOU CAN'T HIDE PT V

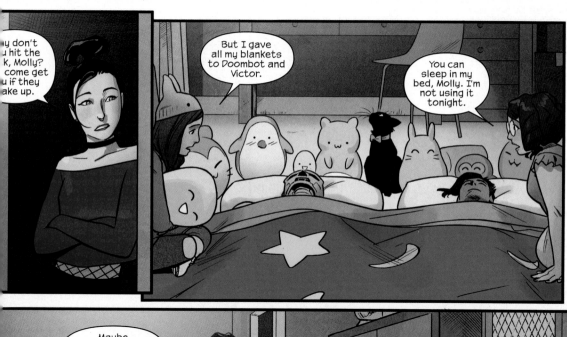

Why don't you hit the rack, Molly? I'll come get you if they wake up.

But I gave all my blankets to Doombot and Victor.

You can sleep in my bed, Molly. I'm not using it tonight.

Maybe we should restrain them while they're both down.

"Them"? Why would we restrain Victor?

Because every time Victor reboots, there's a chance he'll revert to his Victorious programming.

According to who? Are you a programming expert now? Did you consult a manual?

It stands to reason, Gert.

Being Victor's friend doesn't mean pretending he wasn't created by Ultron. Victor himself would *want* us to be cautious.

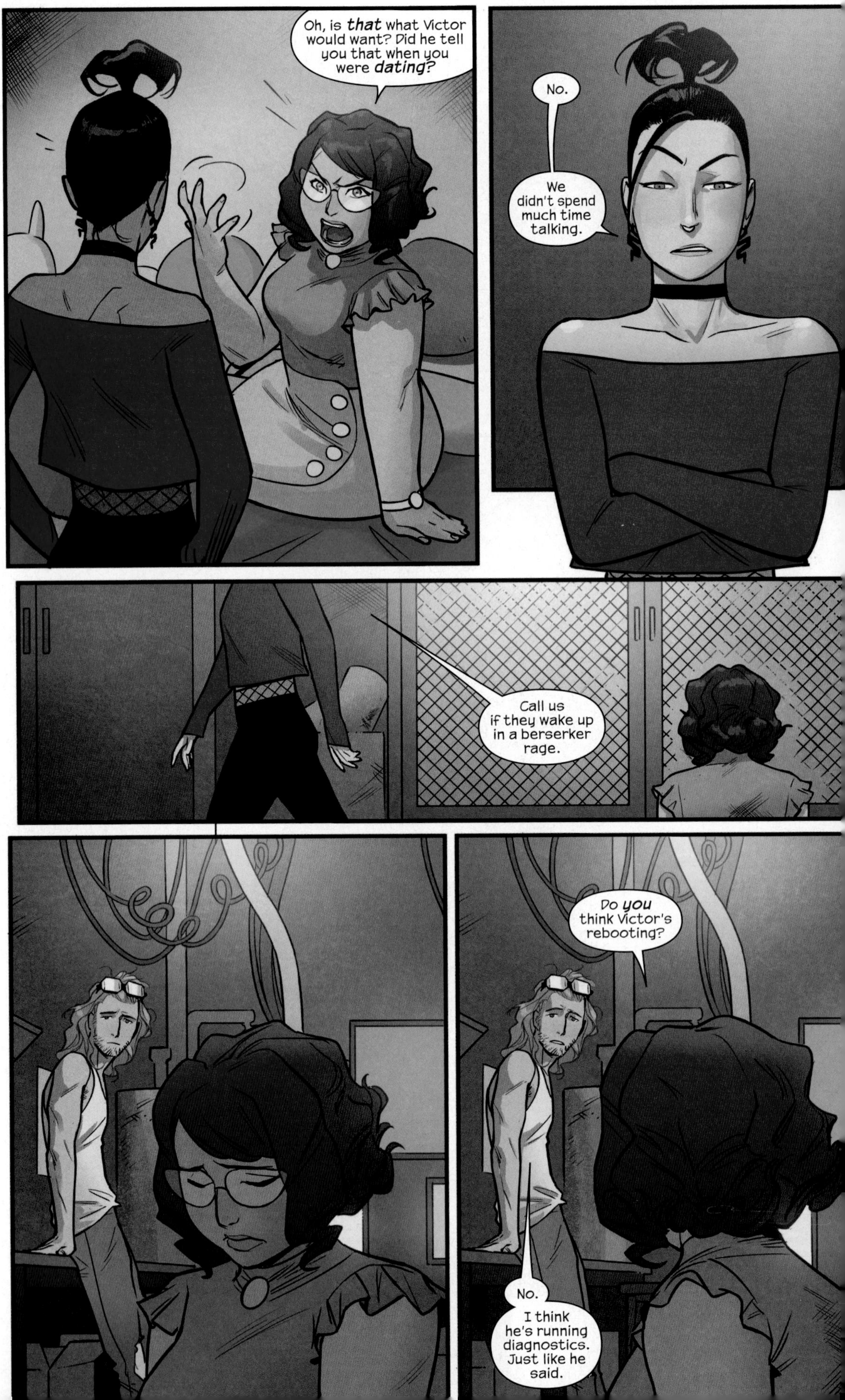
Oh, is *that* what Victor would want? Did he tell you that when you were *dating?*
No.
We didn't spend much time talking.
Call us if they wake up in a berserker rage.
Do *you* think Victor's rebooting?
No.
I think he's running diagnostics. Just like he said.

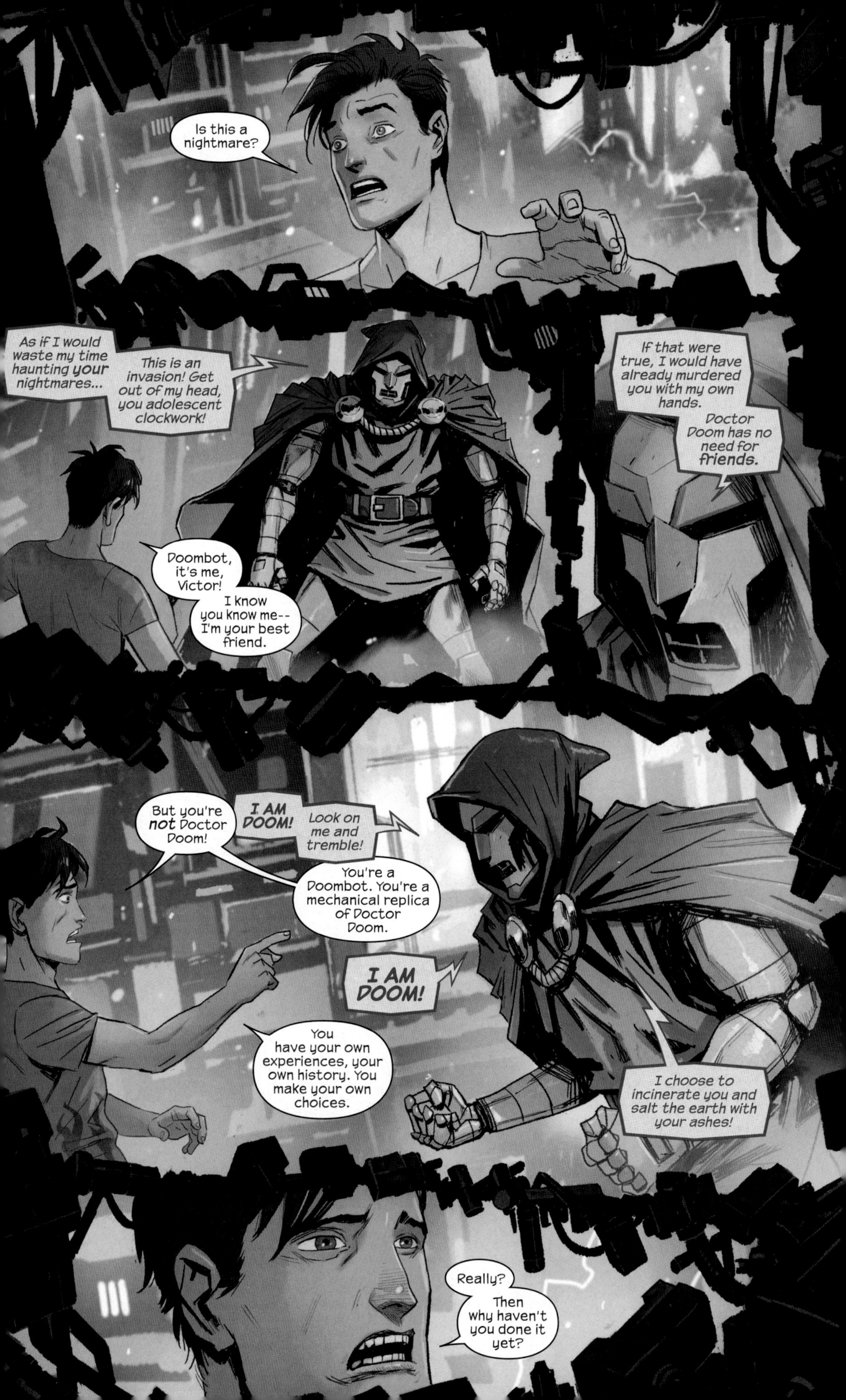
Is this a nightmare?
As if I would waste my time haunting your nightmares...
This is an invasion! Get out of my head, you adolescent clockwork!
If that were true, I would have already murdered you with my own hands.
Doctor Doom has no need for friends.
Doombot, it's me, Victor!
I know you know me-- I'm your best friend.
But you're not Doctor Doom!
I AM DOOM!
Look on me and tremble!
You're a Doombot. You're a mechanical replica of Doctor Doom.
I AM DOOM!
You have your own experiences, your own history. You make your own choices.
I choose to incinerate you and salt the earth with your ashes!
Really?
Then why haven't you done it yet?

Welp, they're both still unconscious. I guess we just hang out at Threat Level Orange.

Gib--I made wonton soup. You can have some.

PRIDELING, I HUNGER.

We're trying our best, Gib. We just don't know what to feed you.

THERE WAS SUPPOSED TO BE A FEAST WHEN WE WOKE UP. BILLIONS OF SOULS. WE WOULD HAVE LIVED OFF THEIR REAPING FOR ETERNITY.

Do cows have souls?

Well, *I* think so.

Great! Gib, I can make you a steak.

THERE MUST BE SACRIFICE. IT IS SACRIFICE THAT SUSTAINS US.

THAT SUSTAINS *ME*, I SHOULD SAY. FOR I AM ALL THAT REMAINS OF THE GIBBORIM.

I mean...*the cow* sacrificed its life so that we could have steak.

DURING WHAT RITUAL?

The global beef-indus ritual. It's v dark.

I FEEL ONLY HUNGER, PRIDELINGS. AND VERY LITTLE HOPE.

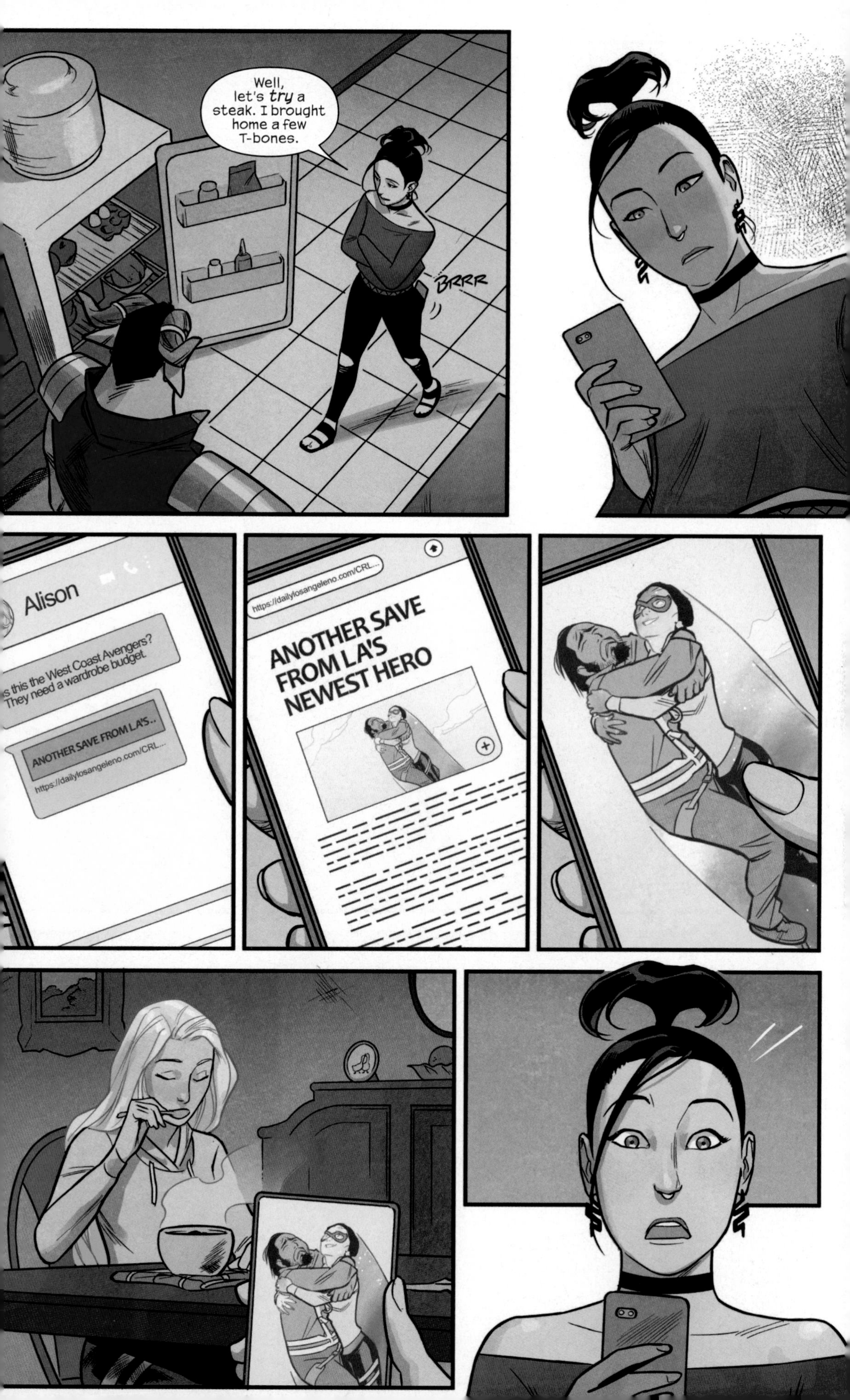

Well, let's *try* a steak. I brought home a few T-bones.
BRRR
Alison
Is this the West Coast Avengers? They need a wardrobe budget.
ANOTHER SAVE FROM LA'S..
https://dailylosangeleno.com/CRL...
https://dailylosangeleno.com/CRL...
ANOTHER SAVE FROM LA'S NEWEST HERO

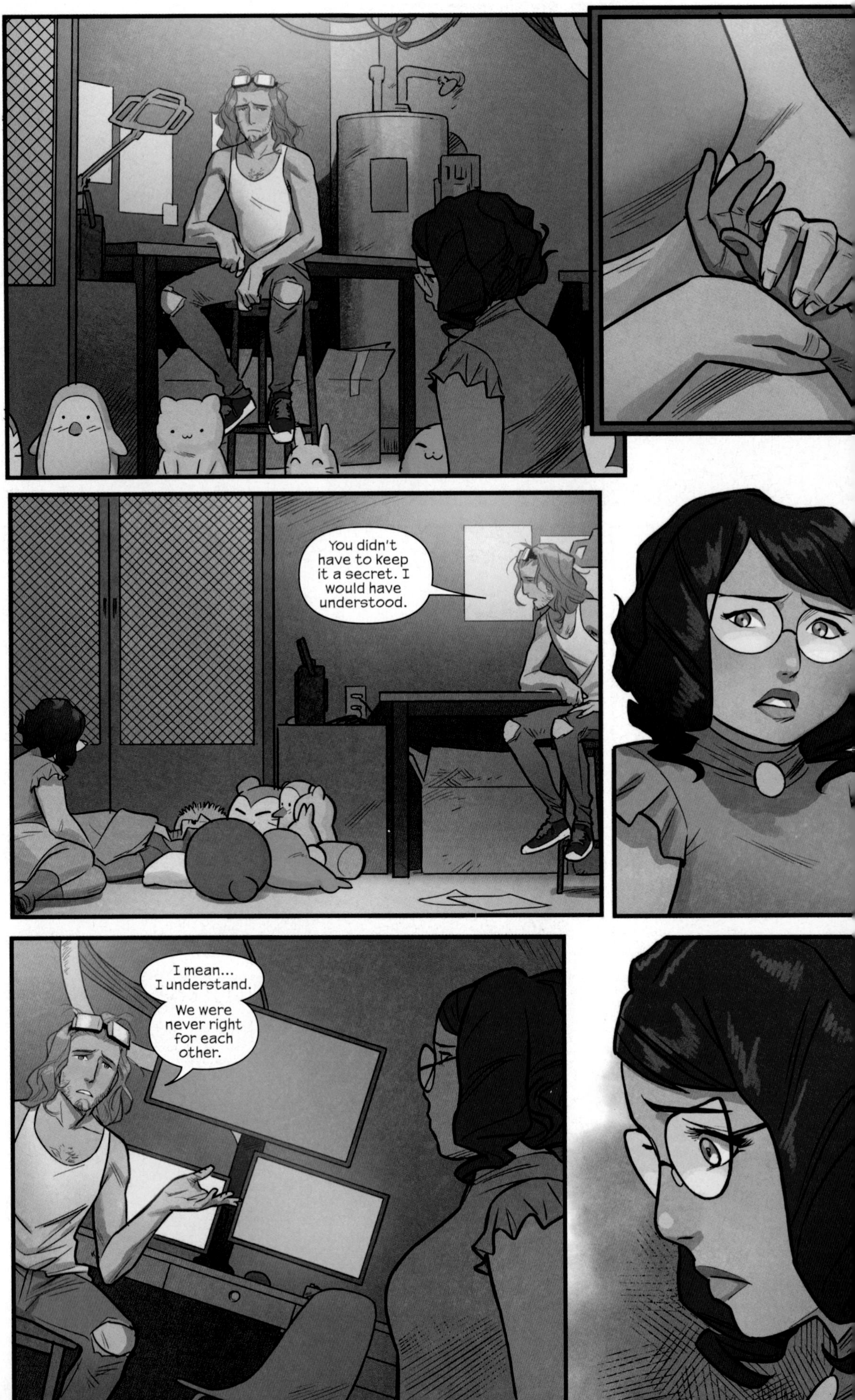
You didn't have to keep it a secret. I would have understood.
I mean... I understand.
We were never right for each other.

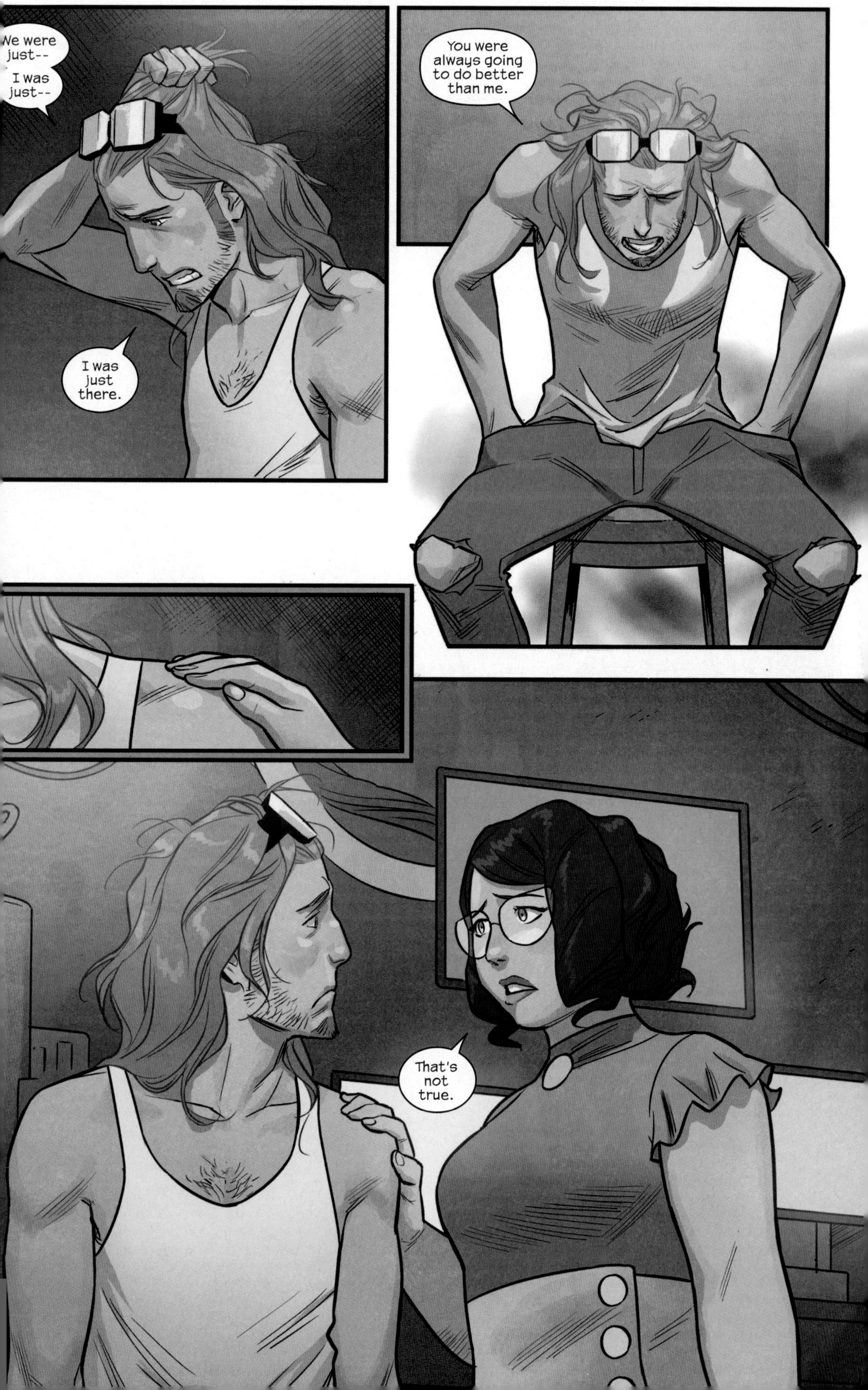
We were just--
I was just--
I was just there.
You were always going to do better than me.
That's not true.

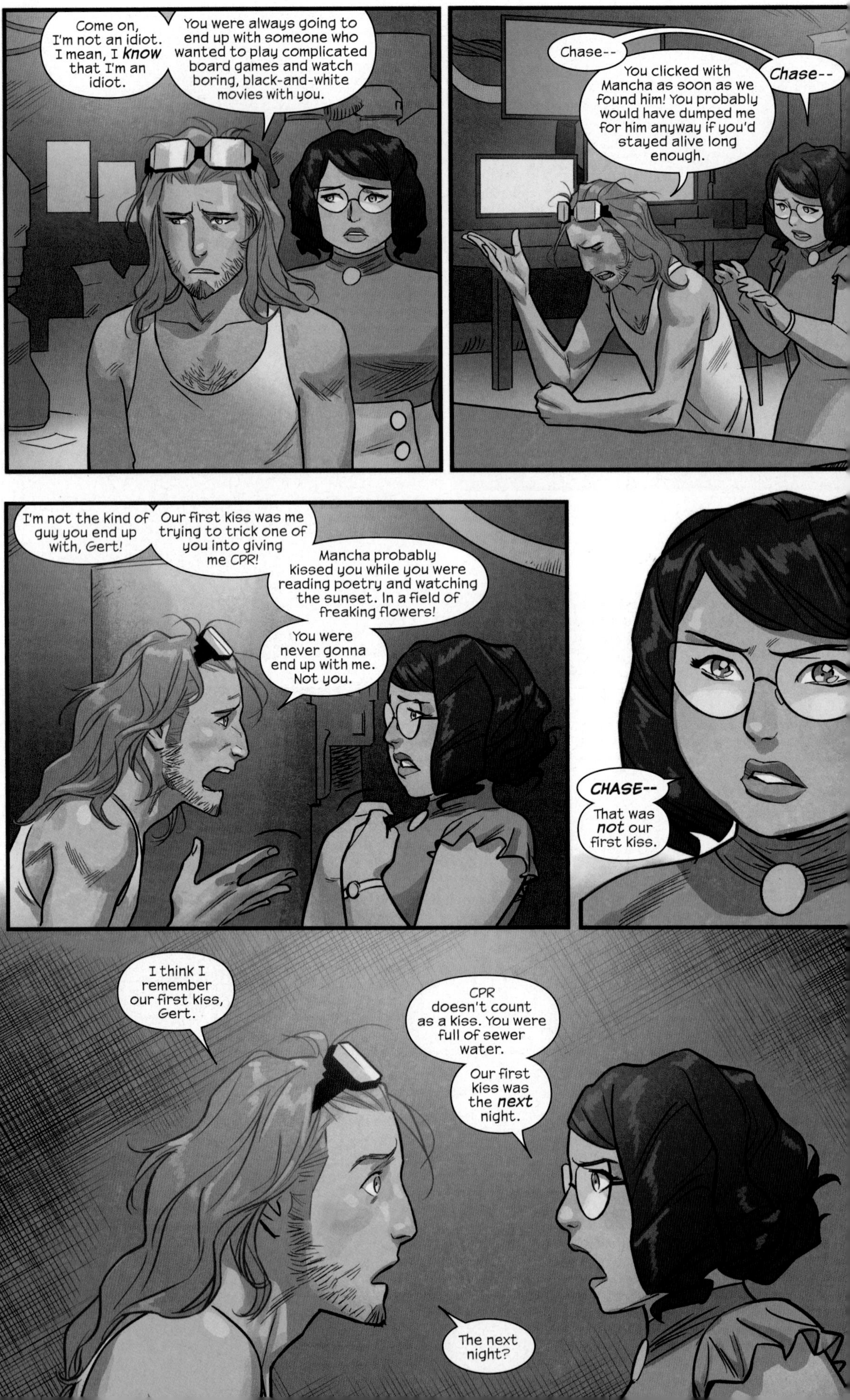
Come on, I'm not an idiot. I mean, I *know* that I'm an idiot.
You were always going to end up with someone who wanted to play complicated board games and watch boring, black-and-white movies with you.
Chase--
You clicked with Mancha as soon as we found him! You probably would have dumped me for him anyway if you'd stayed alive long enough.
Chase--
I'm not the kind of guy you end up with, Gert!
Our first kiss was me trying to trick one of you into giving me CPR!
Mancha probably kissed you while you were reading poetry and watching the sunset. In a field of freaking flowers!
You were never gonna end up with me. Not you.
CHASE--
That was ***not*** our first kiss.
I think I remember our first kiss, Gert.
CPR doesn't count as a kiss. You were full of sewer water.
Our first kiss was the ***next*** night.
The next night?

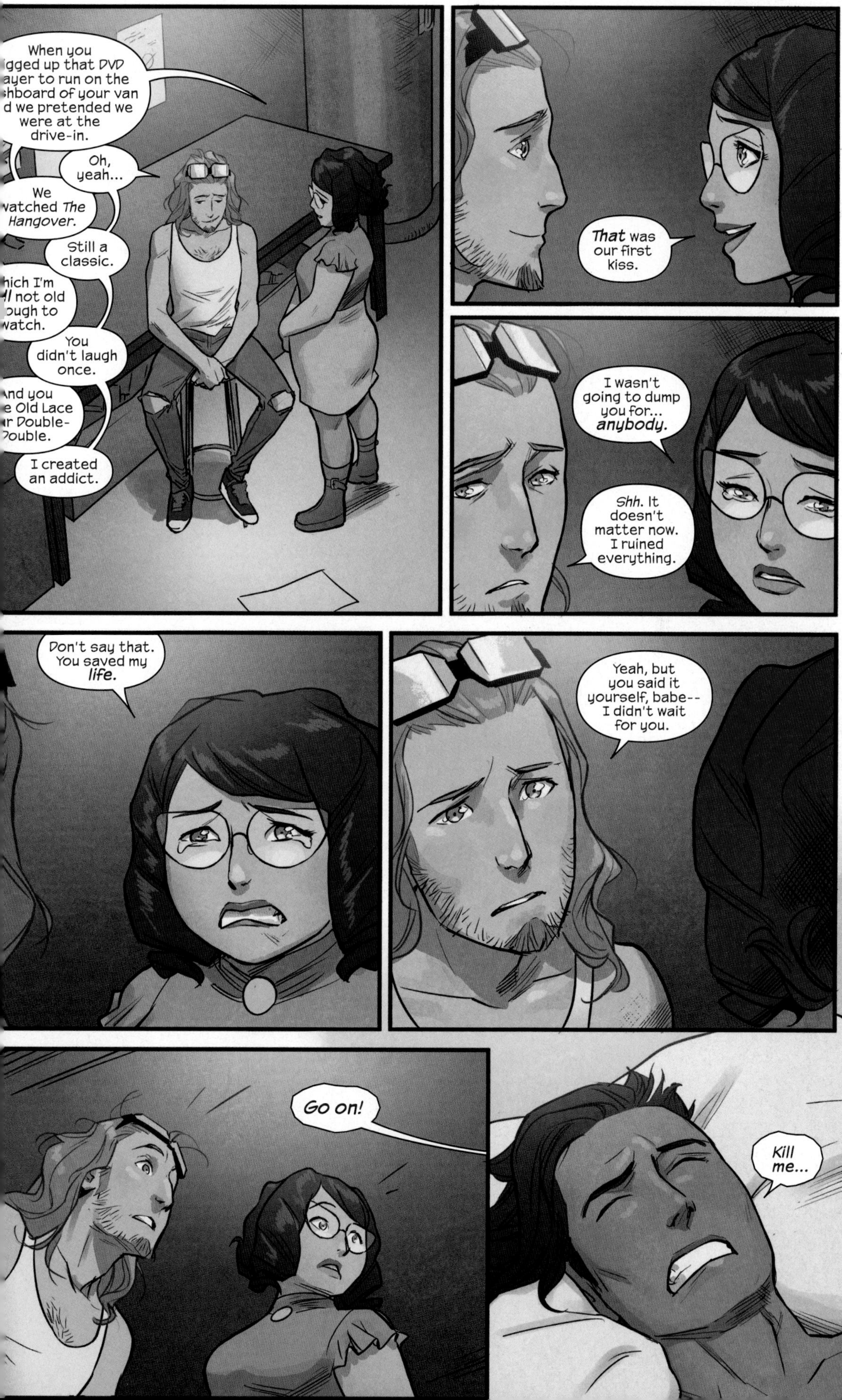

When you
igged up that DVD
ayer to run on the
shboard of your van
d we pretended we
were at the
drive-in.
Oh,
yeah...
We
vatched *The*
Hangover.
Still a
classic.
hich I'm
ll not old
ough to
watch.
You
didn't laugh
once.
And you
e Old Lace
r Double-
Double.
I created
an addict.
That was
our first
kiss.
I wasn't
going to dump
you for...
anybody.
Shh. It
doesn't
matter now.
I ruined
everything.
Don't say that.
You saved my
life.
Yeah, but
you said it
yourself, babe--
I didn't wait
for you.
Go on!
Kill
me...

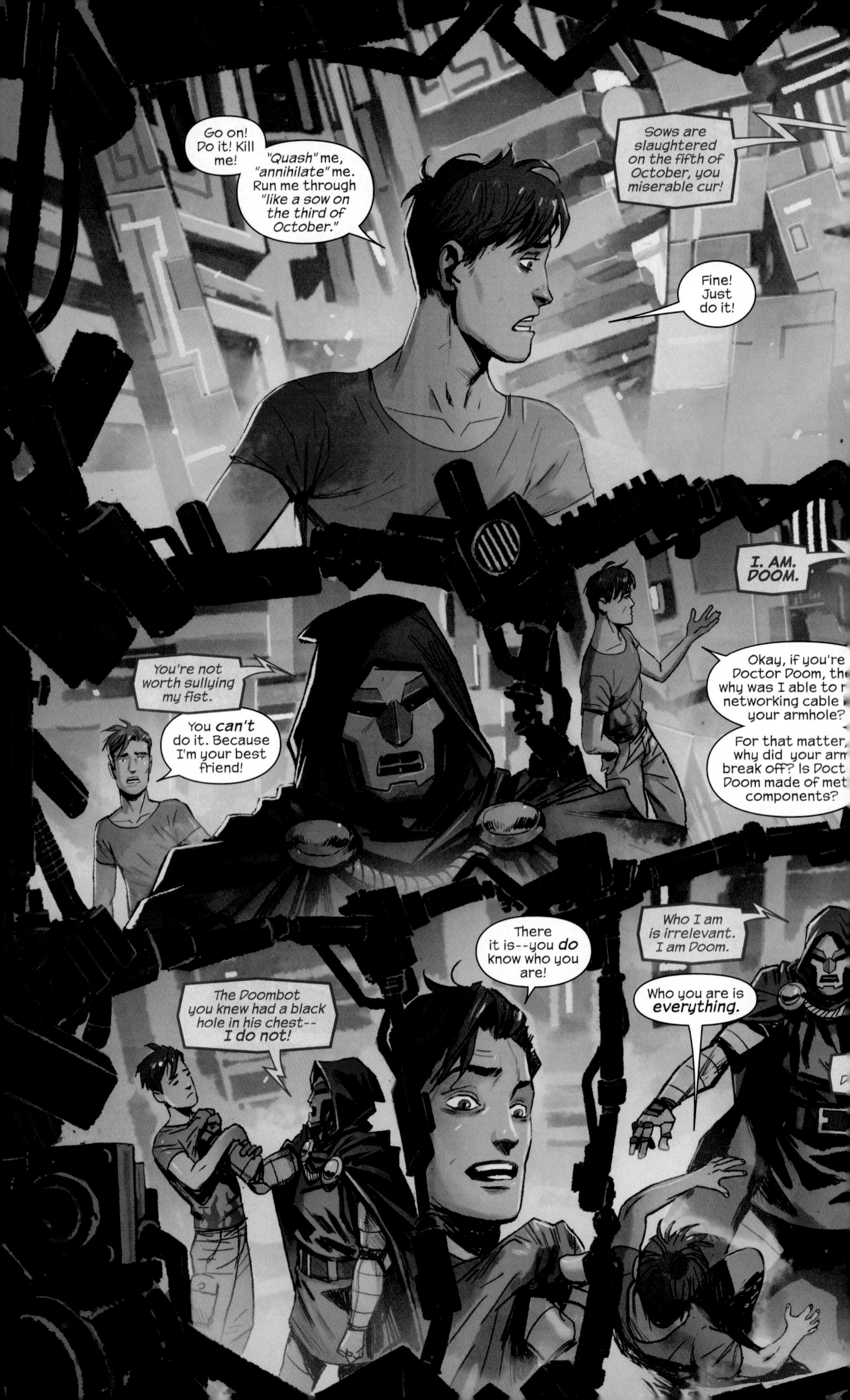

Go on! Do it! Kill me!
"Quash" me, "annihilate" me. Run me through "like a sow on the third of October."
Sows are slaughtered on the fifth of October, you miserable cur!
Fine! Just do it!
You're not worth sullying my fist.
You **can't** do it. Because I'm your best friend!
I. AM. DOOM.
Okay, if you're Doctor Doom, th why was I able to networking cable your armhole?
For that matter, why did your ar break off? Is Doct Doom made of met components?
The Doombot you knew had a black hole in his chest-- **I do not!**
There it is--you **do** know who you are!
Who I am is irrelevant. I am Doom.
Who you are is **everything.**

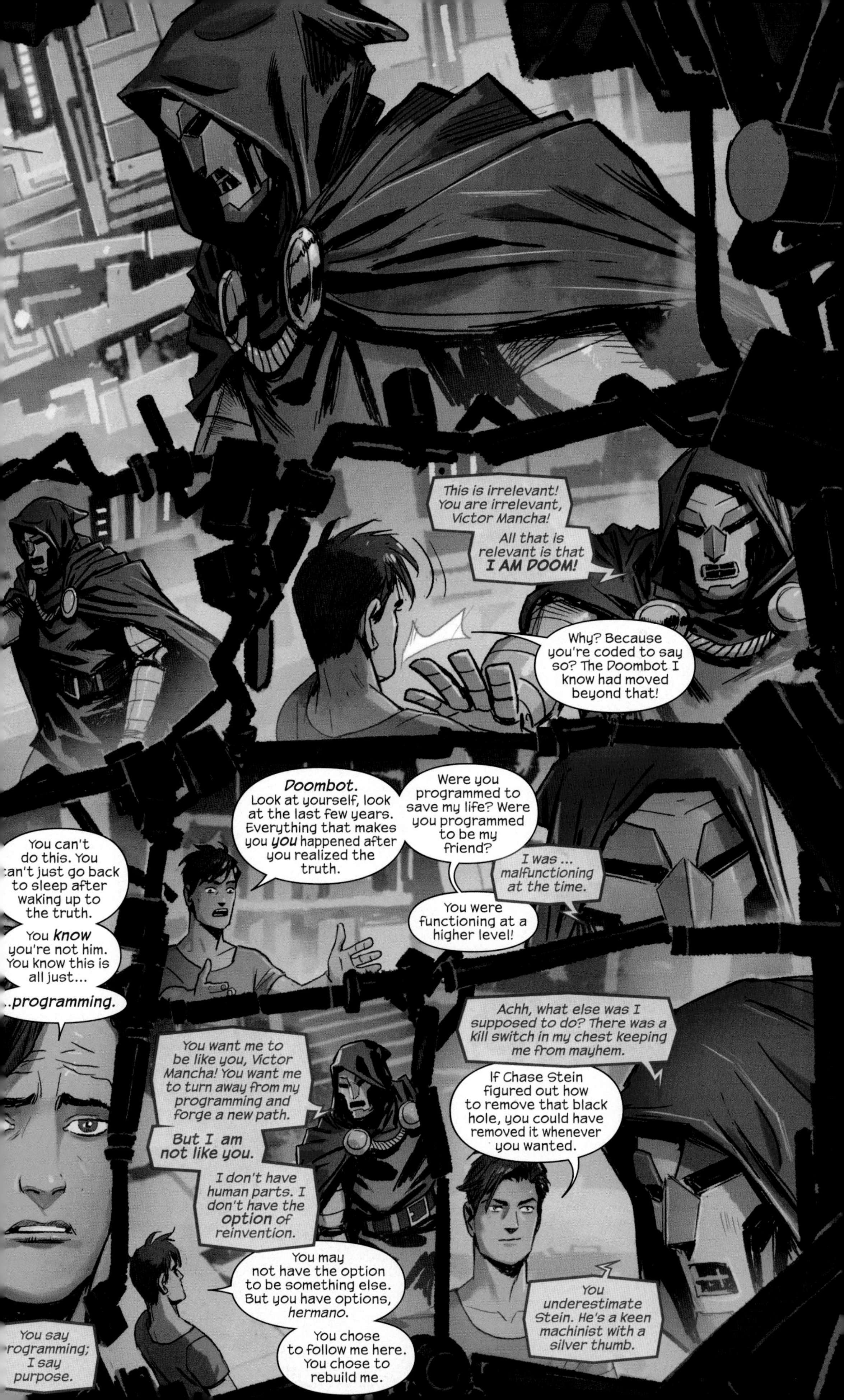
This is irrelevant! You are irrelevant, Victor Mancha!
All that is relevant is that I AM DOOM!
Why? Because you're coded to say so? The Doombot I know had moved beyond that!
Doombot. Look at yourself, look at the last few years. Everything that makes you you happened after you realized the truth.
Were you programmed to save my life? Were you programmed to be my friend?
I was ... malfunctioning at the time.
You were functioning at a higher level!
You can't do this. You can't just go back to sleep after waking up to the truth.
You know you're not him. You know this is all just...
...programming.
You want me to be like you, Victor Mancha! You want me to turn away from my programming and forge a new path.
But I am not like you.
I don't have human parts. I don't have the option of reinvention.
Achh, what else was I supposed to do? There was a kill switch in my chest keeping me from mayhem.
If Chase Stein figured out how to remove that black hole, you could have removed it whenever you wanted.
You underestimate Stein. He's a keen machinist with a silver thumb.
You may not have the option to be something else. But you have options, hermano.
You chose to follow me here. You chose to rebuild me.
You say programming; I say purpose.

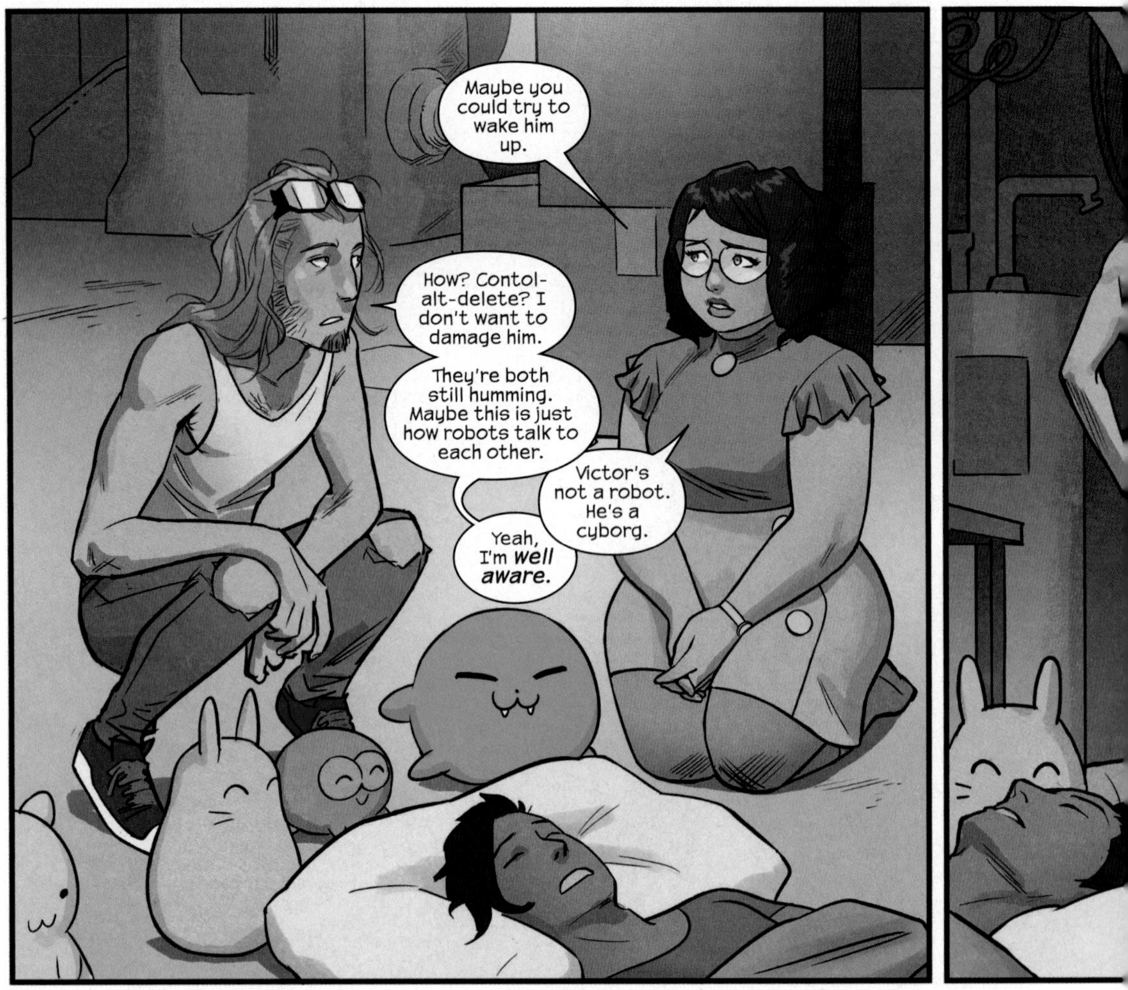
Maybe you could try to wake him up.
How? Contol-alt-delete? I don't want to damage him.
They're both still humming. Maybe this is just how robots talk to each other.
Victor's not a robot. He's a cyborg.
Yeah, I'm *well aware.*

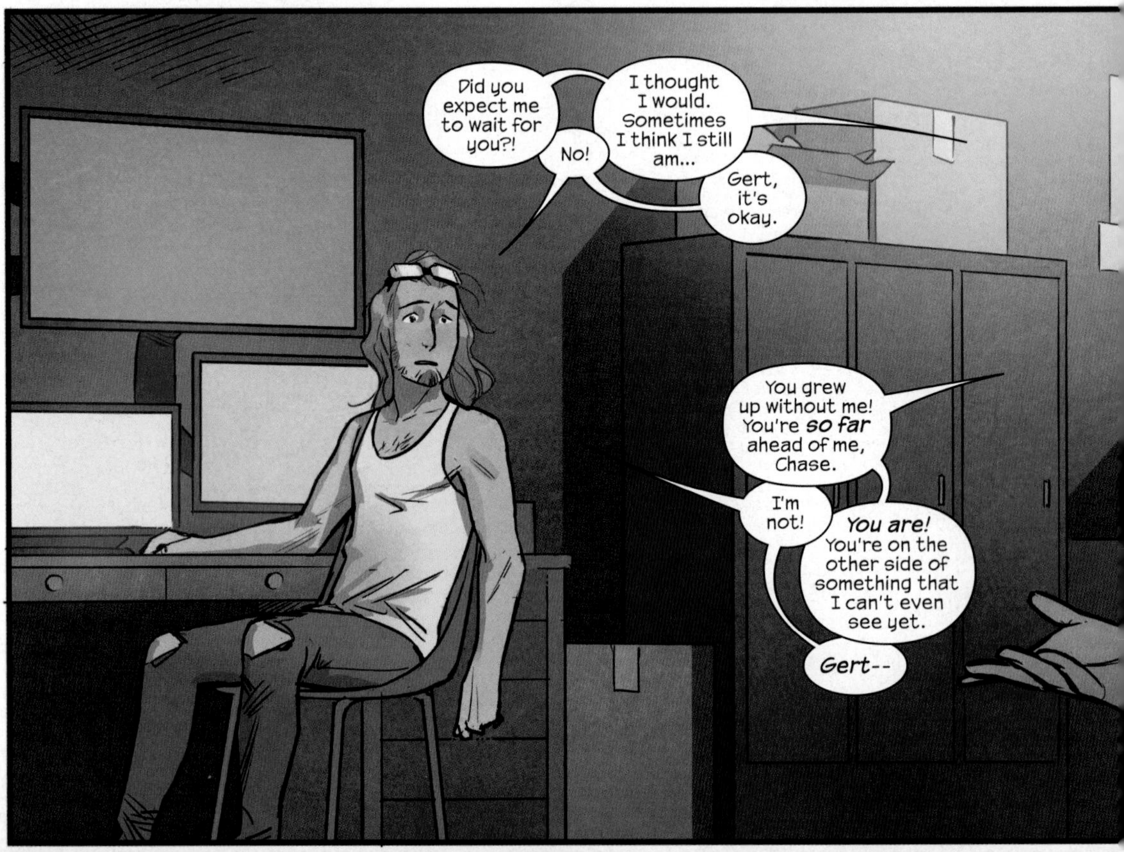
Did you expect me to wait for you?!
No!
I thought I would. Sometimes I think I still am...
Gert, it's okay.
You grew up without me! You're *so far* ahead of me, Chase.
I'm not!
You are! You're on the other side of something that I can't even see yet.
Gert--

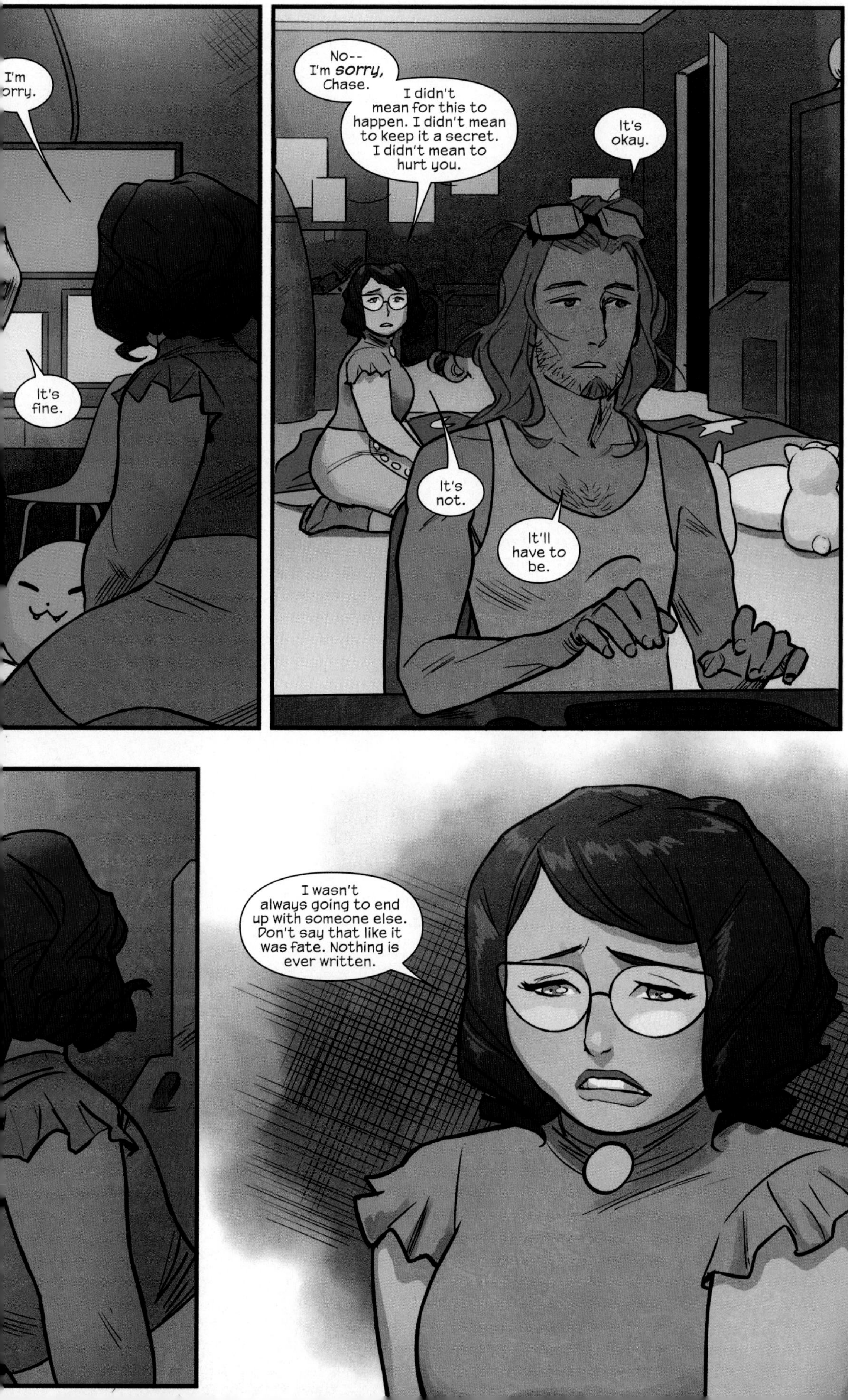
I'm
orry.
It's
fine.
No--
I'm sorry,
Chase.
I didn't
mean for this to
happen. I didn't mean
to keep it a secret.
I didn't mean to
hurt you.
It's
okay.
It's
not.
It'll
have to
be.
I wasn't
always going to end
up with someone else.
Don't say that like it
was fate. Nothing is
ever written.

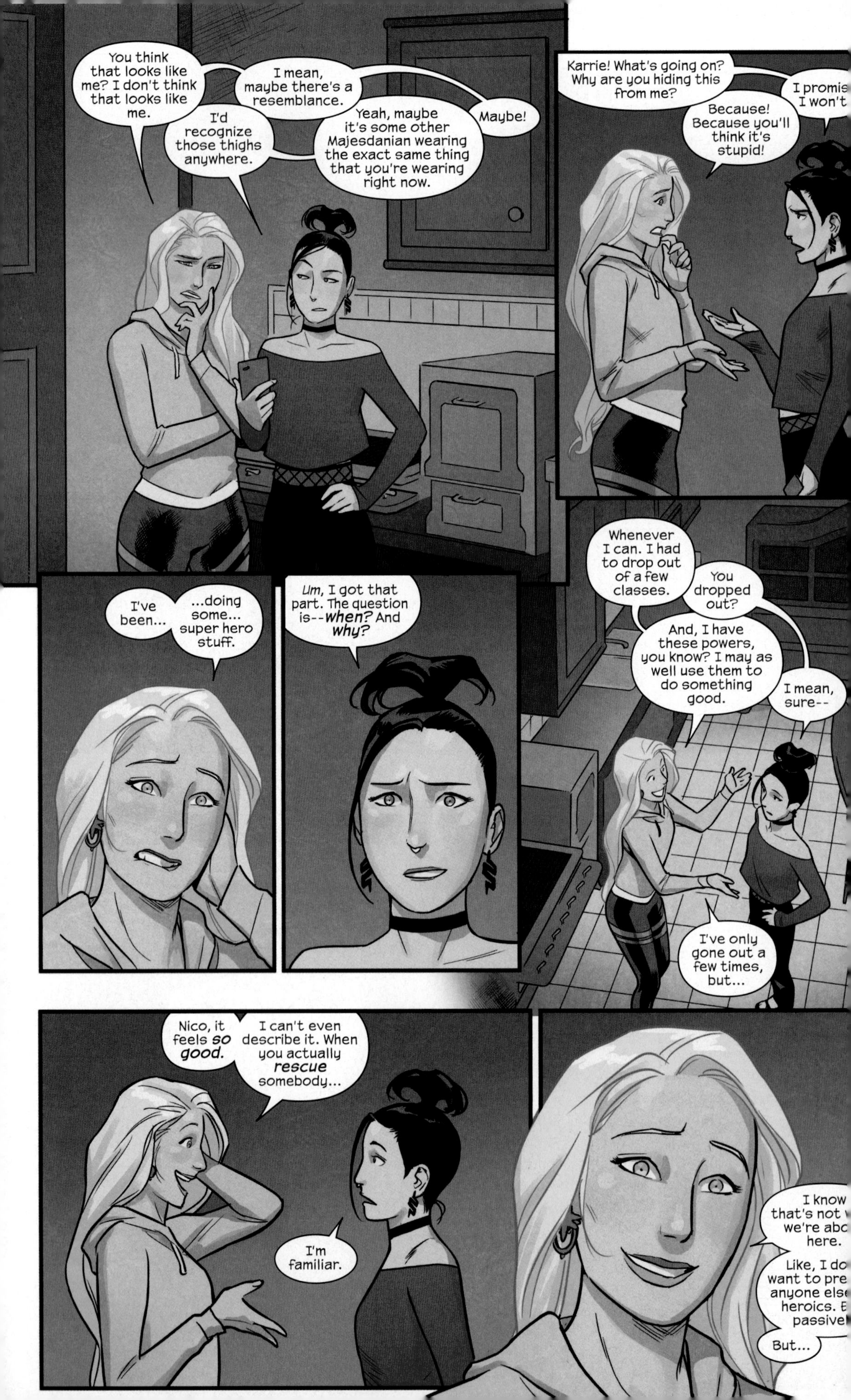
You think that looks like me? I don't think that looks like me.
I mean, maybe there's a resemblance.
I'd recognize those thighs anywhere.
Yeah, maybe it's some other Majesdanian wearing the exact same thing that you're wearing right now.
Maybe!
Karrie! What's going on? Why are you hiding this from me?
Because! Because you'll think it's stupid!
I promis
I won't
I've been...
...doing some... super hero stuff.
Um, I got that part. The question is--when? And why?
Whenever I can. I had to drop out of a few classes.
You dropped out?
And, I have these powers, you know? I may as well use them to do something good.
I mean, sure--
I've only gone out a few times, but...
Nico, it feels so good.
I can't even describe it. When you actually rescue somebody...
I'm familiar.
I know that's not we're abo here.
Like, I do want to pre anyone else heroics. E passive
But...

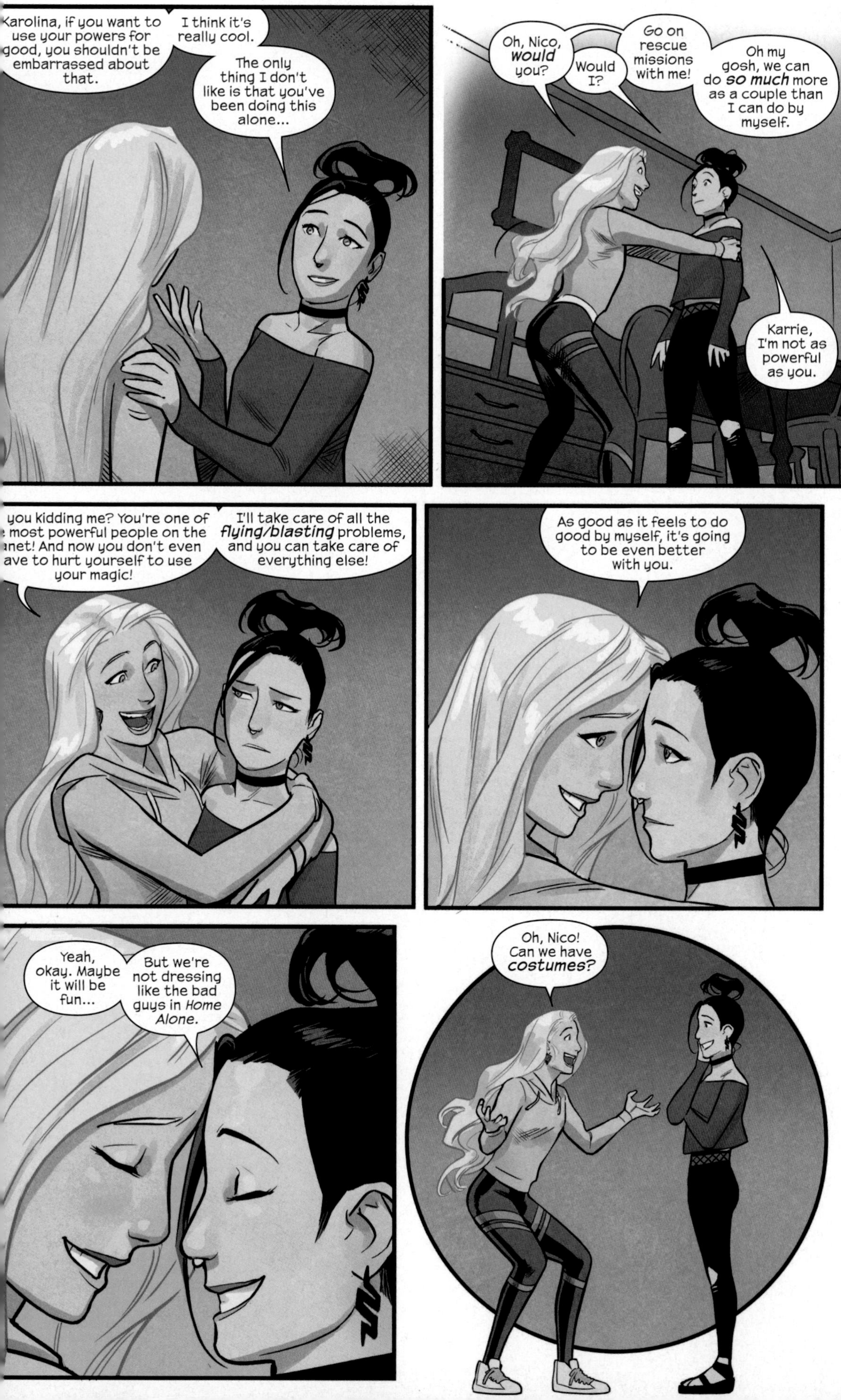

Karolina, if you want to use your powers for good, you shouldn't be embarrassed about that.
I think it's really cool.
The only thing I don't like is that you've been doing this alone...
Oh, Nico, would you?
Would I?
Go on rescue missions with me!
Oh my gosh, we can do so much more as a couple than I can do by myself.
Karrie, I'm not as powerful as you.
you kidding me? You're one of e most powerful people on the anet! And now you don't even ave to hurt yourself to use your magic!
I'll take care of all the flying/blasting problems, and you can take care of everything else!
As good as it feels to do good by myself, it's going to be even better with you.
Yeah, okay. Maybe it will be fun...
But we're not dressing like the bad guys in Home Alone.
Oh, Nico! Can we have costumes?

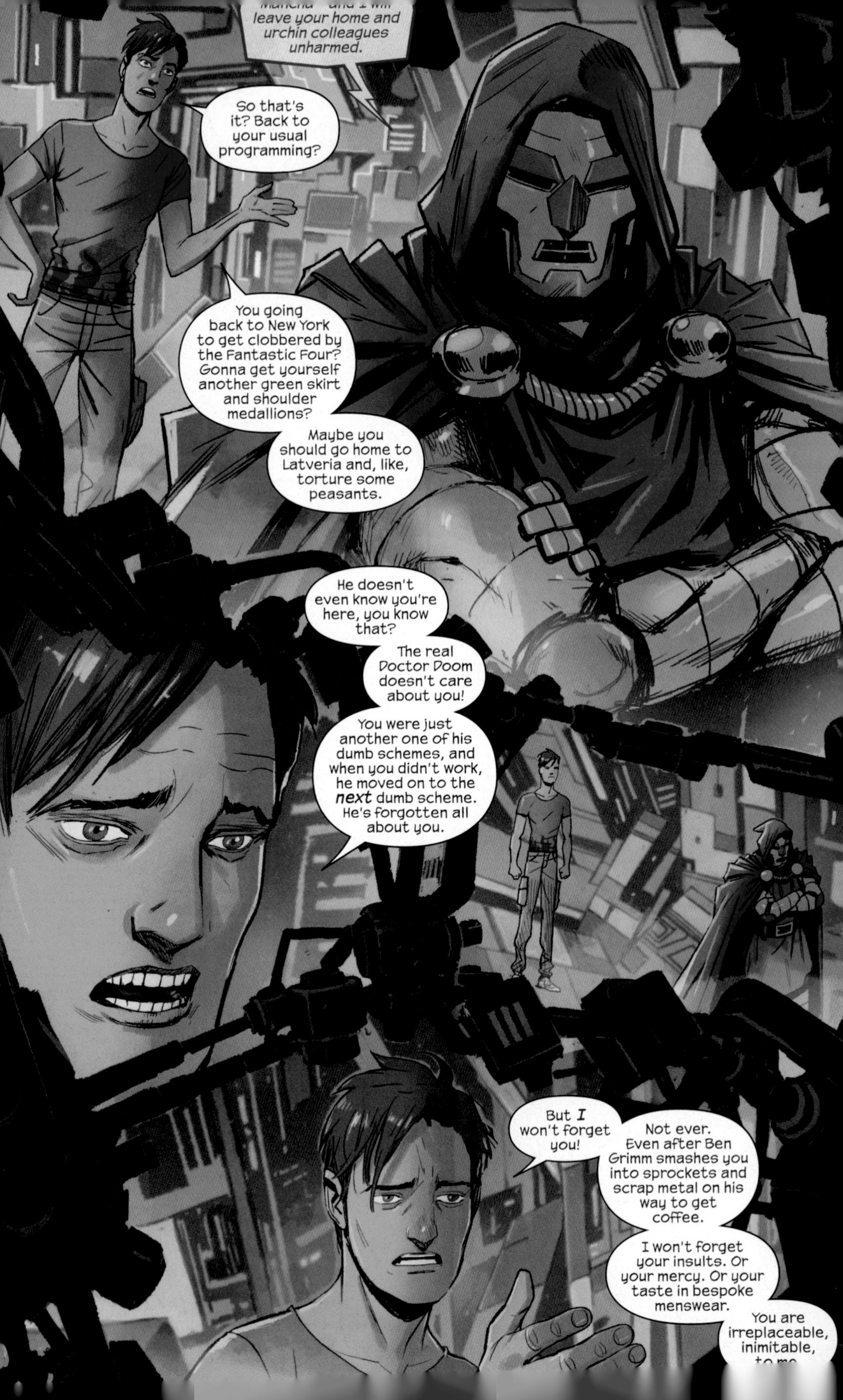
leave your home and urchin colleagues unharmed.
So that's it? Back to your usual programming?
You going back to New York to get clobbered by the Fantastic Four? Gonna get yourself another green skirt and shoulder medallions?
Maybe you should go home to Latveria and, like, torture some peasants.
He doesn't even know you're here, you know that?
The real Doctor Doom doesn't care about you!
You were just another one of his dumb schemes, and when you didn't work, he moved on to the *next* dumb scheme. He's forgotten all about you.
But *I* won't forget you!
Not ever. Even after Ben Grimm smashes you into sprockets and scrap metal on his way to get coffee.
I won't forget your insults. Or your mercy. Or your taste in bespoke menswear.
You are irreplaceable, inimitable,

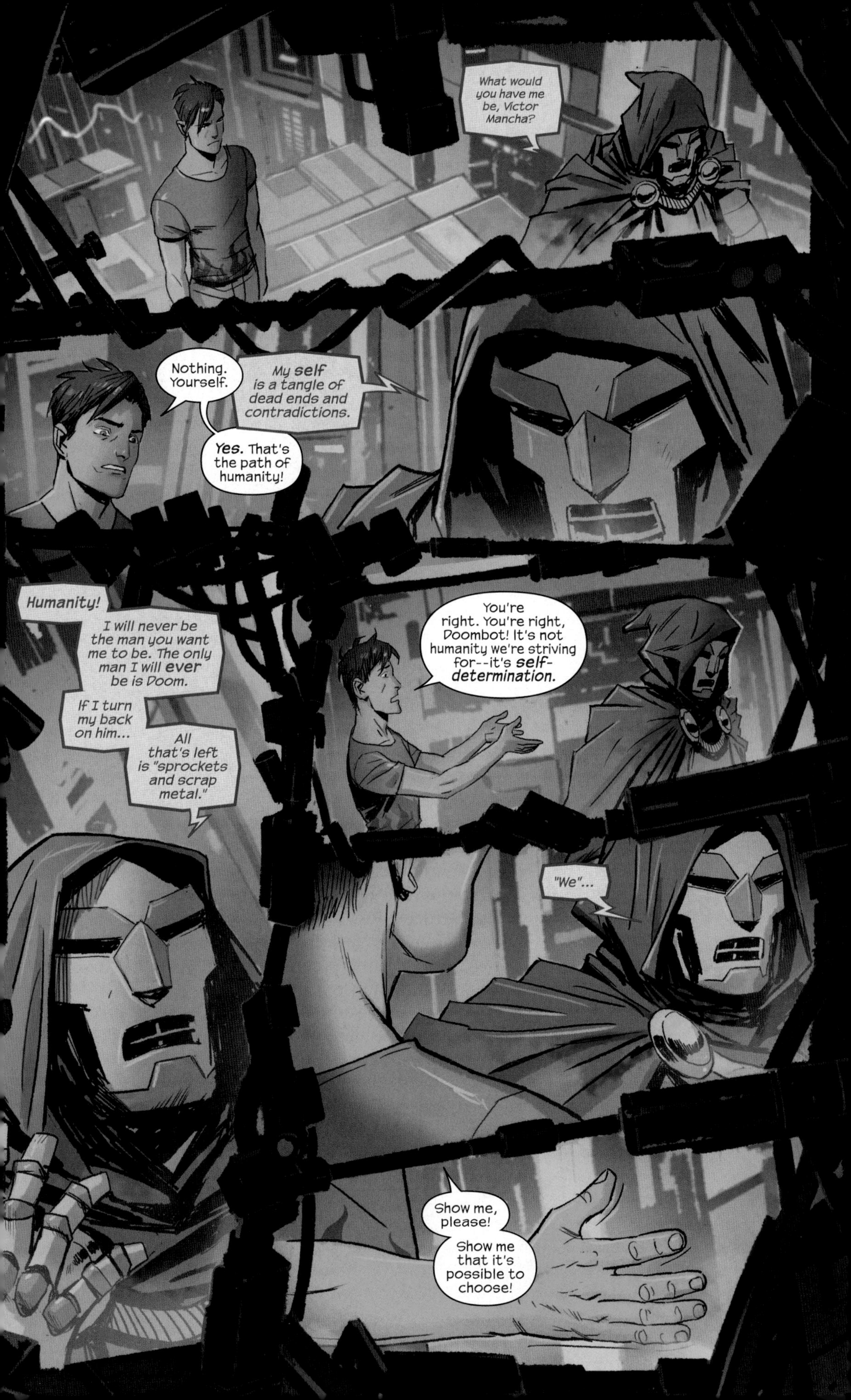
What would you have me be, Victor Mancha?
Nothing. Yourself.
My self is a tangle of dead ends and contradictions.
Yes. That's the path of humanity!
Humanity!
I will never be the man you want me to be. The only man I will ever be is Doom.
If I turn my back on him...
All that's left is "sprockets and scrap metal."
You're right. You're right, Doombot! It's not humanity we're striving for--it's self-determination.
"We"...
Show me, please!
Show me that it's possible to choose!

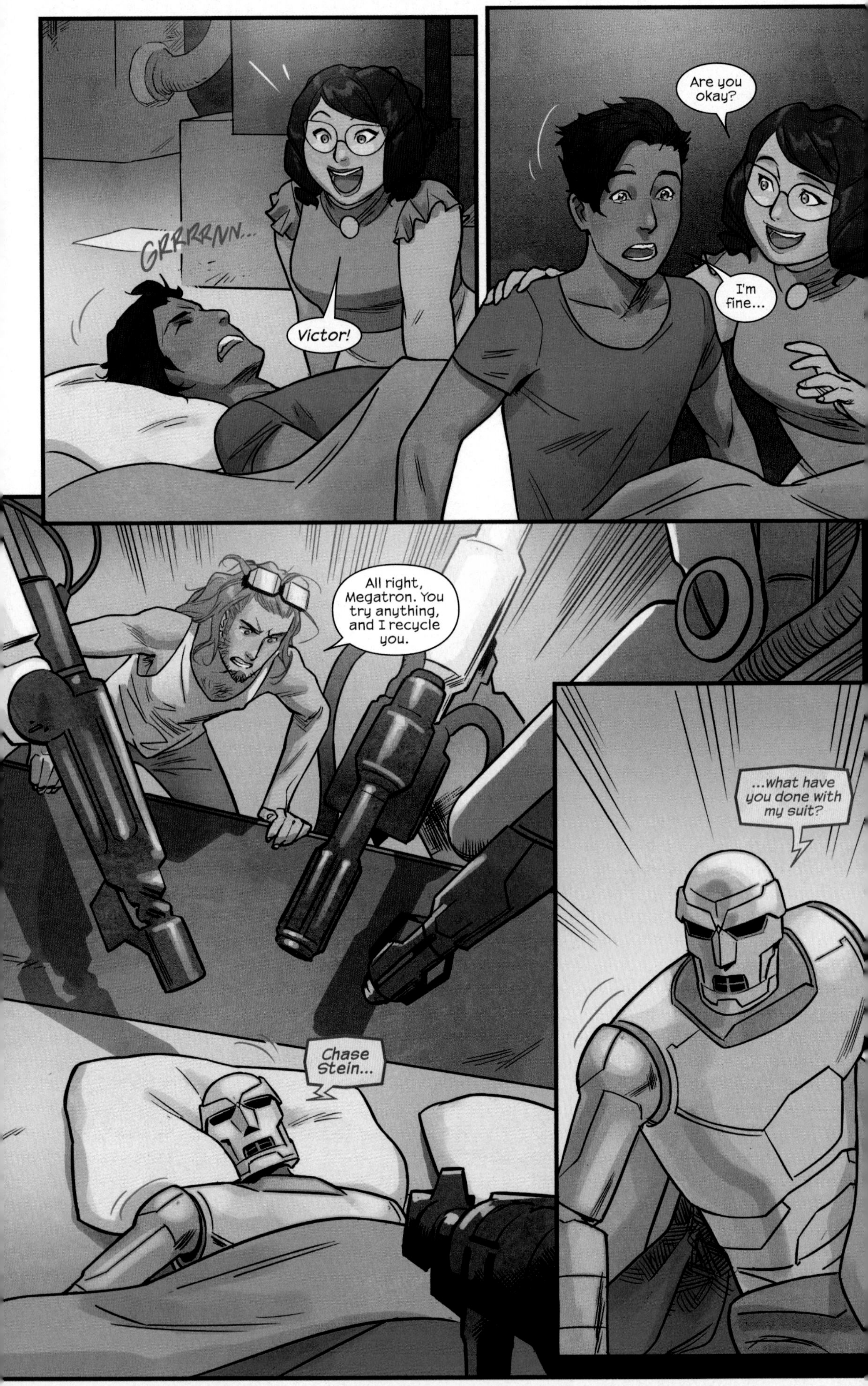
GRRRRNN...
Victor!
Are you okay?
I'm fine...
All right, Megatron. You try anything, and I recycle you.
Chase Stein...
...what have you done with my suit?

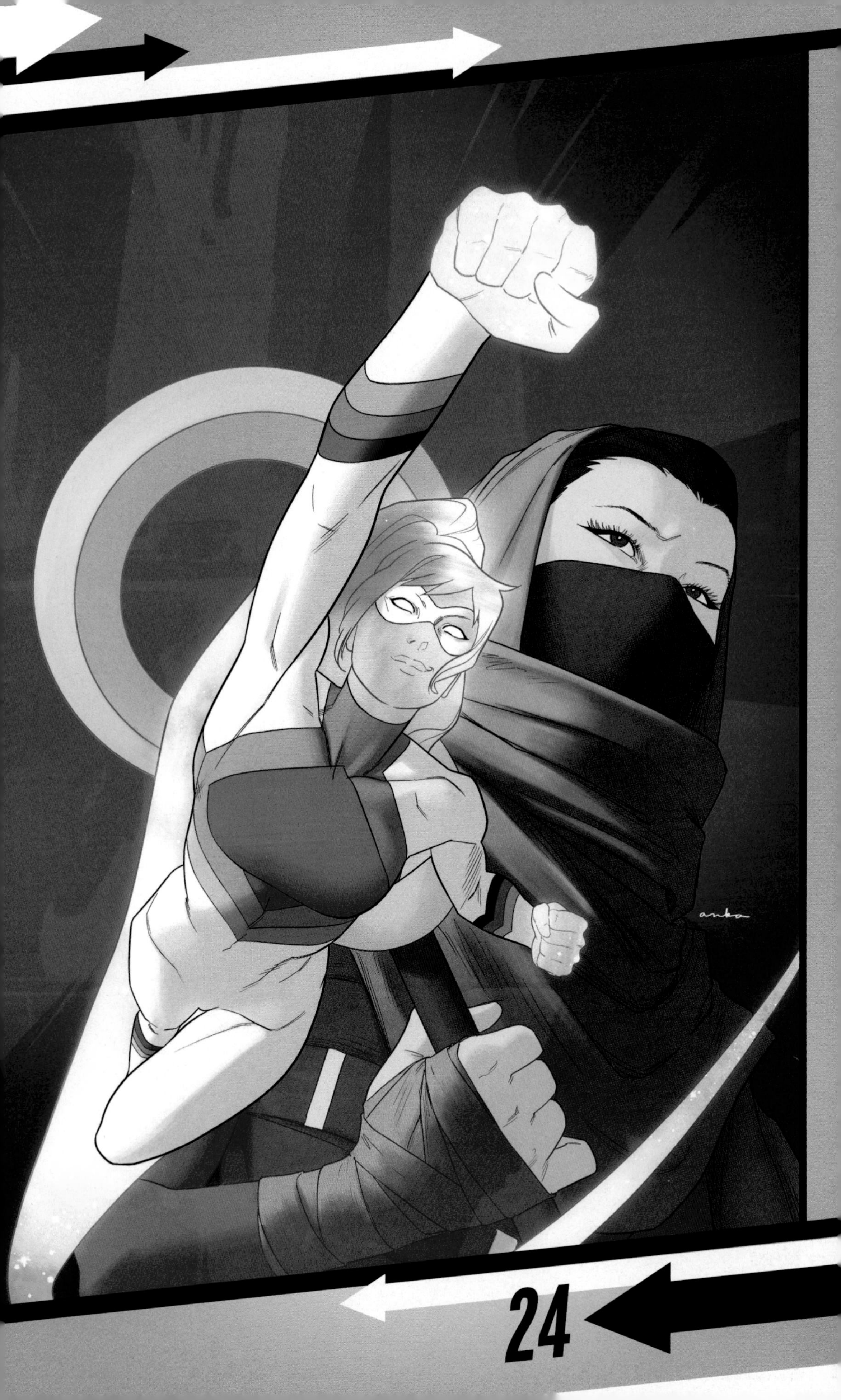
24

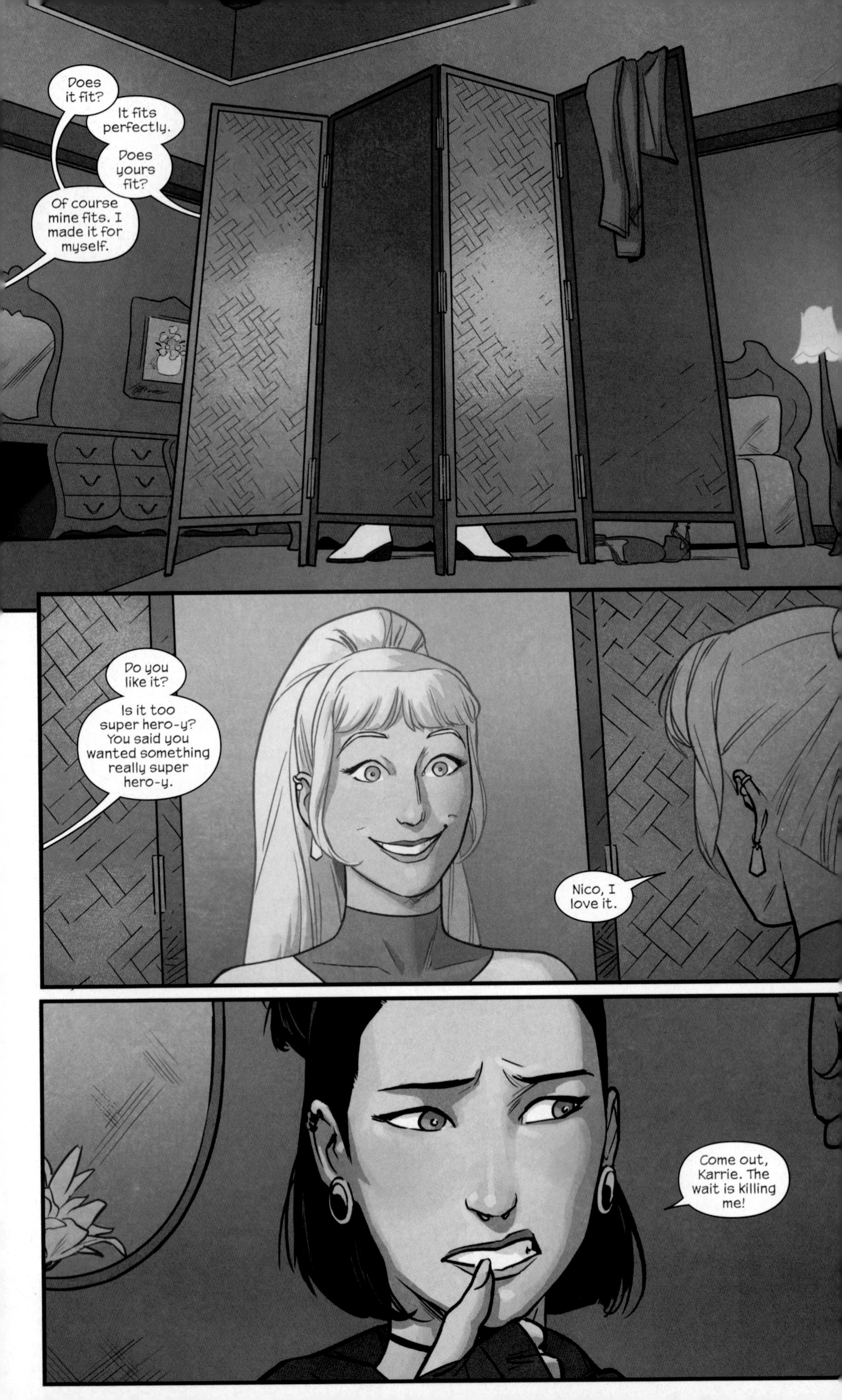
Does it fit?
It fits perfectly.
Does yours fit?
Of course mine fits. I made it for myself.
Do you like it?
Is it too super hero-y? You said you wanted something really super hero-y.
Nico, I love it.
Come out, Karrie. The wait is killing me!

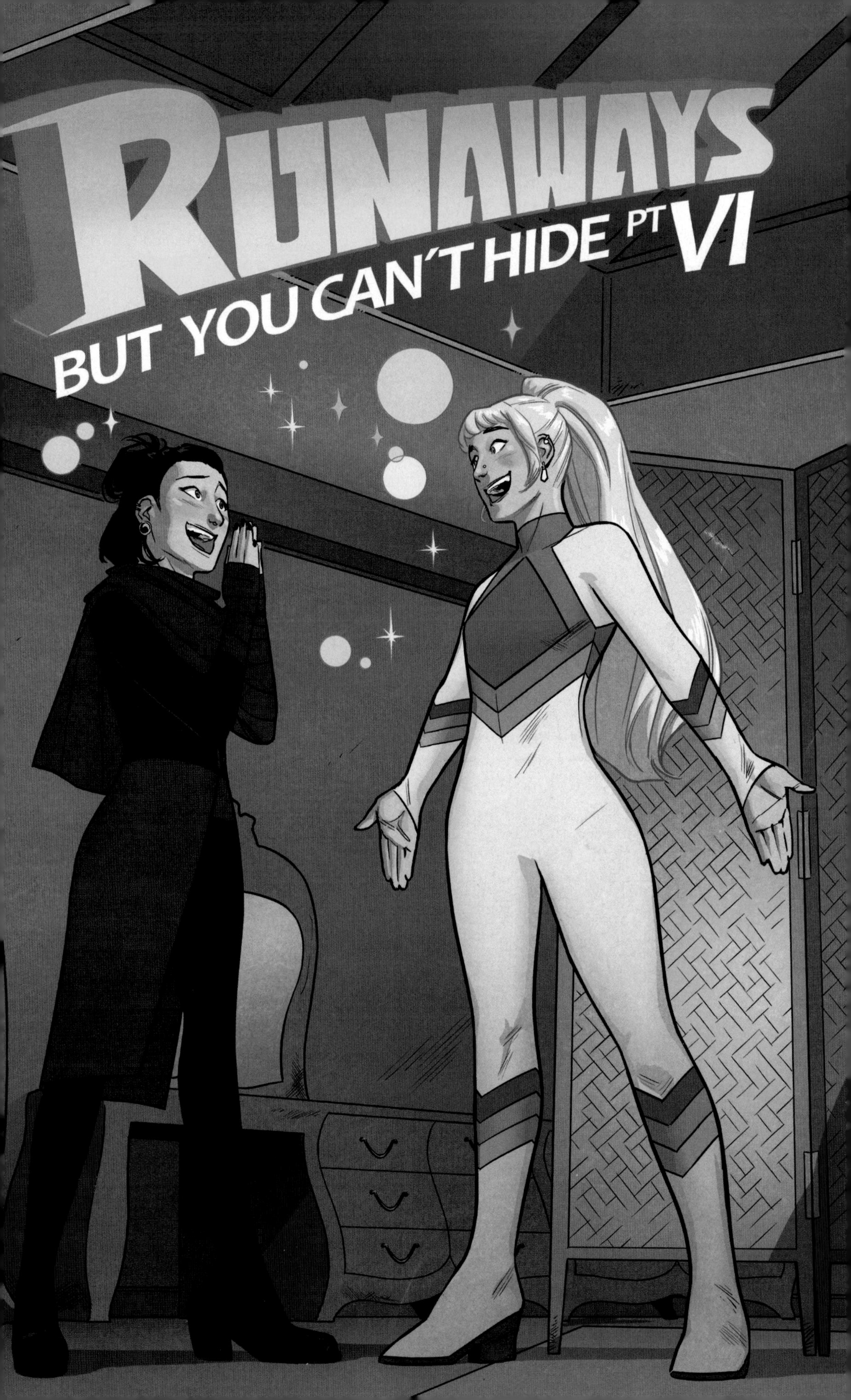
RUNAWAYS
BUT YOU CAN'T HIDE PT VI

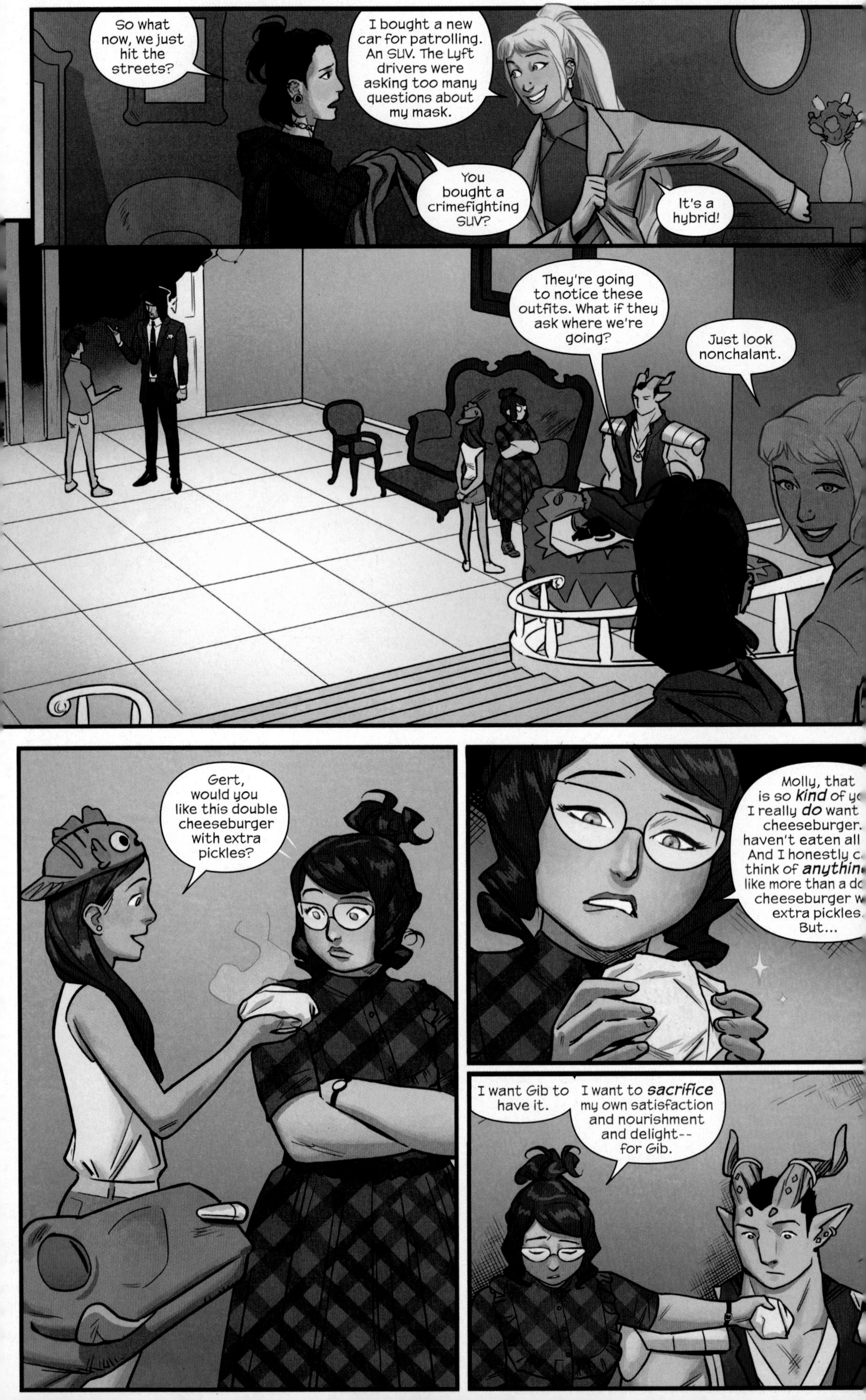
So what now, we just hit the streets?
I bought a new car for patrolling. An SUV. The Lyft drivers were asking too many questions about my mask.
You bought a crimefighting SUV?
It's a hybrid!
They're going to notice these outfits. What if they ask where we're going?
Just look nonchalant.
Gert, would you like this double cheeseburger with extra pickles?
Molly, that is so *kind* of yo
I really *do* want
cheeseburger.
haven't eaten all
And I honestly c
think of *anythin*
like more than a do
cheeseburger w
extra pickles
But...
I want Gib to have it.
I want to *sacrifice* my own satisfaction and nourishment and delight-- for Gib.

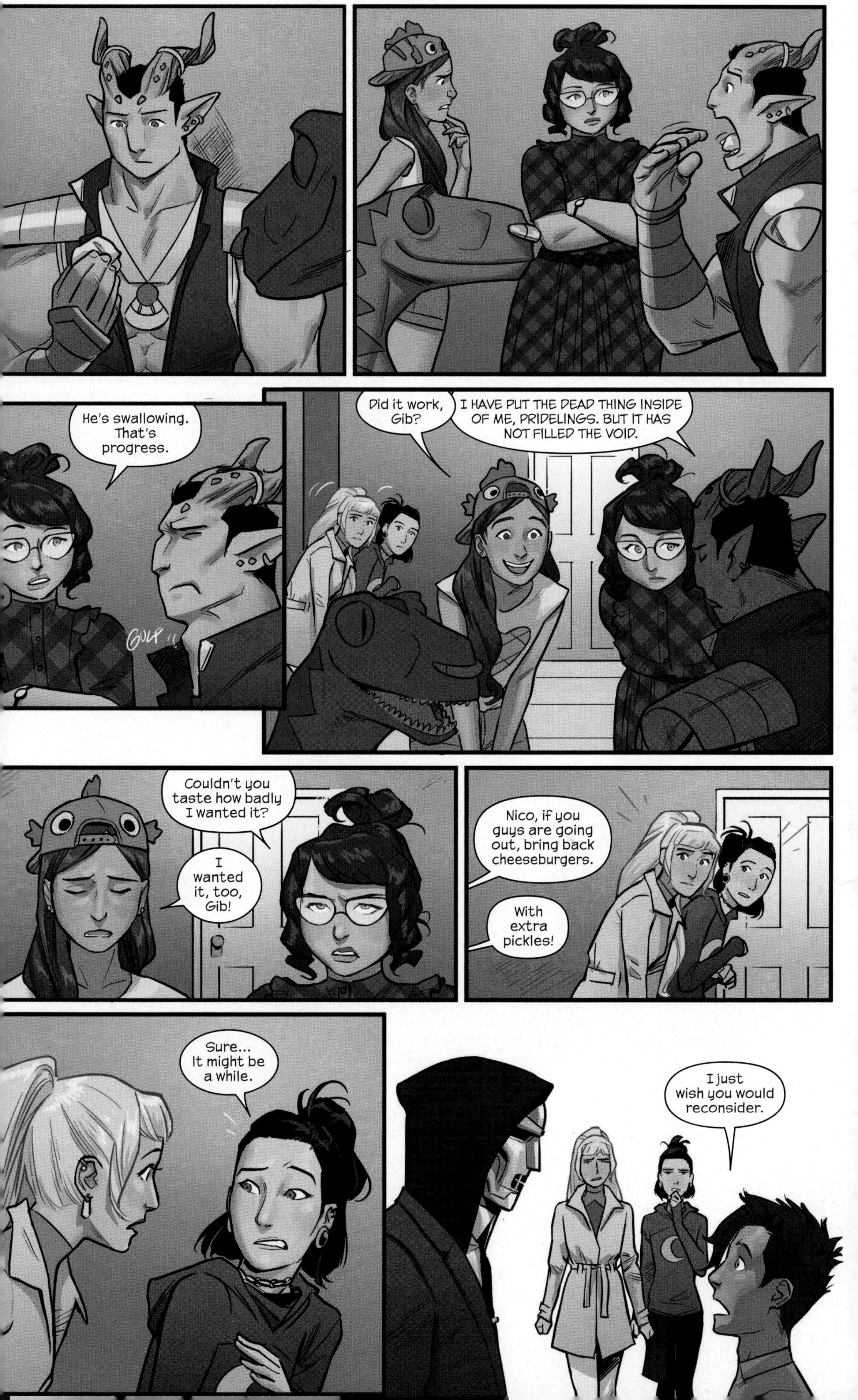
He's swallowing. That's progress.
GULP
Did it work, Gib?
I HAVE PUT THE DEAD THING INSIDE OF ME, PRIDELINGS. BUT IT HAS NOT FILLED THE VOID.
Couldn't you taste how badly I wanted it?
I wanted it, too, Gib!
Nico, if you guys are going out, bring back cheeseburgers.
With extra pickles!
Sure... It might be a while.
I just wish you would reconsider.

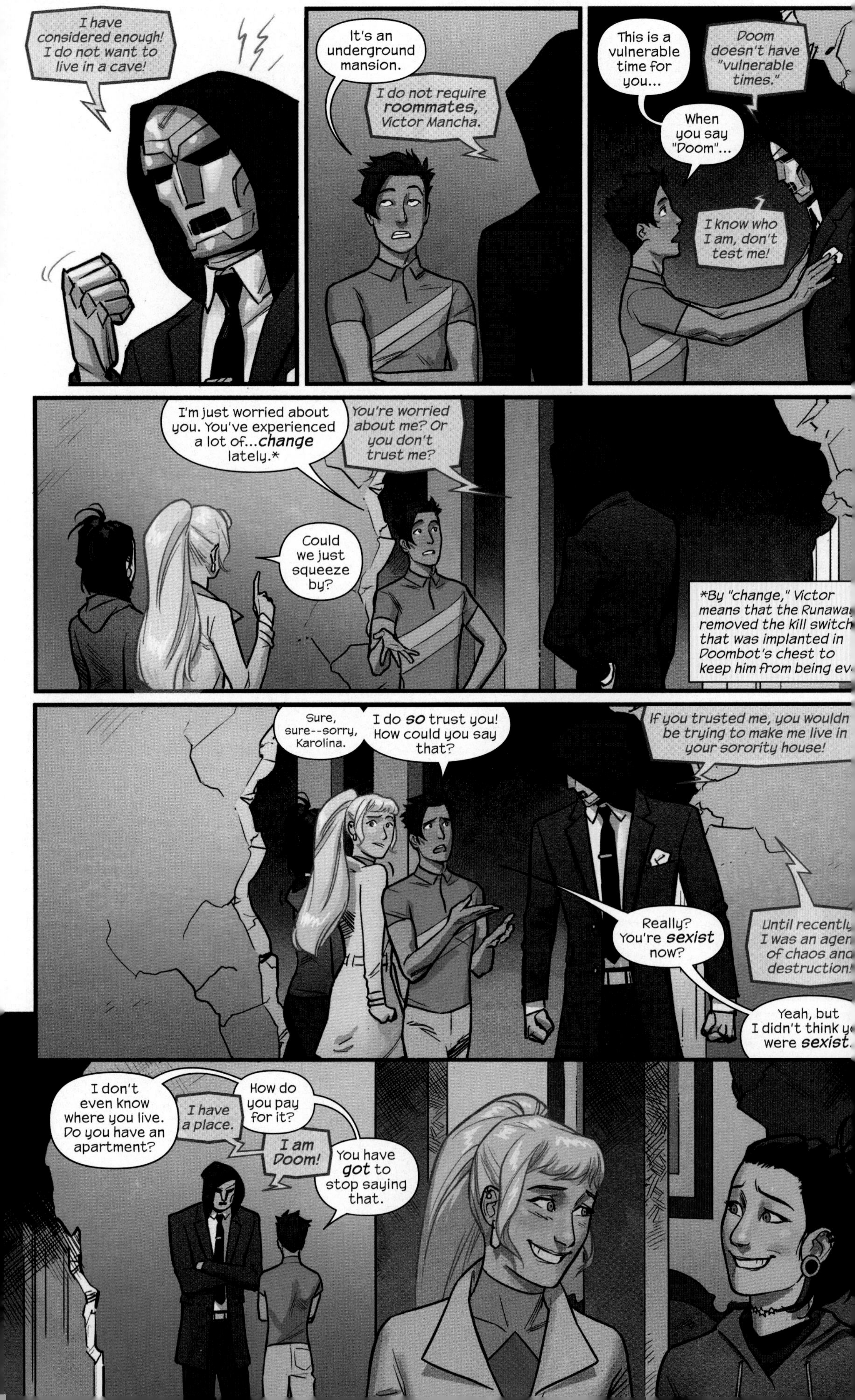
I have considered enough! I do not want to live in a cave!
It's an underground mansion.
I do not require roommates, Victor Mancha.
This is a vulnerable time for you...
Doom doesn't have "vulnerable times."
When you say "Doom"...
I know who I am, don't test me!
I'm just worried about you. You've experienced a lot of...change lately.*
You're worried about me? Or you don't trust me?
Could we just squeeze by?
*By "change," Victor means that the Runawa removed the kill switch that was implanted in Doombot's chest to keep him from being ev
Sure, sure--sorry, Karolina.
I do so trust you! How could you say that?
If you trusted me, you wouldn be trying to make me live in your sorority house!
Really? You're sexist now?
Until recentl I was an agen of chaos and destruction!
Yeah, but I didn't think y were sexist.
I don't even know where you live. Do you have an apartment?
I have a place.
How do you pay for it?
I am Doom!
You have got to stop saying that.

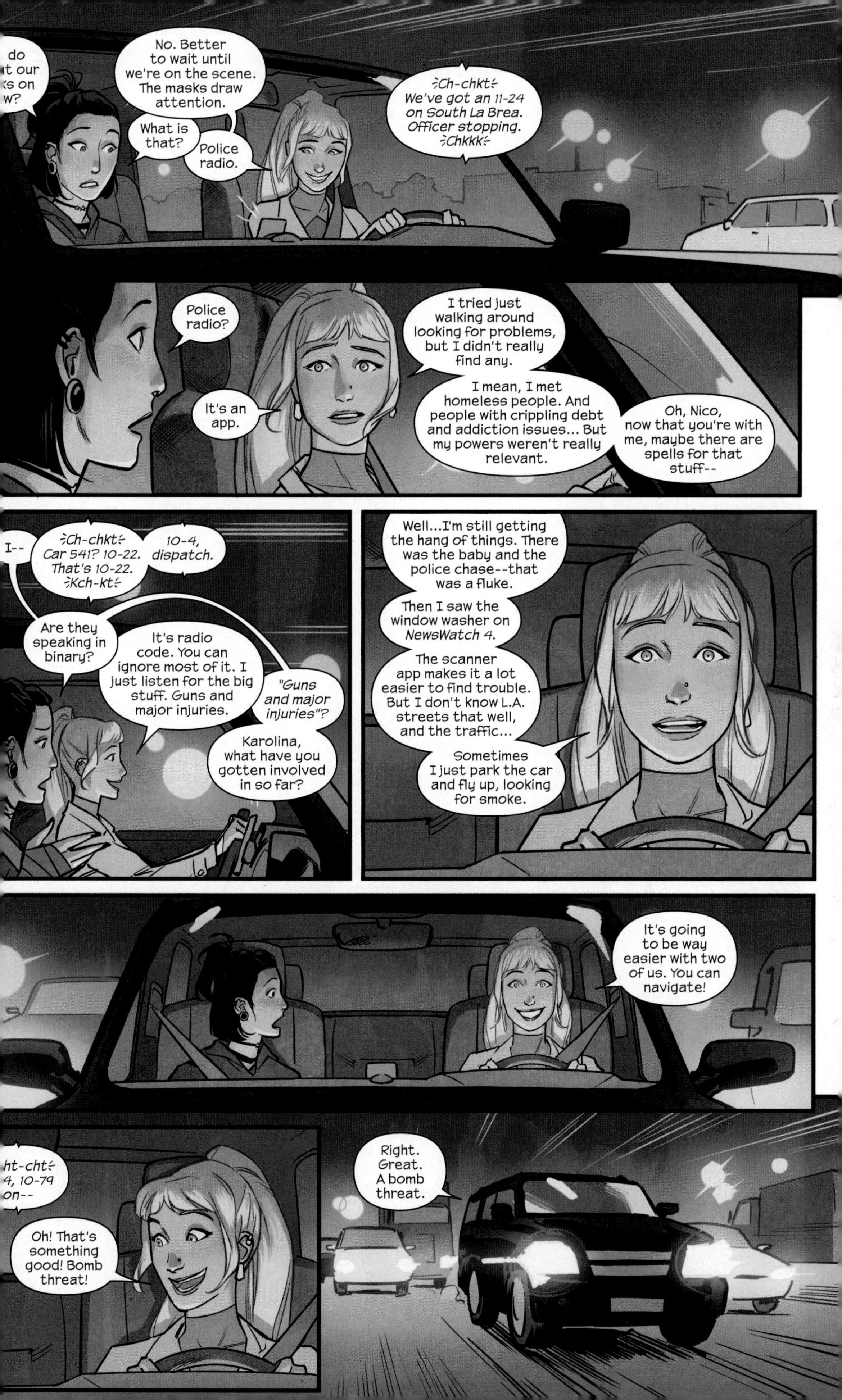

do
t our
s on
w?
No. Better to wait until we're on the scene. The masks draw attention.
What is that?
Police radio.
Ch-chkt We've got an 11-24 on South La Brea. Officer stopping. Chkkk
Police radio?
It's an app.
I tried just walking around looking for problems, but I didn't really find any.
I mean, I met homeless people. And people with crippling debt and addiction issues... But my powers weren't really relevant.
Oh, Nico, now that you're with me, maybe there are spells for that stuff--
I--
Ch-chkt Car 541? 10-22. That's 10-22. Kch-kt
10-4, dispatch.
Are they speaking in binary?
It's radio code. You can ignore most of it. I just listen for the big stuff. Guns and major injuries.
"Guns and major injuries"?
Karolina, what have you gotten involved in so far?
Well...I'm still getting the hang of things. There was the baby and the police chase--that was a fluke.
Then I saw the window washer on NewsWatch 4.
The scanner app makes it a lot easier to find trouble. But I don't know L.A. streets that well, and the traffic...
Sometimes I just park the car and fly up, looking for smoke.
It's going to be way easier with two of us. You can navigate!
ht-cht
4, 10-79
on--
Oh! That's something good! Bomb threat!
Right. Great. A bomb threat.

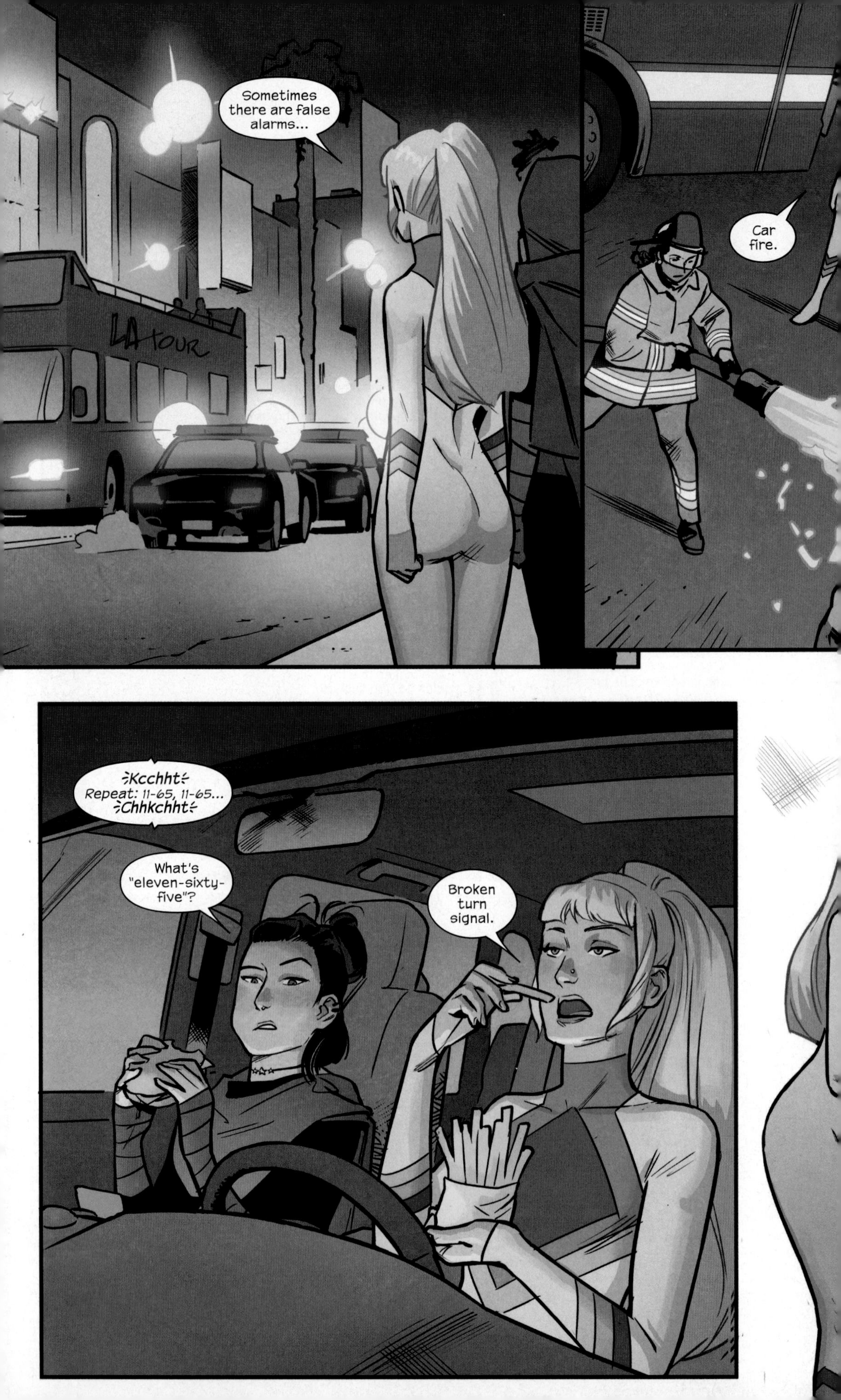
Sometimes there are false alarms...
Car fire.
⚡Kcchht⚡ Repeat: 11-65, 11-65... ⚡Chhkchht⚡
What's "eleven-sixty-five"?
Broken turn signal.

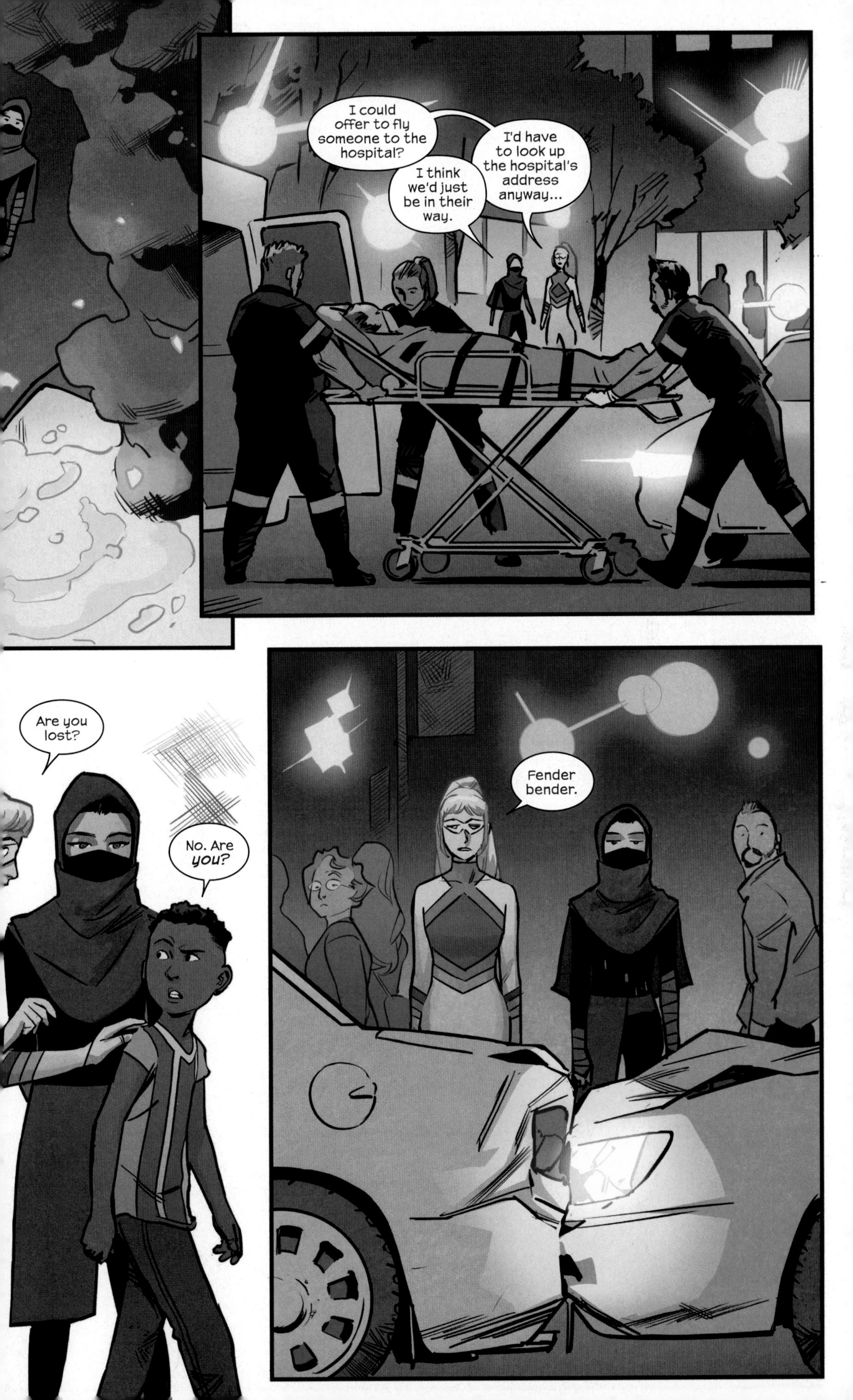
I could offer to fly someone to the hospital?
I think we'd just be in their way.
I'd have to look up the hospital's address anyway...
Are you lost?
No. Are *you*?
Fender bender.

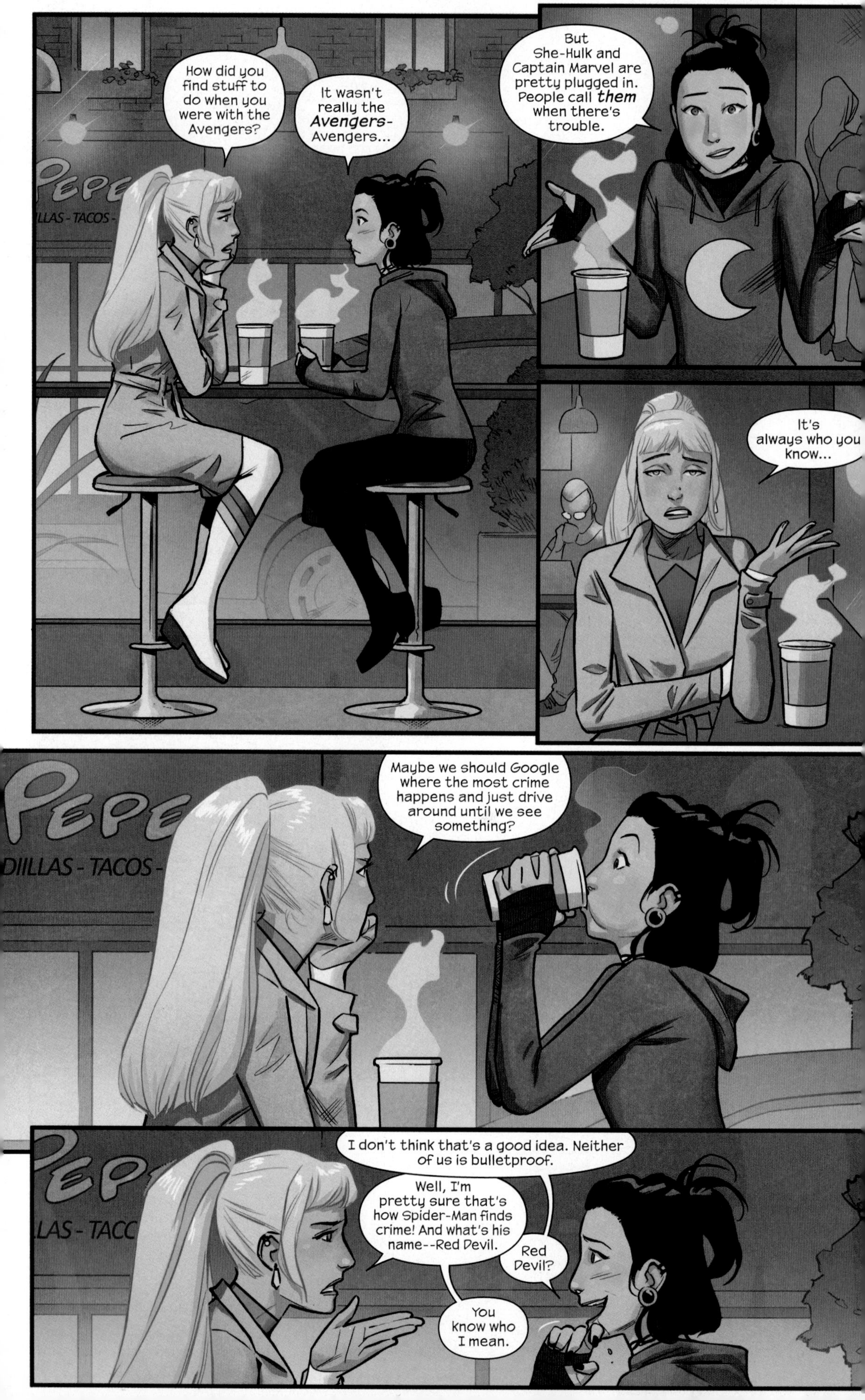
How did you find stuff to do when you were with the Avengers?
It wasn't really the *Avengers*-Avengers...
PEPE
DILLAS - TACOS -
But She-Hulk and Captain Marvel are pretty plugged in. People call *them* when there's trouble.
It's always who you know...
Maybe we should Google where the most crime happens and just drive around until we see something?
I don't think that's a good idea. Neither of us is bulletproof.
Well, I'm pretty sure that's how Spider-Man finds crime! And what's his name--Red Devil.
Red Devil?
You know who I mean.

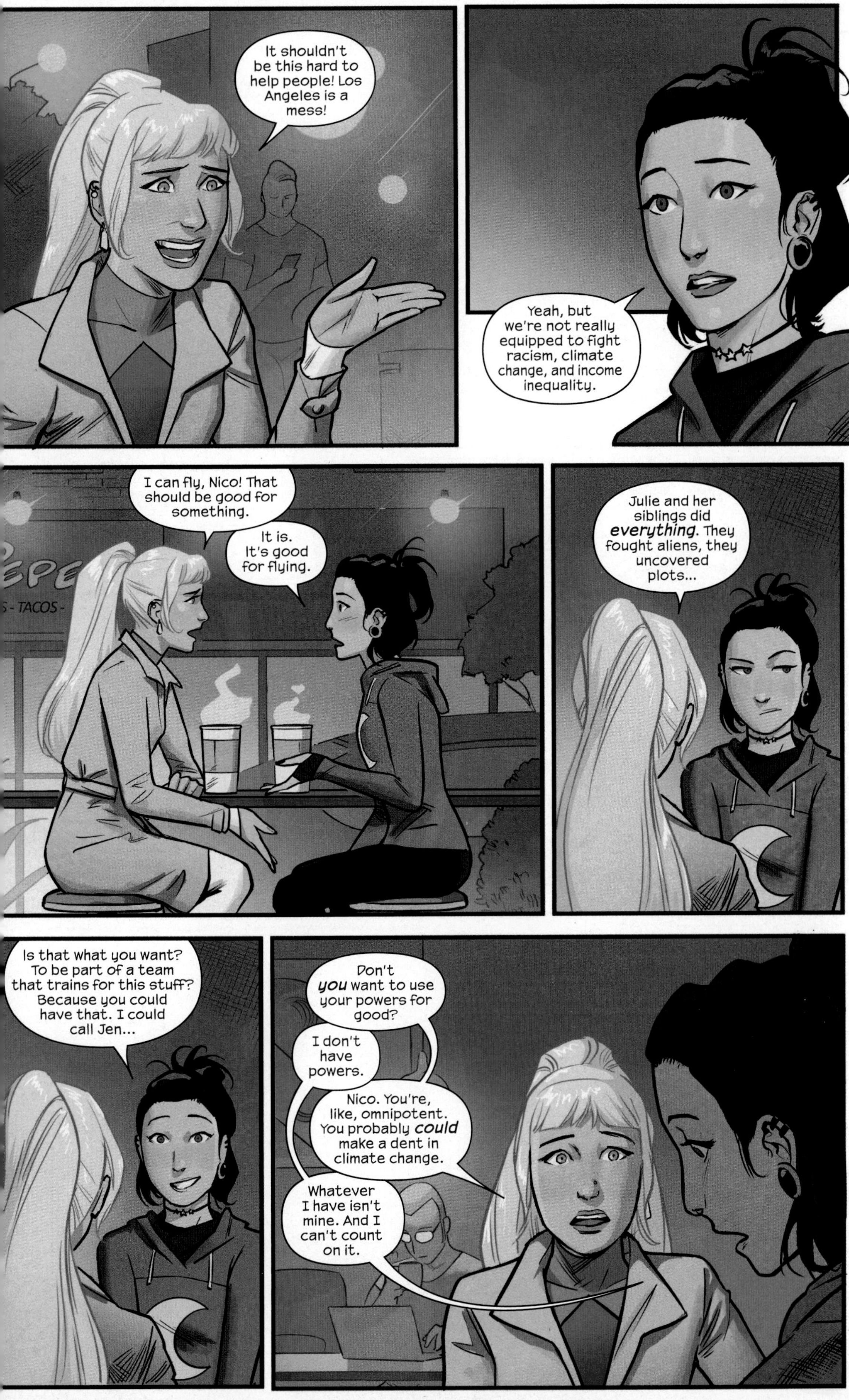
It shouldn't be this hard to help people! Los Angeles is a mess!
Yeah, but we're not really equipped to fight racism, climate change, and income inequality.
I can fly, Nico! That should be good for something.
It is. It's good for flying.
-TACOS-
Julie and her siblings did *everything*. They fought aliens, they uncovered plots...
Is that what you want? To be part of a team that trains for this stuff? Because you could have that. I could call Jen...
Don't *you* want to use your powers for good?
I don't have powers.
Nico. You're, like, omnipotent. You probably *could* make a dent in climate change.
Whatever I have isn't mine. And I can't count on it.

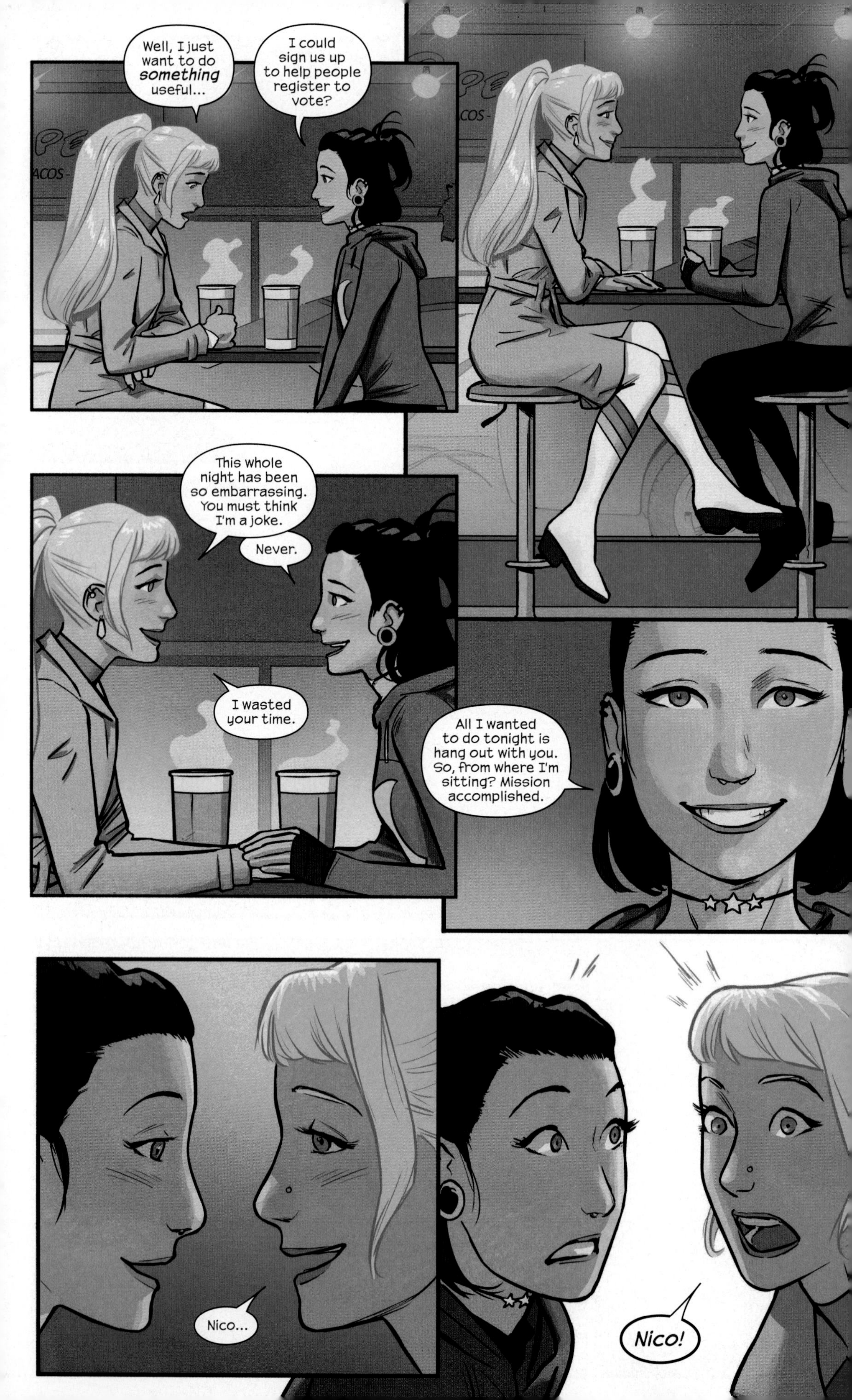
Well, I just want to do *something* useful...
I could sign us up to help people register to vote?
This whole night has been so embarrassing. You must think I'm a joke.
Never.
I wasted your time.
All I wanted to do tonight is hang out with you. So, from where I'm sitting? Mission accomplished.
Nico...
Nico!

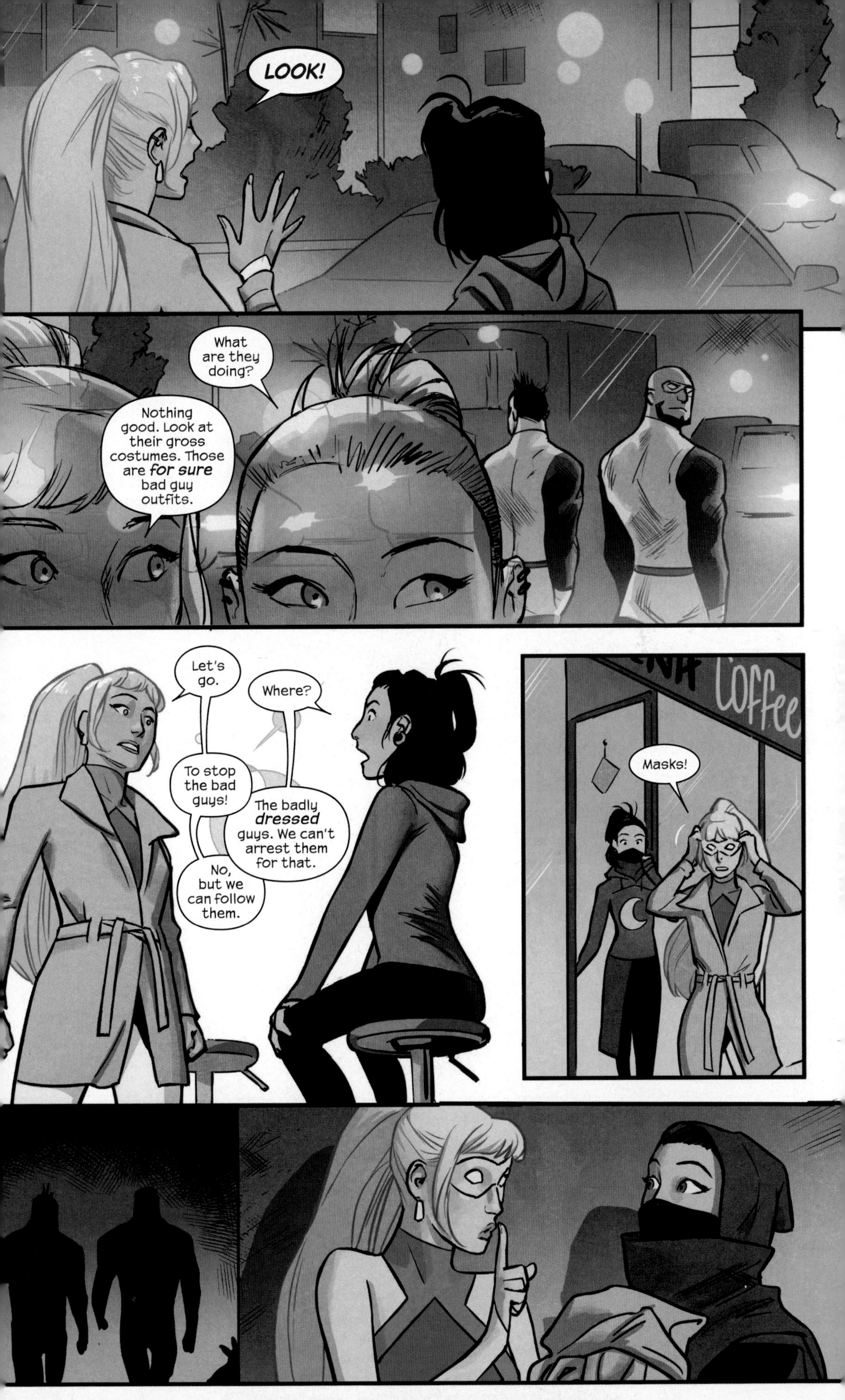
LOOK!
What are they doing?
Nothing good. Look at their gross costumes. Those are *for sure* bad guy outfits.
Let's go.
Where?
To stop the bad guys!
The badly *dressed* guys. We can't arrest them for that.
No, but we can follow them.
Coffee
Masks!

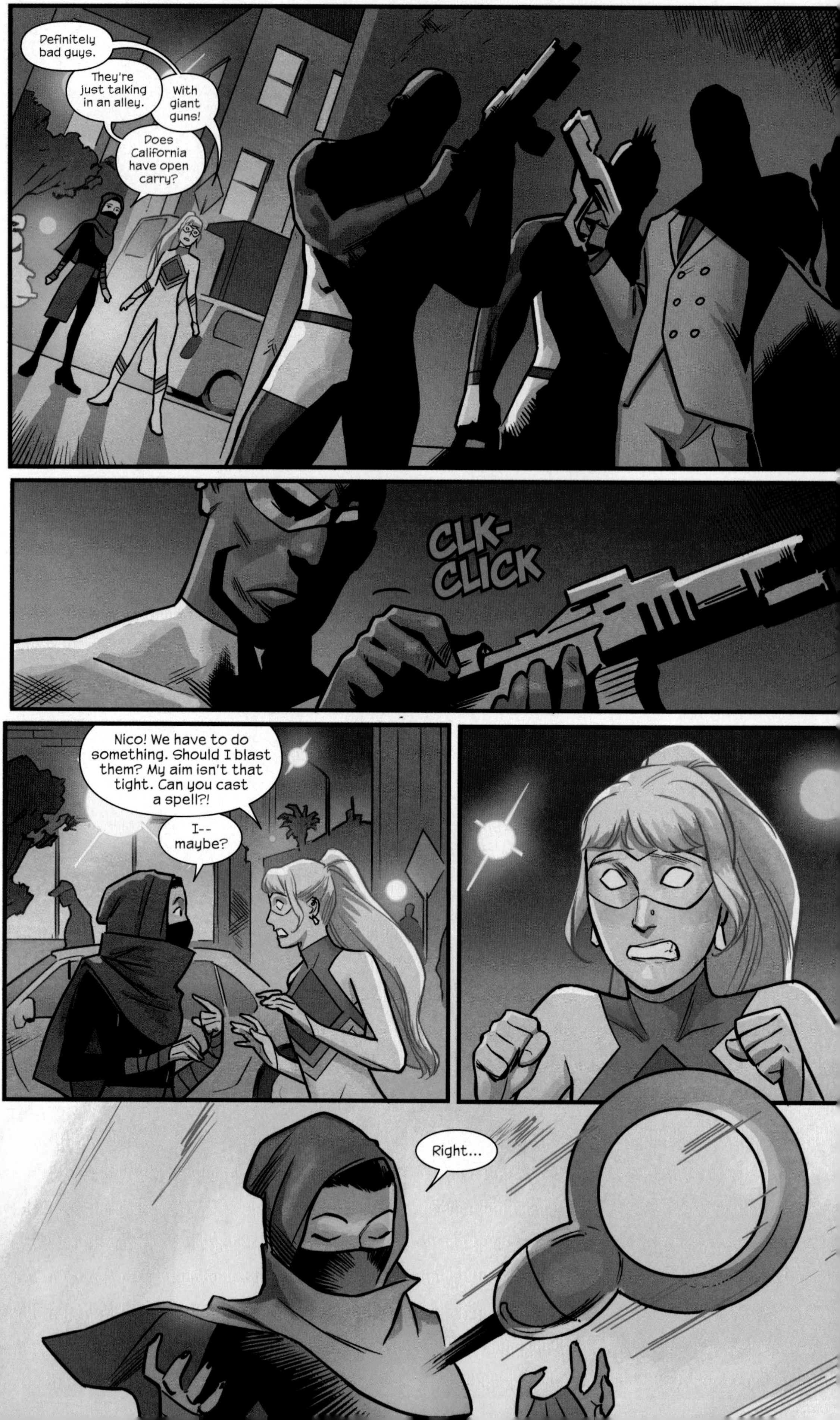
Definitely bad guys.
They're just talking in an alley.
With giant guns!
Does California have open carry?
CLK-CLICK
Nico! We have to do something. Should I blast them? My aim isn't that tight. Can you cast a spell?!
I-- maybe?
Right...

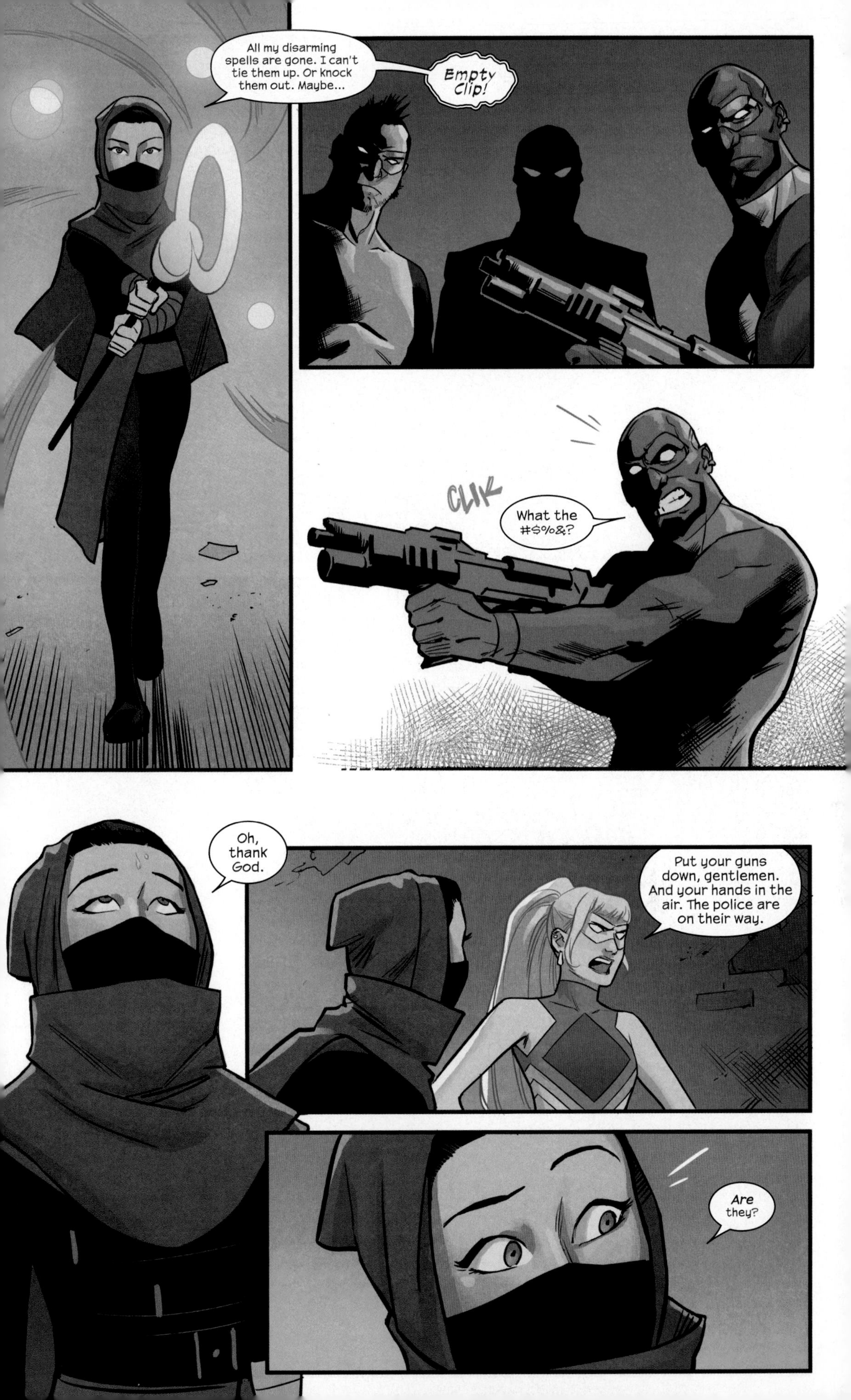

All my disarming spells are gone. I can't tie them up. Or knock them out. Maybe...
Empty Clip!
CLIK
What the #$%&?
Oh, thank God.
Put your guns down, gentlemen. And your hands in the air. The police are on their way.
Are they?

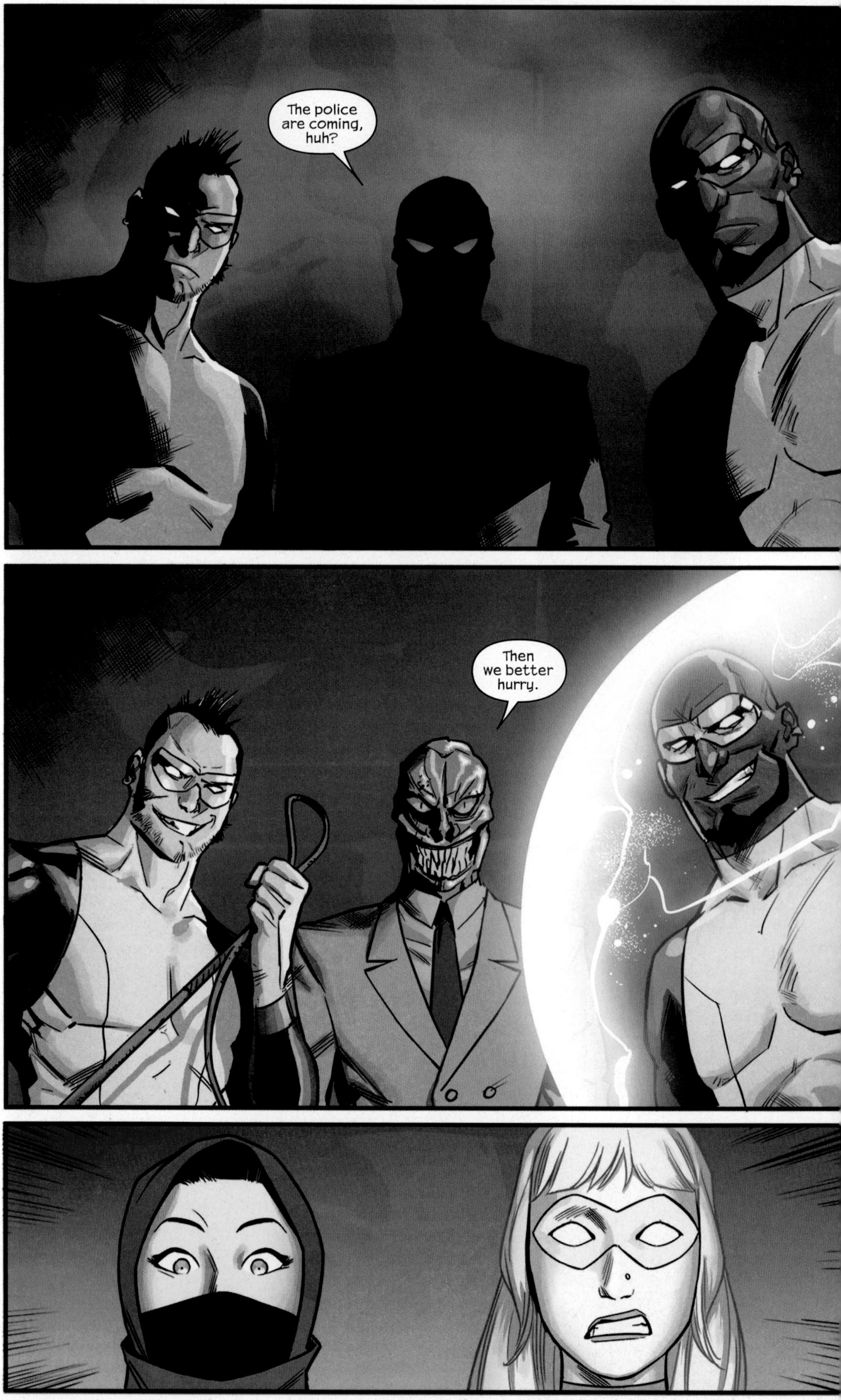
The police are coming, huh?
Then we better hurry.

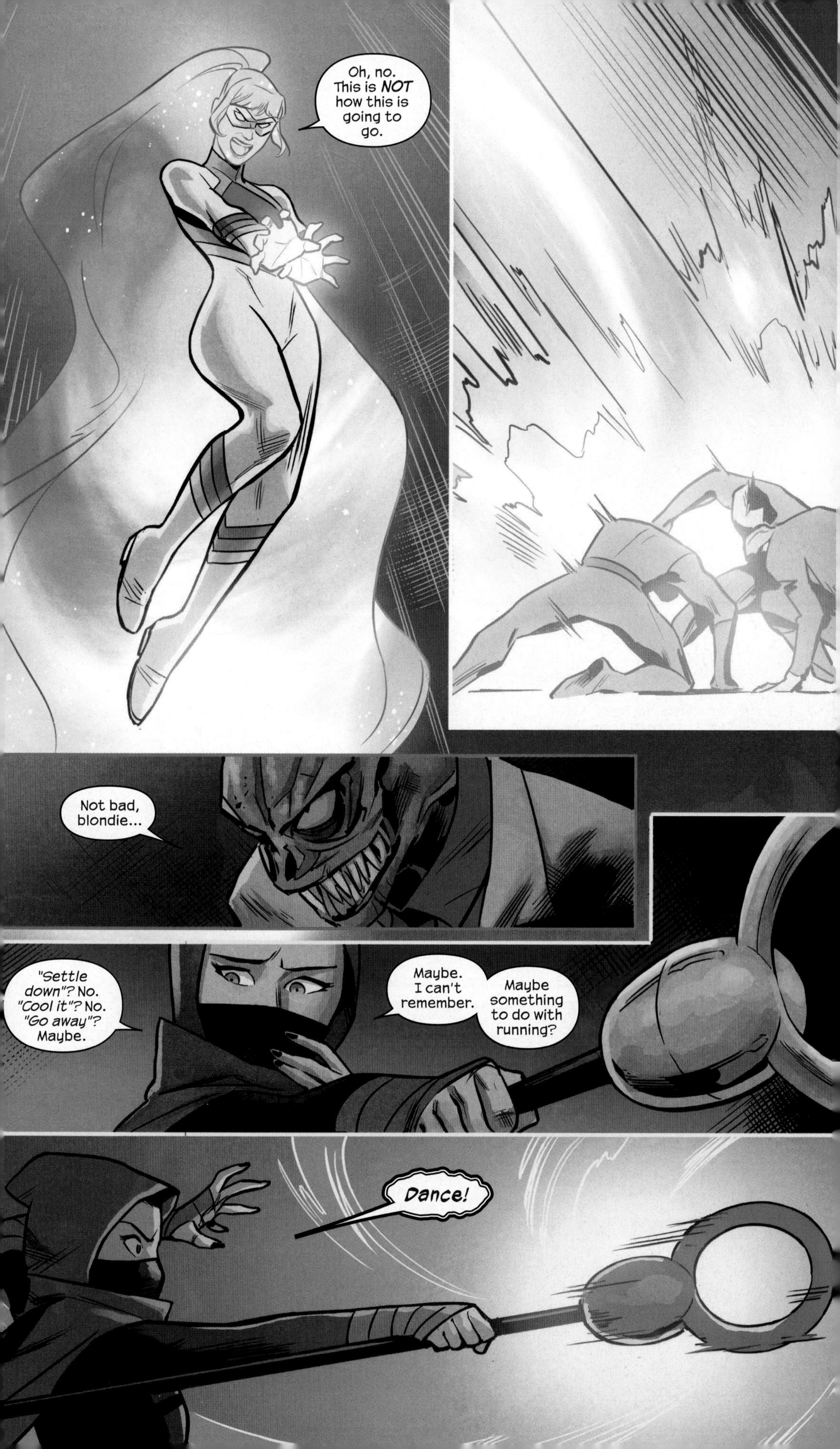
Oh, no. This is *NOT* how this is going to go.
Not bad, blondie...
"Settle down"? No. "Cool it"? No. "Go away"? Maybe.
Maybe. I can't remember.
Maybe something to do with running?
Dance!

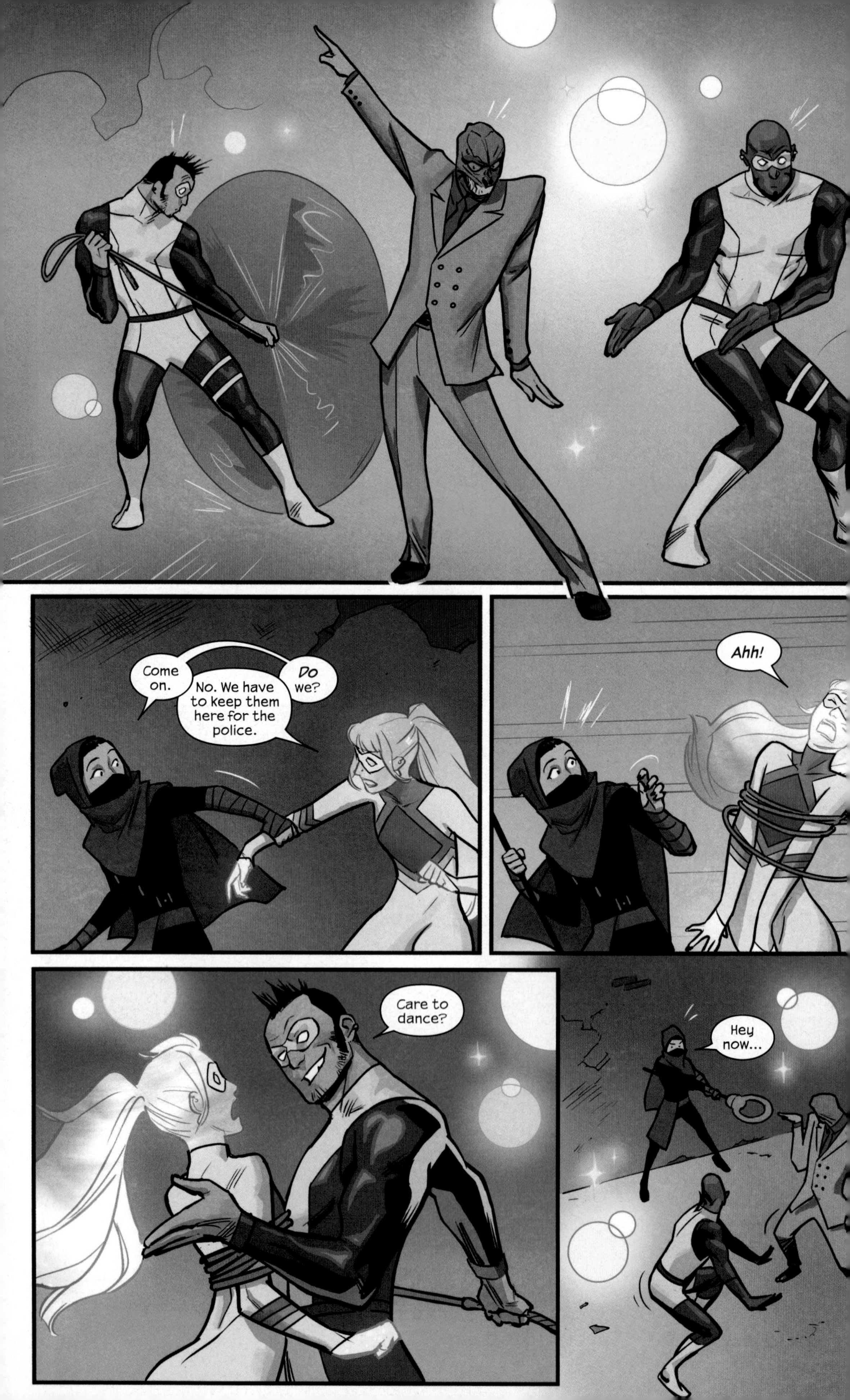
Come on.
Do we?
No. We have to keep them here for the police.
Ahh!
Care to dance?
Hey now...

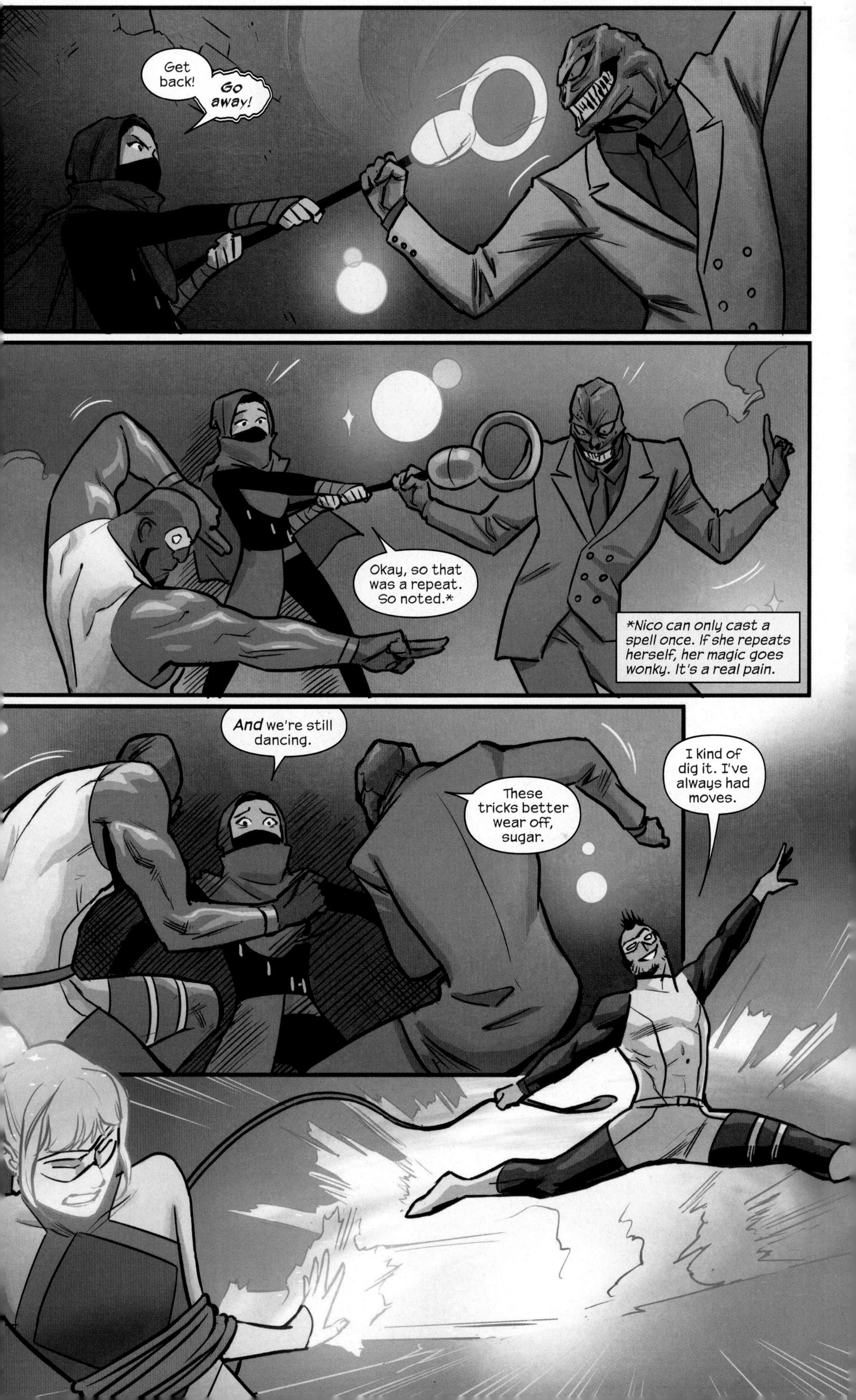

Get back!
Go away!
Okay, so that was a repeat. So noted.*
*Nico can only cast a spell once. If she repeats herself, her magic goes wonky. It's a real pain.
And we're still dancing.
These tricks better wear off, sugar.
I kind of dig it. I've always had moves.

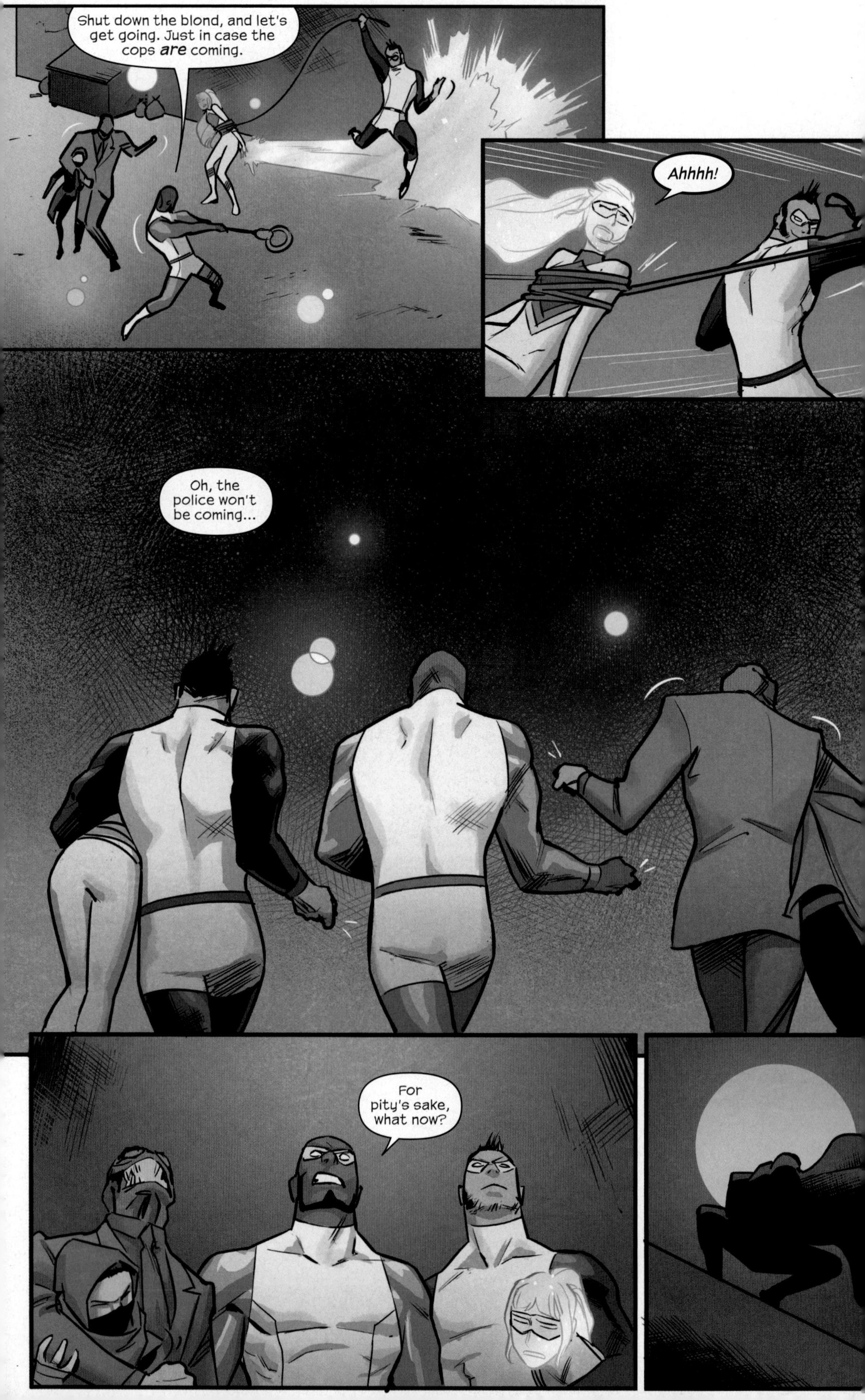
Shut down the blond, and let's get going. Just in case the cops *are* coming.
Ahhhh!
Oh, the police won't be coming...
For pity's sake, what now?

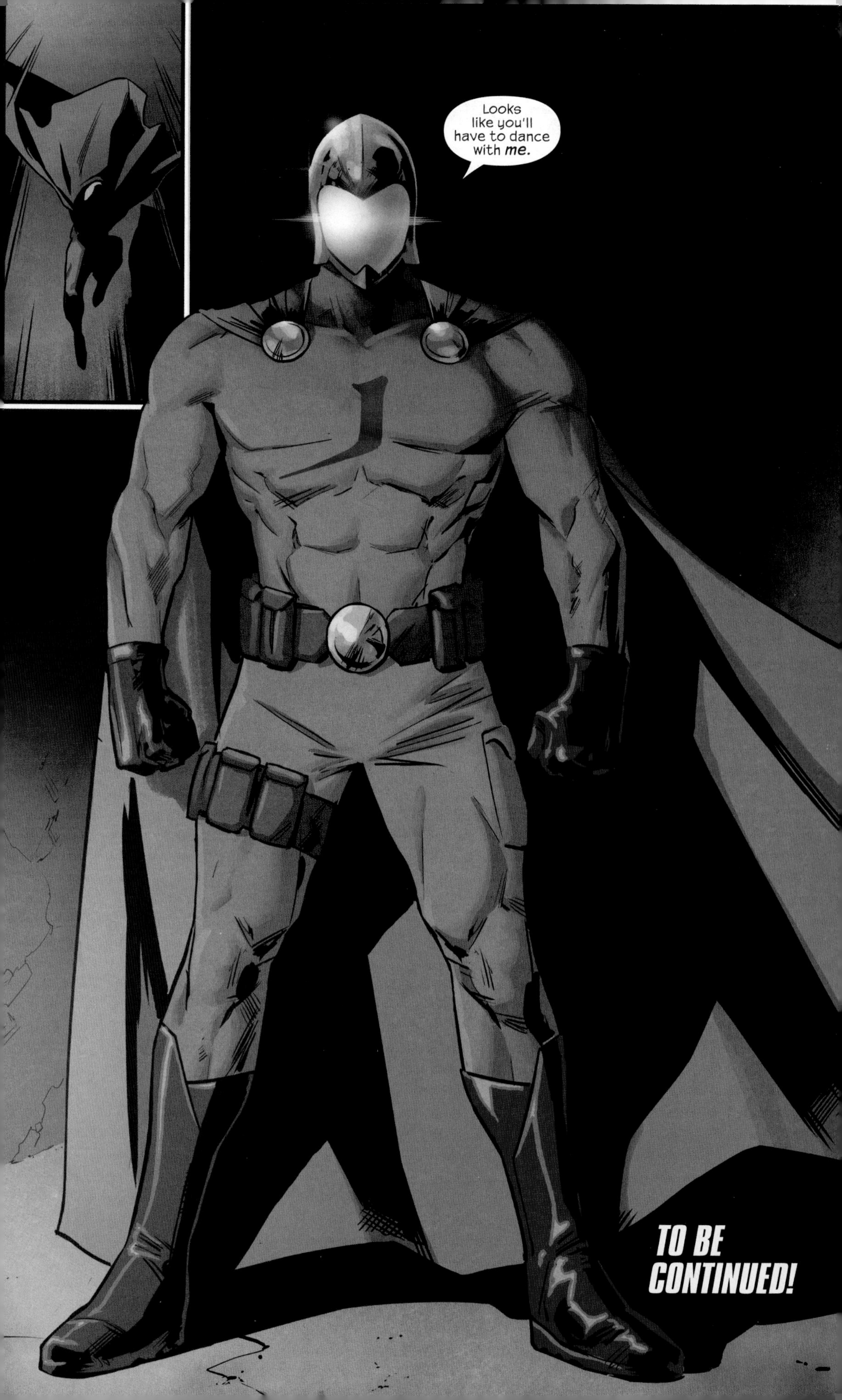

Looks like you'll have to dance with *me.*
TO BE CONTINUED!

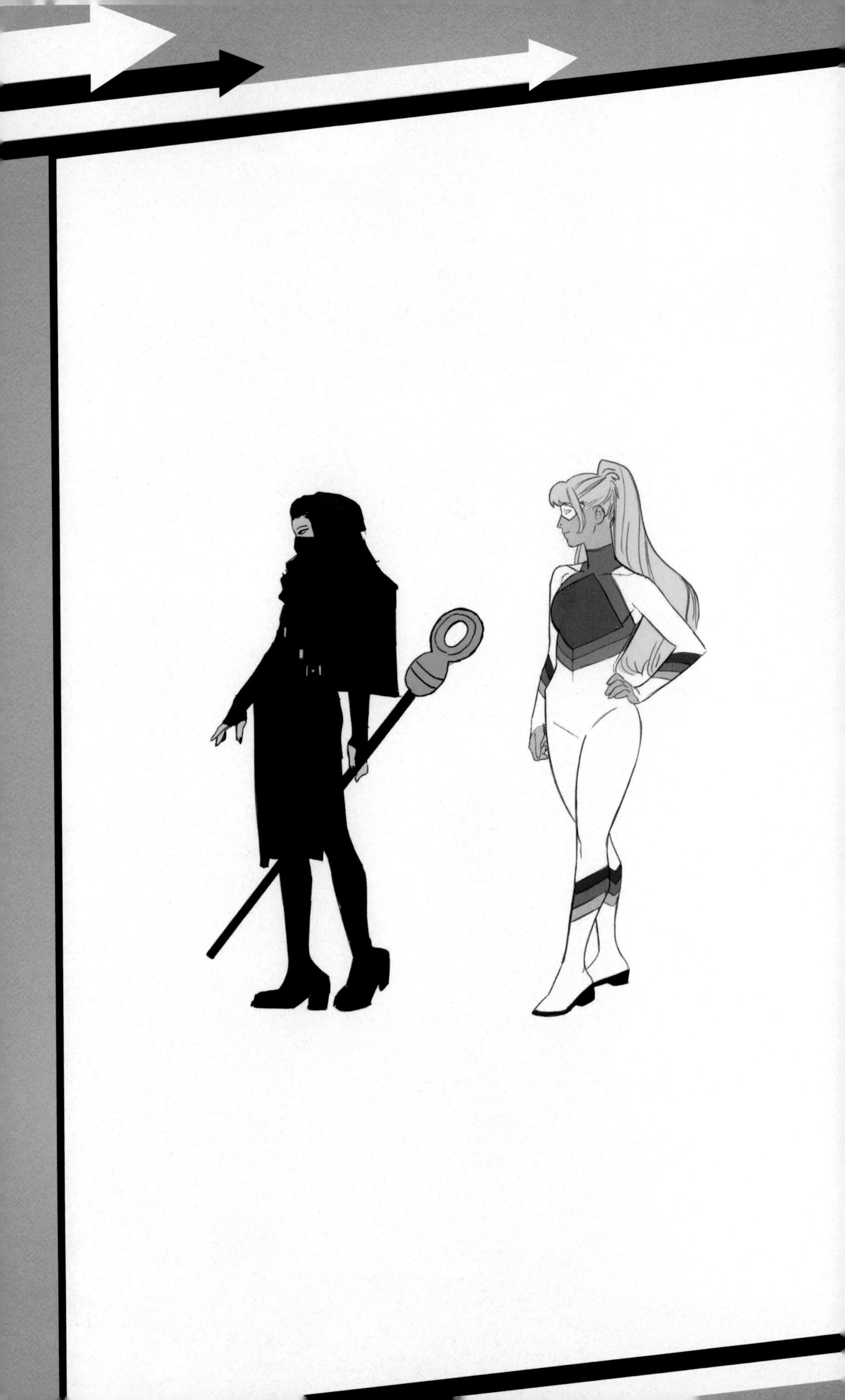

a
b
c

a
b
c

NIKO AND KAROLINA COSTUME DESIGNS BY **KRIS ANKA**

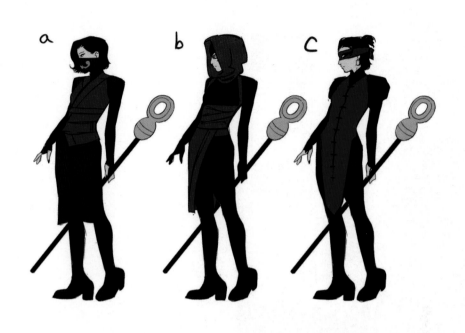

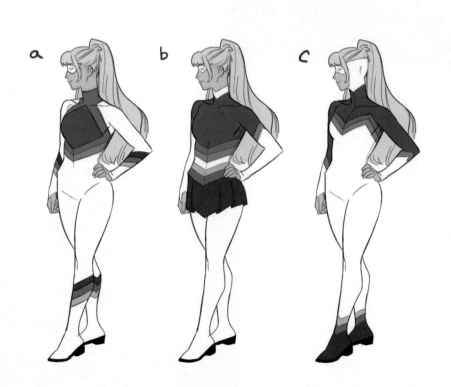

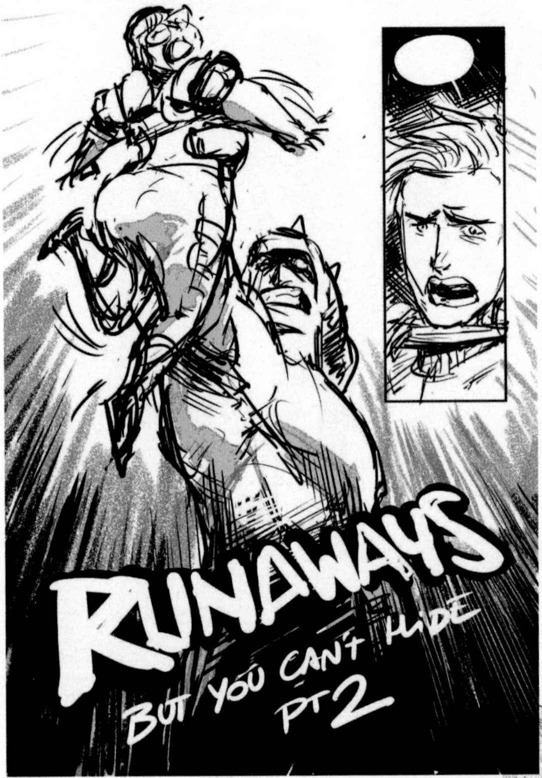
RUNAWAYS
BUT YOU CAN'T HIDE PT 2

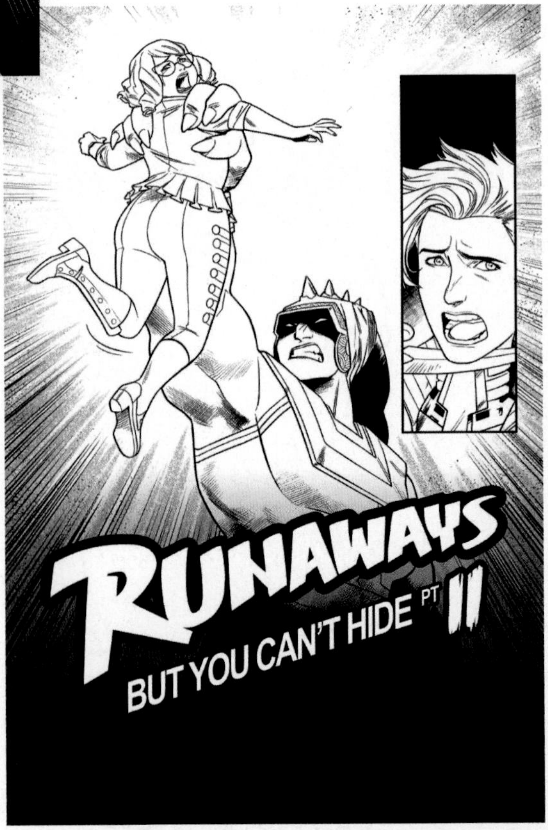
RUNAWAYS
BUT YOU CAN'T HIDE PT II

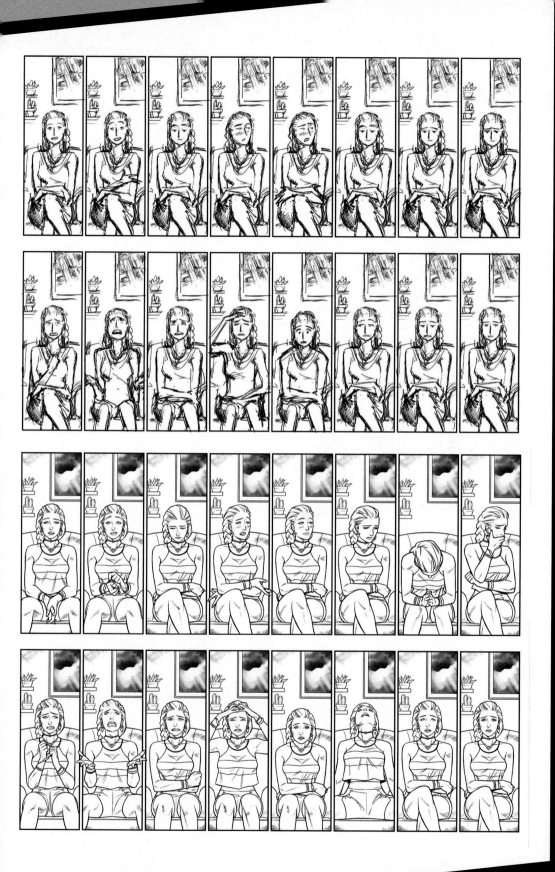

#20, PAGE 1 & #21, PAGE 5-6 LAYOUTS AND INKS BY ANDRÉS GENOLET

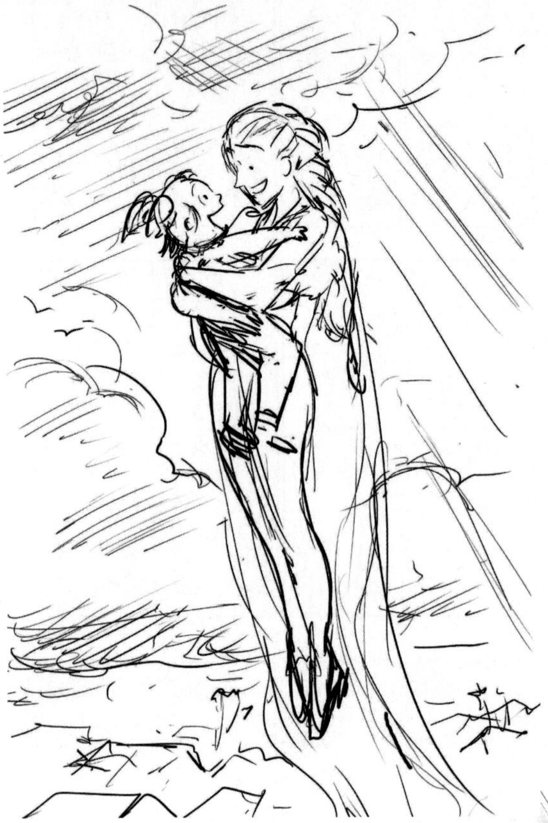

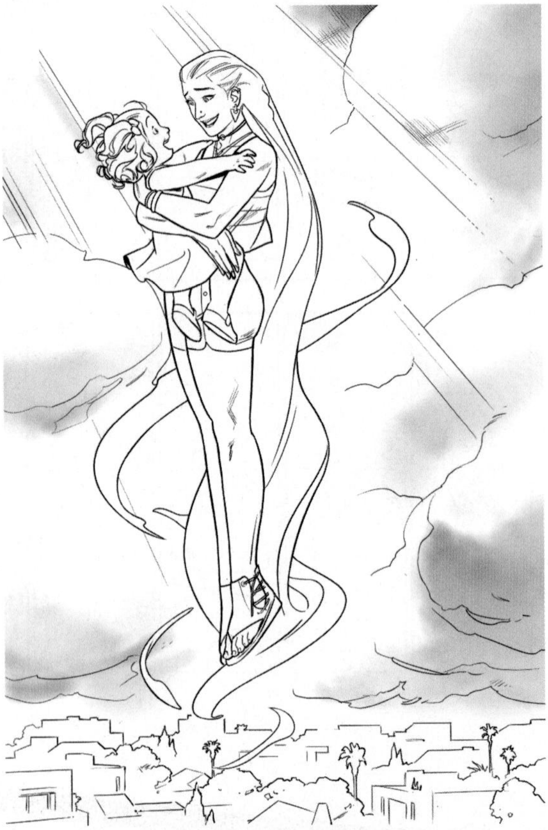

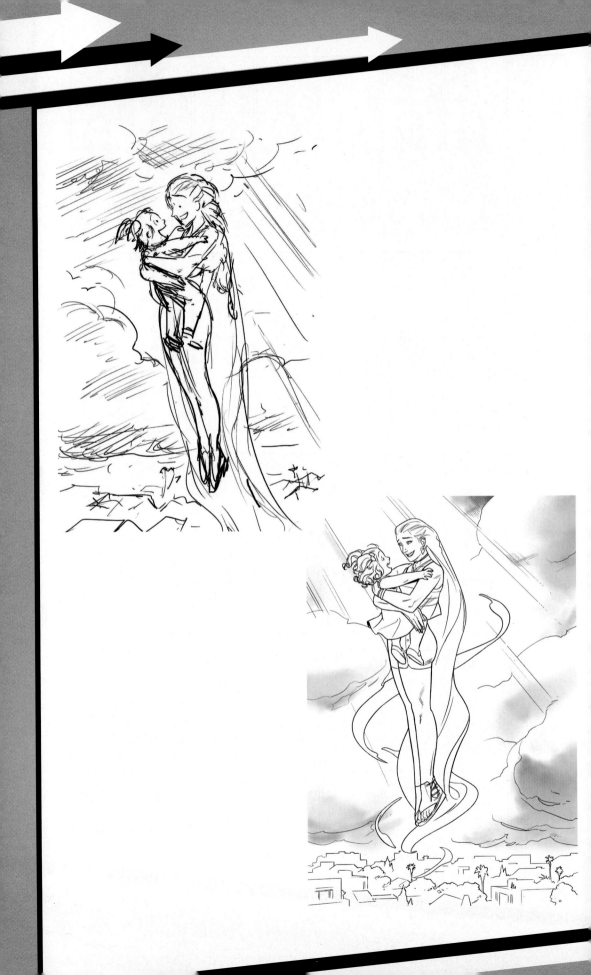

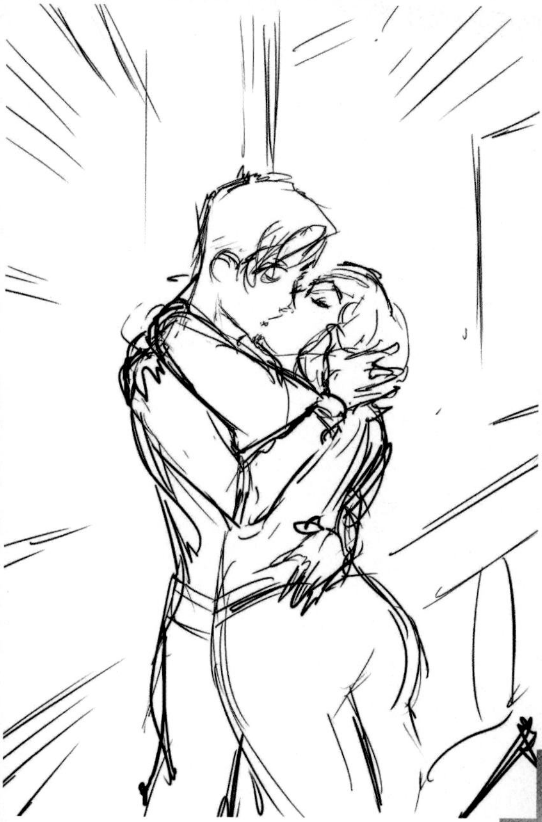

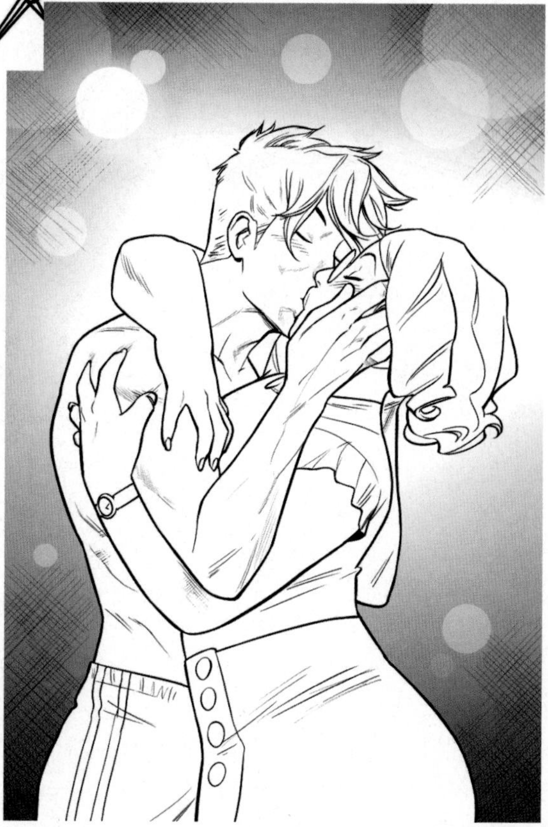

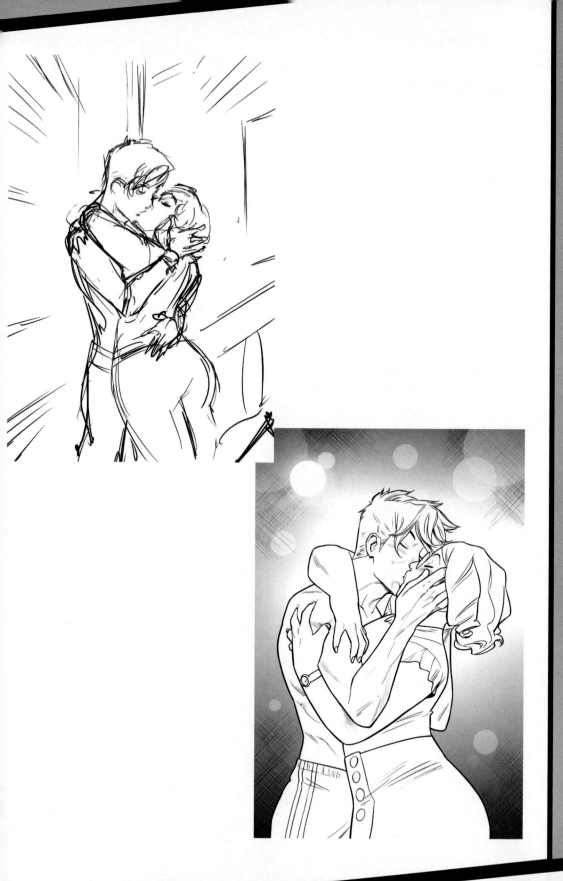

#21, PAGES 10 & 20 LAYOUTS AND INKS BY **ANDRÉS GENOLET**

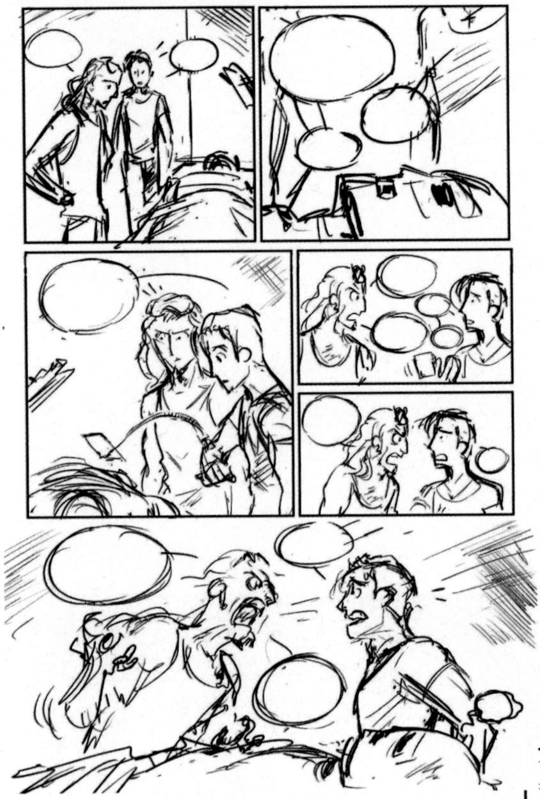

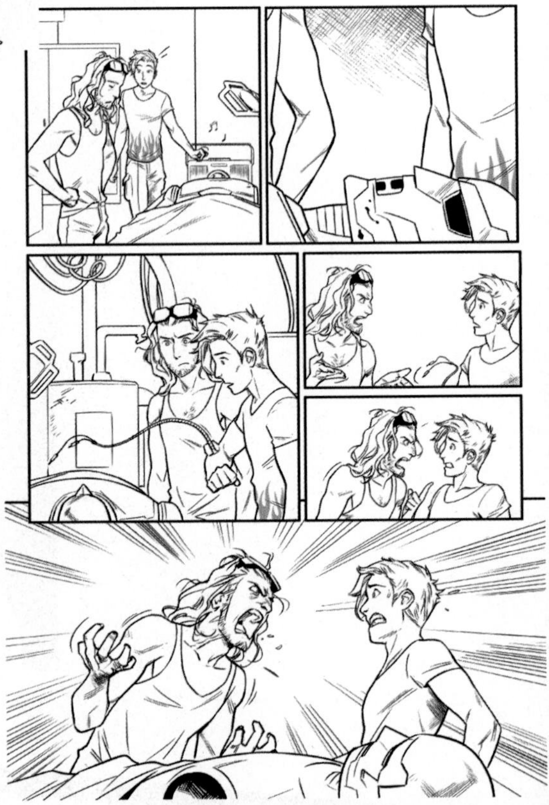

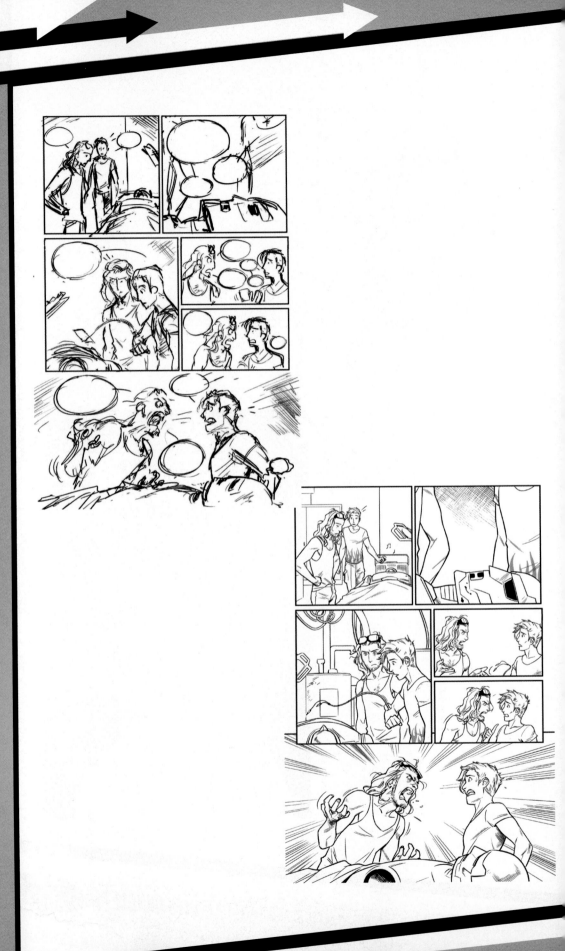

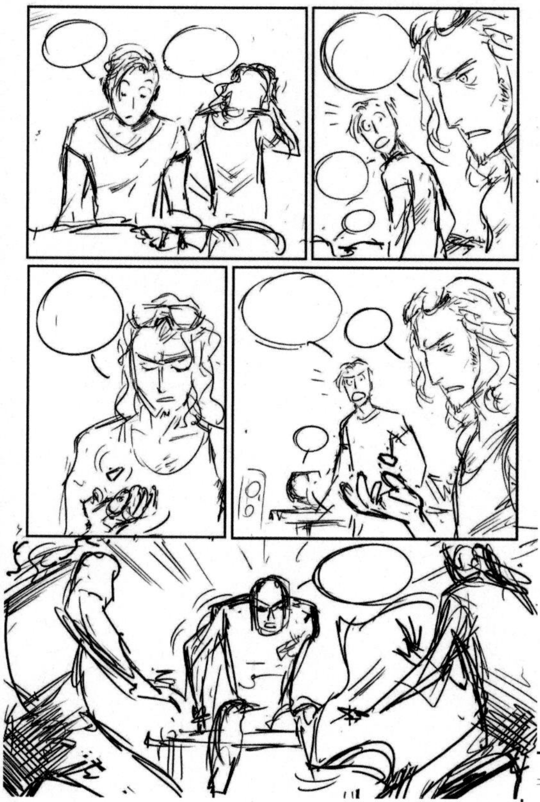

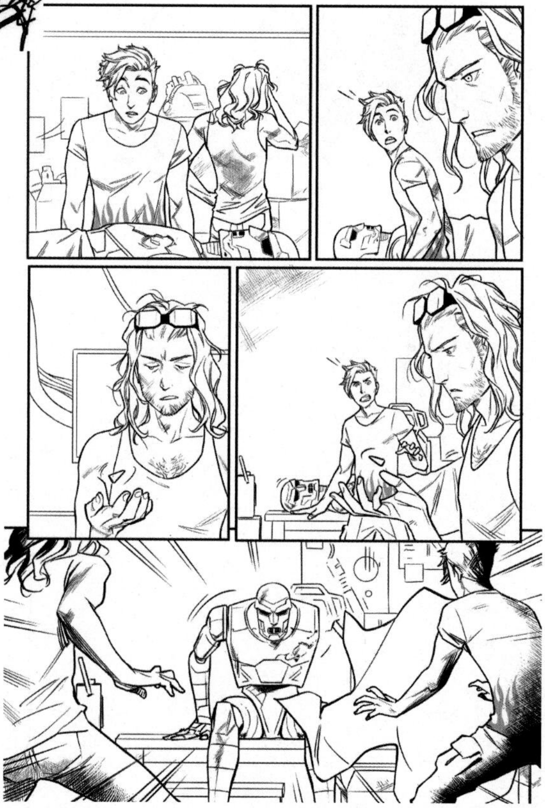

#22, PAGES 12 & 13 LAYOUTS AND INKS BY ANDRÉS GENOLET

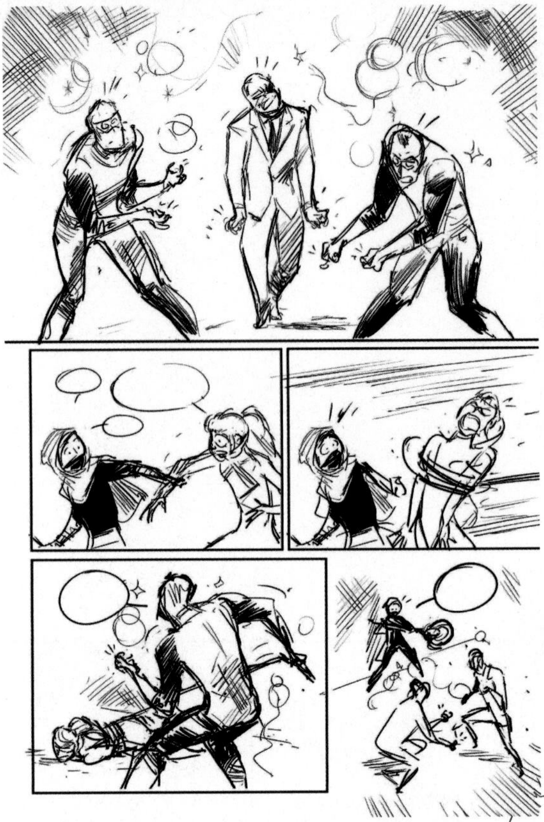

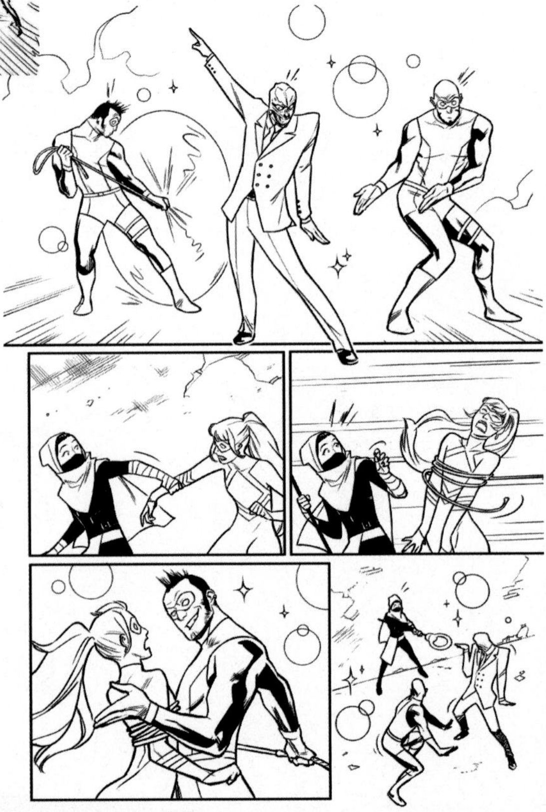

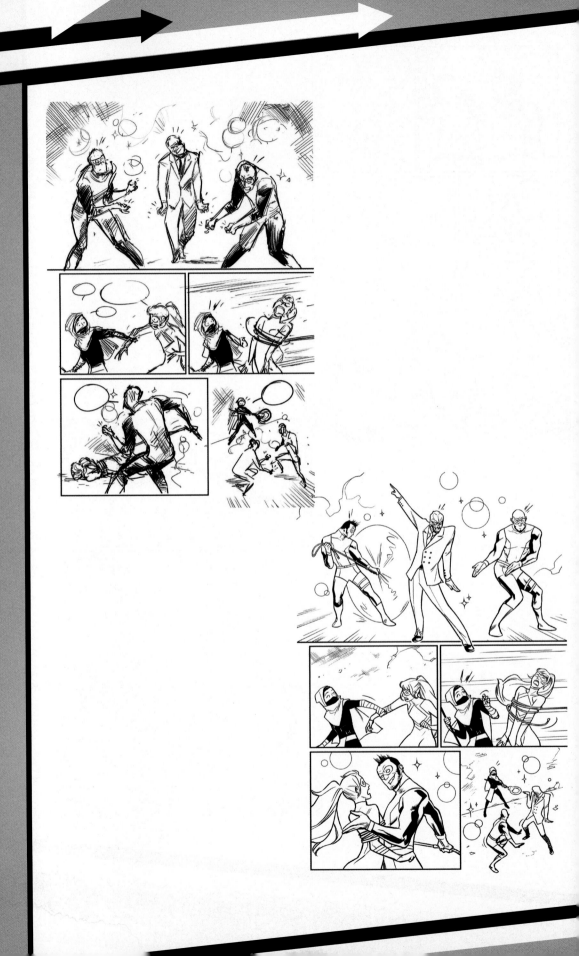

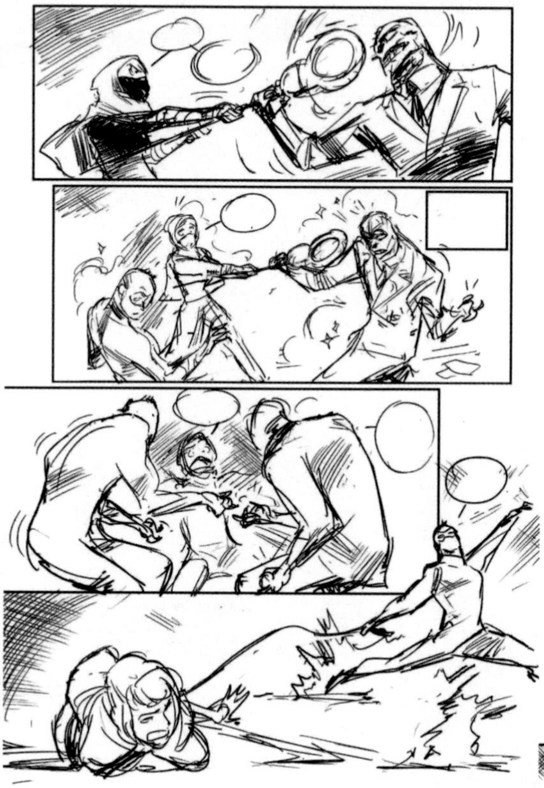

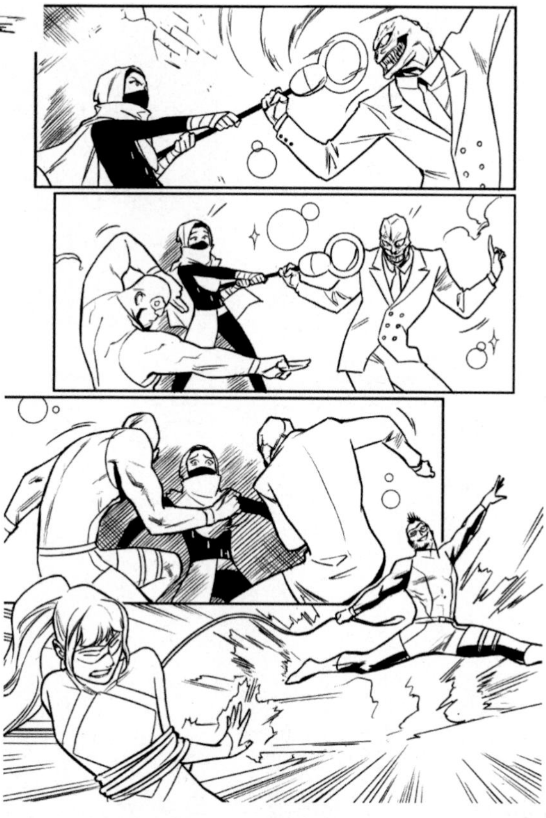

#24, PAGES 17 & 18 LAYOUTS AND INKS BY **ANDRÉS GENOLET**

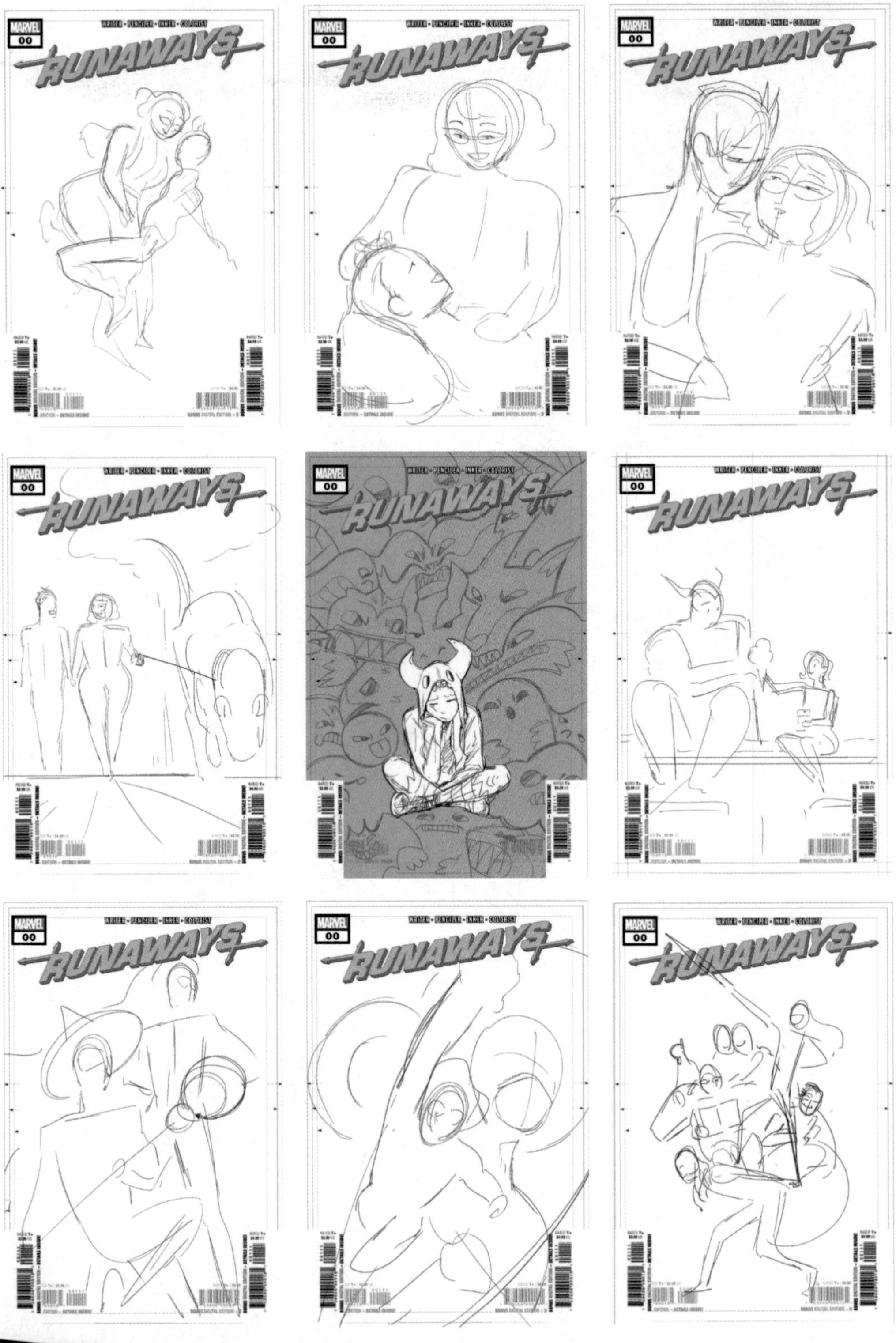
MARVEL
00
WRITER • PENCILER • INKER • COLORIST
RUNAWAYS

COVER SKETCHES BY KRIS ANKA